Transnational Asia Pacific

Transnational Asia Pacific

Gender, Culture, and the Public Sphere

EDITED BY

SHIRLEY GEOK-LIN LIM,

LARRY E. SMITH, AND

WIMAL DISSANAYAKE

With the Assistance of Laura Scott Holliday

University of Illinois Press

URBANA AND CHICAGO

© 1999 by the Board of Trustees of
the University of Illinois
All rights reserved
Manufactured in the United States of America
∞ This book is printed on acid-free paper.

Library of Congress Cataloging-in-Publication Data
Transnational Asia Pacific : gender, culture, and the
public sphere / edited by Shirley Geok-lin Lim,
Larry E. Smith, and Wimal Dissanayake ; with the
assistance of Laura Scott Holliday.
p.   cm.
Includes bibliographical references (p.   ) and index.
ISBN 0-252-02492-3 (acid-free paper)
ISBN 0-252-06809-2 (pbk. : acid-free paper)
1. Sex role—Asia, Southeastern. 2. Sex role—East Asia. 3. Sex
role—Pacific Area. 4. Politics and culture—Asia, Southeastern.
5. Politics and culture—East Asia. 6. Politics and culture—
Pacific Area. 7. Human rights—Asia, Southeastern. 8. Human
rights—East Asia. 9. Human rights—Pacific Area. I. Lim,
Shirley. II. Smith, Larry E. III. Dissanayake, Wimal.
HQ1075.5 A785T73   1999
305.3'095—dc21   99-6055
CIP

1 2 3 4 5 C P 5 4 3 2 1

Contents

Introduction

Shirley Geok-lin Lim and Wimal Dissanayake

THE ASIA PACIFIC REGION is a vast territory encompassing Japan, the newly industrialized states of East Asia and China, the Southeast Asian countries, Australia, New Zealand, the South Sea islands, and the Pacific coast of North America. The past three decades have witnessed rapid and in many ways unanticipated economic developments in these territories. In the opinion of some economists, even the most recent financial crisis will not, in the long run, prevent this region from enjoying higher than average rates of economic growth. These changes have resulted in shifts and instabilities in the economic and political center of gravity in the world.

Many analyses of the Asia Pacific region focus largely on economic and political issues to the virtual exclusion of the sphere of culture, leading to a partial understanding of the dynamics of the region. The objective of this volume is to rectify this imbalance by focusing on questions of cultural production and globalization and to explore how they are vitally imbricated with the region's future development.

The identity of the "Pacific Rim" as a topographical entity took shape only in the mid-twentieth century, consequent upon newer political, economic, and cultural forces exerting their influence in the world. During the fifteenth century, when Europeans first arrived in East Asia, the Pacific was merely a geographical name. The elements that were later to form a recognizable region remained unconnected. When commercial capitalism initiated by the Europeans made its presence felt in East and Southeast Asia, one could not identify the "Pacific Rim" as an entity because there was no regional community to which one could readily refer. There were no diplomatic, trade, or cultural interlinkages and institutional structures and processes that would indicate the presence of such a community.

As a term of identification and evaluation, the "Pacific Rim" came into prominence only after the Japanese attack on Pearl Harbor in 1941. The Pacific war, a later development in World War II, gave currency to this term. The defeat of Japan resulted in a greater military presence of the United States in the region. For a brief period, it must be remembered, Japan occupied many of the former European colonies, from Indochina to Indonesia. Subsequent to the defeat of Japan in the Pacific war, these colonies obtained their independence, and the United States emerged as the dominant power in the region. The involvement of the United States in both security matters and trade began to expand, and the wars in Korea and Vietnam served to bring large numbers of American citizens into the region. According to the historian James C. Hsiung, "The rise of multipolarity on the global level is to be repeated on the Asia Pacific regional level."[1]

The cold war, which soon extended to the Asia Pacific region, took the form of a U.S.-Soviet rivalry across the board—in the Korean Peninsula, in Indochina, over China, and, furthermore, over waters in the Pacific stretching all the way to the Indian Ocean. That the Soviet Pacific Fleet was the largest of the Soviet naval forces was perhaps a good indicator of the intensity of the U.S.-Soviet conflict in the Pacific. Equally, the United States's bilateral mutual security pacts with Japan, South Korea, the Republic of China (Taiwan), and the Philippines, along with ANZUS (the security pact encompassing Australia, New Zealand, and the United States), and SEATO (Southeast Asian Treaty Organization)—all of these were a measure of the cold war conflict. The identity of the Asia Pacific region was thus abetted by its emergence as a security community. Increased trade and other contacts among its members, which developed after the 1960s, further sharpened the region's identity.[2]

After the 1960s, a constellation of factors served to focus on the importance of the Asia Pacific region. From the mid-1960s onward, the Vietnam War had the effect of foregrounding this region in the imagination of the world. In addition, the period witnessed rapid and unprecedented growth of global market economies. Japan emerged as the dominant economy in the region, accounting for about half of the region's income. The emergence of Hong Kong, Singapore, Taiwan, and South Korea as countries with great trade and industrial strength served to intensify the attention paid to this region. These countries successfully launched new programs of economic structural transformations that resulted in the emergence of powerful export-driven economies. During the last two decades, countries such as Malaysia, Thailand, and Indonesia have also joined this "club." Hsiung argues that "by virtue of its phenomenal economic success and rapid growth rates, which are expected to continue well into the twenty-first century, Asia Pacific will stand out as the most crucial region for the United States in comparison with other groupings of nations."[3] Despite the economic collapse and woes of Asia Pacific nations such as Indonesia, Thailand, and Malaysia in 1998–99, geoeconomic interests in the region continue to remain significant.

The importance of this region, then, is undeniable. However, a mere description does not address some of the crucial problems, both conceptual and pragmatic, that beset this region. The very discursive production of the term "Pacific Rim" generates a number of problematic issues. As Arif Dirlik has pointed out, the relationships that give rise to the question of the "Pacific Rim" are neither coextensive with the entirety of the area connoted by that term nor necessarily restricted to that area delineated in physical terms. In the production of cultural discourse, there is no "Pacific Rim" that is an "objective" given. Rather, a competing set of ideational constructs projects upon that location on the globe the interest, power, and vision of these historically produced relationships, one of the most crucial being constituted through the Asia Pacific region's participation in a geoeconomic system in which capitalism is dominant. Dirlik notes:

> Capitalism has indeed become universal, based not only on the globalization of commodity exchange and financial transactions but, most importantly, on the transnationalization of production through a "new international development of labor." . . . Whereas earlier capitalist development led to the emergence of Europe as the core of a capitalist world economy, the contemporary transnationalization of capitalism, by creating nodes of capitalist development around the globe, has decentered capitalism, put an end to Euro-American domination of the world, and has abstracted capitalism for the first time from its Eurocentrism.[4]

Asia Pacific has risen to prominence in this "new economic configuration of the world . . . described as a 'global regionalism' or a 'global localism.'"[5]

The discursive dynamics of what might be better termed the "transnational Asia Pacific" region merit closer analysis. To treat the region as a geographical given, and to ignore the various forces that have traversed the terrain and the discourses that have served to invent the terrain, is to turn a blind eye to the issues central to the region. The region has to be understood in terms of colonialism, postcolonialism, multinational capitalism, globalization, the complex and multifaceted interplay between the Asia Pacific and the Euro-American Pacific, and their diverse and intersecting discursive productions. The "Pacific Rim" was not a pure success story, as some economists held prior to the 1998 economic collapse. Transnational Asia Pacific is not a unitary and cohesive entity either. The situation in the region is far more complex and subject to contradictory forces than such a characterization would posit. Questions of domination and subjugation, development and peripheralization, exploitation of labor, issues of gender, class and ethnicity, and cultural and ecological destruction must be examined to arrive at a more just estimate of the nature and significance of the region.

* * *

This volume focuses on an important aspect of contemporary globalization, namely, the complex ways in which cultural production is reconceptualized in a postnationally reconstructed world and in an era of transnational capitalism. We cannot conceptualize globalism as a homogenizing and universal force, nor can we consider localism as an endangered particular. At a superficial level, it may appear as though we are witnessing the rise of a homogenized global culture and a transnationalized discursivity. However, this newly emergent global culture is not a magnification of the culture of the nation-state. As evidenced by the essays in this volume, a complex dynamic operates at a number of different levels of social and cultural formation, giving rise to newer cultural postmodernities and discrepant cosmopolitanisms. The surprising ways in which transnational culture intersects with high-capitalist poetics as well as local rhetorics are as important as they are fascinating.

In exploring the discourse of localism and globalism, the essays in this volume critique simplistic binaries—for example, globalism as a totalizing force that undermines and eventually obliterates localism—to argue that localism and globalism are complicated and mutually constitutive. The production of locality is also largely a result of globalism. The central question here thus focuses on the imbrication of these two forces. Localism cannot be projected as a counterpoint to the global but is itself a significant dimension of globalization. Paradoxically, globalization has led to a strengthening of local ties, allegiances, and identity politics within different nation-state formations, even though what may emerge is a version of the local that has been thoroughly reshaped by the global and operates largely within its logic.[6]

The global/local dialectic has another important implication for the transnational Asia Pacific region. The imagined community of the nation-state that took shape in response to a felt need to create a coherent modern identity based on religion, patriotism, nationalistic symbols, and language is being rapidly undone by the onslaught of the heteroglossic interplay between the local and the global; and the once-accepted national metanarratives are increasingly subject to interrogation. Hence, as we discuss and explore the sites of cultural production in the transnational Asia Pacific, the linkages, fissures, disjunctures, and fractures brought about by the interface of the local and the global must be investigated.

Many of the gifted and sensitive writers from the transnational Asia Pacific region are deeply cognizant of this problematic. Their writings seek to come to terms with these newer historical conjunctures. The Hong Kong poet Leung Ping-kwan muses,

> How shall I translate into a moon of La Jolla
> Hong Kong's moon?
> Could one keep those concrete Tang images
> in another, a Western language,
> and not get lost without tenses and parts of speech,
> without settling all the time on syntax?
>> It's getting chilly
>> the leaves on the trees are red.
>> We stroll the streets
>> remembering friends in other places,
>> the sky darkening steadily,
>> hiding the natural images in Tang poems.
>
> Lighted before us are concrete, foreign names:
> Taco Bell,
> Jack-in-the-Box
> Safeway.
>> We walk on
>> all the chillier.
> Which are more frequent here
> the old Tang chrysanthemums or orchids?[7]

This poem, translated from the Chinese, voices the challenges facing writers in the transnational spaces of the Asia Pacific region as they try to negotiate the competing and contradictory logics of localism and globalism. The hybridity of the spaces traversed, the interpenetration of tradition and modernity, the diverse cultural values in play in the poem image the complex terrain that is the Asia Pacific region.

* * *

The concept of public sphere allows us to understand better the nature of cultural production in the transnational Asia Pacific region at the present historical conjuncture and to explore the ways in which cultural products make interventions into ongoing debates regarding culture, politics, and society. The pioneering work of Jürgen Habermas has resulted in widespread interest in the concept of the public sphere, which works to foreground issues of democratization, public participation, and oppositionality.[8] Habermas has delineated a set of forces and institutions that emerged in the late seventeenth and eighteenth centuries in Europe that he sees as vital to a comprehension of democratic discourse and the emergence of oppositionality. He terms this set of forces the "bourgeois public sphere," a discursive space that is distinct from the state and from civil society. Later commentators, such as Oskar Negt and Alexander Kluge, expand Habermas's concept of the public sphere by pointing out the power of mass media, such as cinema, as sites of contestation of meaning and as significant cultural practices.[9] Negt and Kluge probe the troubling question of the public in an increasingly technological-ly saturated public sphere where democratic self-realization and communi-ty participation are becoming more and more problematic. Kluge—himself a distinguished filmmaker—succeeds in calling attention to the distinctive nature of cinema in relation to the public sphere.

This notion of the public sphere as separate from state and civil society is central to the project of this volume. By investigating issues of gender, cul-tural identity, sites of resistance, and public negotiations of meaning, the essays gathered here focus on the vitally important public sphere in the trans-national Asia Pacific region. The contributors have sought to thematize and theorize the cultural dynamics of the region in its diversity of interests, strug-gles, and locations. Gender is very much at the heart of these dynamics. In exploring gender as particularities and specificities of historical, cultural, ethnic, and class situatedness, the contributors avoid essentializing the sub-jects of their study. Many of the chapters are interdisciplinary in approach and explore a number of significant subjects drawn from transnational Asia Pacific studies, ranging from food to music. The concept of the body as a symbolic construct that bears the diverse cultural inscriptions and interplay of power also figures prominently in this volume. Drawing on poststructur-al semiotics, these studies map social experience in the Asia Pacific nations. The conjunction of such diverse studies illustrates certain exciting theoreti-cal questions concerning the relation of gender to development, education, and culture that are being raised about this economically volatile region: the psychosocial and linguistic processes through which women's "selves" and roles are constructed, for example; or the ways in which historical and con-temporary state ideologies have responded to the stresses of modernization and the operations of global capitalism, as well as the consequences of these responses on the lives of men and women; and the role of popular culture and of mass media in the formation of "new" identities shaped within more conservative social communities.

Together, the chapters in this volume exhibit an exuberant plethora of rich-ly and differently nuanced, densely supported, and original studies on the major categories of culture, gender, class, and globalization as they inflect the sociopolitical phenomena emanating from Asia Pacific regions and countries. They offer individual, separate investigations on topics that concern schol-ars, citizens, and policymakers alike. In Asia Pacific territories such as Aus-tralia and Singapore, for example, movements are generally keyed to issues that possess global resonance and origins yet take on indigenous cultural shapes.

The essays concentrate first on gender features of the public sphere in transnational Asia Pacific societies, analyzing the interplay between the ideological and material as these forces are seen to operate economically and socially. At times the attempt to make sense of the processes of localization and globalization can result in cultural and linguistic resistance that foregrounds the intersection of body, space, and identity. The first three chapters, examining very different topics—third-world factory labor, Filipina mail-order brides, and prostitution—argue that women's bodies form the transnational site for political struggle. More than floating signifiers, women's bodies, historically and plangently in the development issues that have risen in these Asia Pacific countries, are materially contested "objects" and subjects.

In his rigorously argued opening chapter, Pheng Cheah suggests that human rights discourse, as it is deployed in Asia Pacific international relations, takes place as a "performative contradiction." More important, he argues, its "contaminated normativity" further suggests that global capitalism is not a totality, as most economists would have us believe, but "a sheaf of differential processes" and that the positive effects of human rights arise at just these unpredictable moments when the totalizing structure of global capitalism is opened by particularistic forces. Rolando B. Tolentino examines the geopolitics of Filipina bodies inscribed in transnational space. His essay focuses on the problem of the mail-order bride phenomenon as a social and political practice, placing the problem in a historical context and within a politics of location: "How and why women are here or there instead of elsewhere; . . . why place and placelessness are vital issues for women who choose to be relocated outside the national space." Lynn Thiesmeyer's chapter on the West's "comfort women" analyzes the ways in which Western discourses on the sex trade in Asian countries erases the active role played by Western interests in such abuse. Placing the United States as an Asia Pacific territory, Thiesmeyer's analysis of the gaps in Western media and political and governmental resolutions that offer a rhetoric of liberation while evading responsibility for the traffic of bodies points to a larger theme, namely, the imbalance of power between colonial power and colonized body.

This volume also focuses on the politics of representations of gender as well as on the politics of the gendered body. The later chapters illustrate this hypernuancing of social and identity categories that a globally circulating, mass, techno-, and popular culture requires.[10] In Asia Pacific territories such as Hawaii and Singapore, for example, movements manifest global and indigenous cultural origins and forms. Rob Wilson acutely contrasts the hegemonizing global imagination at work in popular Hollywood films such as *South Pacific* and *Blue Hawaii* with the "oppositional regionalism" that is constructed in cultural texts produced by indigenous and local writers. C. J. W.-L. Wee's chapter on the Singapore-based pop singer Dick Lee demonstrates how national and subgroup resistances to Western-style modernity are set up at the same time assimilation to globalized technoculture is occurring. Treating the ways in which the Japanese language and its symbolic representations are inflected by structures of gender domination and subordination, Fukuko Kobayashi clarifies the ways in which the Japanese gender system is constituted as a "cultural construction," resulting in the maintenance of stereotypes that "unwittingly participate in the oppression of Japanese women."

In the penultimate chapter, Sneja Gunew offers a fascinating entry into the study of writing by ethnic minorities in Australia. Investigating the popularity of the "multicultural food festival" in Australian ethnic literature, Gunew argues that it provides "an accurate metaphoric and metonymic delineation of the ideology at the heart of postwar migration in Australia and the various attempts to manage it." Finally, Susan Fulop Kepner offers a comprehensive survey and analysis of Thai women's writing that focuses on the challenges of representing the sexual body facing Thai women authors writing from a rigidly conventional and moral society. In this chapter and throughout the volume the authors' crossnational, transcultural perspectives draw richly upon national cultural materials while remaining sensitive to the complex cultural-embeddedness of their subjects.

Notes

1. James C. Hsiung, "Asia Pacific in the Post–Cold War Order," in *Asia Pacific in the New World of Politics*, ed. James C. Hsiung (Boulder, Colo.: Lynn Rienner Publishers, 1993), 6.

2. See ibid., 1–20.

3. Ibid., 8.

4. Arif Dirlik, *After the Revolution: Waking to Global Capitalism* (Hanover, N.H.: Wesleyan University Press, 1994), 62.

5. Ibid., 63.

6. Stuart Hall writes: "One of the things that happens when the nation-state begins to weaken, becoming less convincing and less powerful, is that the response seems to go in two ways simultaneously. It goes above the nation-state, and it goes below it. It goes global and local in the same moment. Global and local are the two faces of the same movement from one epoch of globalization, the one that has been dominated by the nation-state, the national economies, the national-cultural identities, to something new" ("The Local and the Global: Globalization and Ethnicity," in *Dangerous Liaisons: Gender, Nation, and Postcolonial Perspectives*, ed. Anne McClintock, Aamir Mufti, and Ella Shohat [Minneapolis: University of Minnesota Press, 1997], 178).

7. Ping-kwan Leung, *City of the End of Time* (Hong Kong: University of Hong Kong Comparative Literature Department, 1992), 127.

8. Jürgen Habermas, *The Structural Transformation of the Public Sphere: An Inquiry into a Category of Bourgeois Society* (Cambridge, Mass.: MIT Press, 1989).

9. Oskar Negt and Alexander Kluge, *Public Sphere and Experience: Toward an Analysis of the Bourgeois and Proletarian Public Sphere* (Minneapolis: University of Minnesota Press, 1993).

10. See the discussions on related topics in Armand Mattelart, *Transnationals and the Third World: The Struggle for Culture,* trans. David Buxton (South Hadley, Mass.: Bergen and Garvey, 1983); Arjun Appadurai, "Disjuncture and Difference in the Global Cultural Economy," *Public Culture* 2 (1990): 1–24; Immanuel Wallerstein, *Geopolitics and Geoculture: Essays on the Changing World System* (Cambridge: Cambridge University Press, 1991); Inderpal Grewal and Caren Kaplan, eds., *Scattered Hegemonies: Postmodernity and Transnational Feminist Practices* (Minneapolis: University of Minnesota Press, 1994).

1. Posit(ion)ing Human Rights in the Current Global Conjuncture

Pheng Cheah

IN THE CURRENT CONJUNCTURE of global capitalism, the deployment of human rights discourse by various key actors on the stage of Asia Pacific international relations takes the general form of a performative contradiction. Existing human rights discourses claim a normative force that is unconditional. Yet within the international frame of their invocation, these practical claims become radically contaminated and stretch the theories of normativity that have so far governed our understanding of human rights to the point where they become untenable. Does the contaminated normativity of human rights necessarily lead to nihilism, cynical pragmatism, or relativism? Or can normativity be unconditional and contaminated at the same time? In this essay, I suggest that the theoretical significance of the internationalization of human rights—the work that it does in the house of theory—is that it enjoins us to think of normativity as a response/responsibility to original contamination.

Orientations

Human rights are a crucial part of politics and international relations, of ethical and political philosophy and law, and even of comparative history and anthropology if we are concerned with the cultural or historical origins of the concept. Several preliminary clarifications are therefore necessary to orient the reader to my approach in this essay. The debate over human rights in international relations should be wrenched away from the common but mistaken approach that juxtaposes the plurality of cultures with the universal validity that makes human rights normative. Such a view suggests that if human rights are inalienable entitlements that should belong to all individ-

uals for the sole reason that they are human, then irresolvable tensions inevitably arise from the fact that individuals also exist as members of a plurality of collectives called "cultures," which have their own unique norms and
rules. Such an argument can function to expose universalizing modes of
thought as cultural forms of imperialism that serve the interests of a hegemonic culture. Thus, unwittingly or consciously, critiques of the ideological
abuse of the doctrine of universal human rights show the influence of the
early Karl Marx's early critique of the formalism of bourgeois civil rights.[1]
They argue that the *Universal Declaration of Human Rights* (1948) sets forth
a vision of rights that "reveal[s] a strong Western bias" and regards "human
rights ahistorically and in isolation from their social, political and economic milieu."[2] Phrased even more sharply, the Universal Declaration qua doctrinal basis for the U.S. government's drive for international human rights
is denounced as a mask for realpolitik because it incorporates "all human
beings across nations and cultures into an abstract universal community of
which the U.S. government is the champion."[3]

This is also the view of many Asian governmental actors in contemporary
global politics. For instance, in his statement at the Vienna World Conference
on Human Rights entitled "The Real World of Human Rights," the foreign
minister of Singapore argued that "the extent and exercise of rights . . . varies
greatly from one culture or political community to another . . . because [rights]
are the products of the historical experiences of particular peoples."[4] He cautioned against a harmful universalism, an artificially imposed and stifling una-
nimity that "is used to deny or mask the reality of diversity." This staged resistance to Northern or Western imperialism is representative of the position of
Asian states on human rights (see the Bangkok Declaration adopted by ministers and representatives of Asian states). The ostensible opposition between
universalism and cultural relativism expressed here is also the insular focus of
the greater part of cultural studies and postcolonial discourse analysis.

We would, however, be wrong to interpret this scene in terms of the ster-
ile opposition between universalism and cultural relativism for at least two
reasons. First, the critique of the historical limits of the Western concept
of human rights is also a universalistic argument because it remains within a human rights framework. The concept of human rights is by no means
monolithic since it includes first-, second-, and third-generation rights.[5]
The Asian governmental position about the cultural limits of the Western
vision of human rights is invariably linked to an argument about the need
to subordinate political and civil rights to the right to development. As such,
it depends on an assertion of the universal right to self-determination of
all peoples. Second, the claim to cultural difference by Asian states is itself
questionable since the figured face of statist cultural difference is not identical to the cultural diversity of its peoples. The very governments that claim

to be the custodians of Southeast Asian cultures are responsible for the destruction of the cultures of indigenous peoples who stand in the way of the deforestation and mining projects of state-supported capitalist development. Therefore, the question should not be whether universal human rights exist. Instead, we should focus on the nature and limits of the normative claims being made by various actors—northern and southern states and nongovernment organizations (NGOs)—when they appeal to human rights within the theoretical framework of established human rights discourse.

A third reason makes the attempt to move beyond universalism versus cultural relativism particularly important. We are currently witnessing the spectacular economic growth of the Asia Pacific region and the rise of the so-called East Asian paths of development as competing models of global capitalism.[6] Some Asian conglomerates are outperforming U.S. and European multinationals in private sector investment in the Asia Pacific region.[7] The message in the business pages of the *New York Times* is that U.S. companies should "plug themselves into local conditions" by "finding the right partner, someone to guide you through the maze of Asia,"[8] much like Ariadne guided Theseus. (But then we know what befell Ariadne after she served her purpose.) After the correct moans and groans have been made about East Timor, the Clinton administration is wooing President Suharto of Indonesia to support market-opening progress at the 1995 Asia-Pacific Economic Co-operation (APEC) meeting in Osaka: "'He's our kind of guy,' a senior Administration official who deals often on Asian policy, said. . . . 'this is the kind of relationship we want to have with China.'"[9] This oddly conjugal vocabulary indicates that what is at stake in the elaborately media-staged skirmishes between states over international human rights is not really Western or Northern imperializing universalism versus Eastern or Southern cultural difference. The two poles of that binary opposition are complicitous. The fight is between different globalizing models of capitalist development attempting to assert economic hegemony.[10] The coding of this fight in terms of cultural difference diverts our attention from the subtending line of force of global capital that brings the two antagonists into an aporetic embrace *against* the possibility of other alternatives of development, feminist or ecological-subalternist. Hence, any analysis of the normative claims of appeals to human rights within established discourse ought to ask: What do we mean when we posit human rights? How are these various positings positioned in or by the current global conjuncture?

As I argue in the concluding section, the irreducible imbrication of all claims to human rights within the force field of global capitalism requires us to rethink the theory of normativity that is the basis of existing human rights discourse. Here, let me offer a schematic working definition of "normativity" for the nonspecialist reader. Simply put, normativity is that which confers the status of norm upon a maxim of action or a desired state of affairs. It is the being-normative of norms, that which makes a norm normative. Thus, normativity is the quality that makes us regard ourselves as obligated to bring about a certain state of things or as being bound—etymologically speaking, obligation derives from ligature—by an imperative commanding or restraining a certain course of action.

In contemporary Western thought, there are different criteria for the rational determination of different sources of normativity, just as there are different types of normativity. The common analytical distinctions are between legal, ethical, and moral normativity. According to legal positivism (the dominant position in analytical jurisprudence), a specific rule is legally normative or valid if it conforms to an internalized, rationally accepted set of social standards that operates within a territorial political community.[11] Such conformity makes the rule a rule of law because its enforcement by coercive mechanisms will be upheld by popular social sanction. However, as morally evil laws (such as Nazi laws) illustrate, legal normativity is distinguishable from ethical and moral normativity because it is concerned with the day-to-day operations of a legal system. It is not concerned with the moral value of that system beyond the minimum content of natural law that is fundamental to the social life of a particular political community (e.g., some prohibition of killing, provision of basic resources, and protection of property).[12]

By contrast, the normativity of morality (*Moralität*) is unconditional. After Kant, a maxim is said to possess moral force, to be morally binding, only if it is universally valid for all rational creatures or humanity in general. But as Hegel astutely points out in his critique of Kant, the problem with the unconditional, atemporal, "pure" normativity characterizing morality is twofold. First, because it is articulated at such an abstract level of universality, the moral law is deprived of all determinate objective content. Furthermore, the abstraction "humanity," the collective carrier and agent of morality's norms, cannot be politically effective because it is not embodied in a sociocultural, institutional context in which meaningful action can take place. (Thus, for Hegel, morality risks degenerating into the bad infinity of destructive absolute subjectivism, typified by the terror of the French Revolution.) The third type of normativity—ethical normativity—can be seen as a bridge that mediates between mere legality and abstract universal morality. As distinguished from morality, ethical normativity (*Sittlichkeit*) refers to binding substantive forms of ethical self-understanding that are arrived at through consensual procedures of law enactment and political decision making. Thus, at the same time the procedural consensus of their articulation (procedural justice) reflects universal rationality, ethical norms also express and give objective embodiment to the concrete life of a political community, thereby reconciling the universal and the particular. The ethical realm has also been characterized as the political morality of the state or its (national) public sphere (*Öffentlichkeit*).[13] It is the site where morality can exert an influence over the political and legal processes of the state. The important point to note, however, is that, notwithstanding their differences, these three types of normativity all compute normativity in terms of *rational* obligation. Legality, morality, and ethical life are respectively determined by and express legal-political rationality, universal reason, and the ethical self-understanding of the national political community. Indeed, legality, morality, and ethics are interrelated and form a continuum only because they share this rationalist determination of normativity.

This working taxonomy of normativity helps us position international human rights practical discourse more exactly. The anomalous status of international human rights is well known. On the one hand, international human rights instruments are regarded as part of public international law.[14] They are commonly invoked to justify humanitarian intervention in areas under the jurisdiction of sovereign states on the grounds of illegality under the provisions of international treaties. Thus, their normativity would appear to be legal in nature. "Public international law" is, however, a misnomer. Within the current interstate system, nation-states largely retain their sovereignty. In the absence of a supranational executive body capable of enforcing decisions independently of the compliance of individual nation-states, public international law cannot be law in the strict sense. On the other hand, to the extent that humanitarian interventions also invoke the universality of human rights, they might be seen as examples of moral normativity. Yet, unlike moral claims, human rights claims have a normative force which is institutionally grounded. Since these claims are codified in the U.N. Charter and other international covenants and resolutions, human rights claimants can rightfully expect to rely on the limited policing mechanisms that are available to ensure that the claimed rights are being observed. Consequently, it may be more appropriate to regard international human rights practical discourse as expressing a kind of political morality on an international scale.[15] Indeed, transnational human rights NGO networks regard themselves as forming an international public sphere. Primarily deriving its normative force from quasi-formal codifications that center around and elaborate the Kantian principle of moral respect for humanity, such an emergent transnational *Sittlichkeit,* or ethical community, would seek to influence the actions of particular states.

We see from this that theories of political morality in classical German philosophy are far from obsolete. They have become institutionalized and continue to exert a tenacious influence through the operational logics of states and other collective actors. As I later suggest, Asian states that assert sovereignty in defense against foreign intervention over human rights issues take a position that is not unlike Hegel's communitarian critique of Kant's notion of cosmopolitan right. The claim that transnational human rights networks constitute an international public sphere should therefore be understood as a response to a Hegelian communitarian critique of neo-Kantian human rights talk. Yet these philosophies of normativity also find themselves deformed in their historical performance in contemporary globalization. I suggest that arguments about the existence of an international public sphere or transnational political morality are implausible because they are grounded in a rationalist conception of normativity that the actually existing capitalist world-system renders untenable. But against neo-Hegelian statism I also argue that international human rights have a very real normative force and do not merely take "the form of an ought-to-be."[16] The question, then, is how to think about this normative force, how to philosophize otherwise.

One final clarification on the genre of this essay. The preferred mode of philosophical discourse on human rights is deontological. But formal philosophizing inevitably ends up confirming the rationalist determination of normativity that we ought to question because it presupposes ideal rational actors. Hence, I have chosen to approach the philosophical question of normativity by way of a sociohistorical analysis of the human rights practices of finite institutional actors within the text of global capitalism. It should be clear, however, that I am not suggesting that human rights practical discourse in global capitalism is bereft of any normative element. That would be a lapse into sociological determinism and historicist relativism. My wager is that normativity should be thought of as being outside both historicist relativism and rationalist-teleological conceptions of history.

The Three Voices of Existing Human Rights Practical Discourse and Their Philosophical Basis

Existing human rights practical discourse can be divided into three voices: what I call the first voice is the position of governments in constitutional democracies in the economically hegemonic North or West; the second voice refers to the position of Asian governments; and the third voice refers to the position of human rights NGOs in the South. My taxonomy is meant to be heuristic, and its immediate frame of reference is the assertion of cultural difference by Asian governments in response to charges of human rights violations in Asia Pacific international relations. I have not considered the position of former Eastern bloc countries in a post–cold war scenario, although it is arguable that they have been assimilated into the South. My concern here is with the universal validity of human rights in general, the normative force claimed by the three voices of human rights. This is not quite the same as the validity of specific human rights. The latter refers to the determinate negative or positive rights laid out in conventions, covenants, or declarations; the former refers to something more primary and more difficult to determine, namely, the right to human rights. Obviously, any articulation of why the constitution of humans gives them a right to rights will influence the specific rights that flow from this universal entitlement. But the crucial point is that unlike specific rights, which can be challenged, the right to rights is not contestable because it has no specific historical, political, or cultural content.

Indeed, if the United States prides itself on having contributed the most famous articulation and justification of the idea of rights to international human rights discourse—that is, the justification of rights by natural law in the Preamble to the Declaration of Independence[17]—the eminent human rights scholar Louis Henkin points out that universal human rights instruments reflect no particular political philosophy: "International human rights instruments do not affirm rights as 'natural.' They do not necessarily assume that a person is originally, or in principle, autonomous, that rights antecede society and government. . . . As justification for human rights, they simply assert truths—or rhetoric—that no one has bothered to question. Rights derive from the 'inherent dignity of the human person.'"[18] The phrase "dignity of the human person" comes from the Preamble and Article 1 of the Universal Declaration of Human Rights. The Preamble begins with the statement that the recognition of "the inherent dignity and of the equal and inalienable rights of all members of the human family is the foundation of freedom, justice and peace in the world." Article 1 elaborates this inherent dignity in terms of an anthropological thesis: "all humans are born free and equal in dignity and rights. They are endowed with reason and conscience and should act towards one another in the spirit of brotherhood."

The minimal philosophical justification of the human entitlement to rights in these sections of the Universal Declaration seems to be as follows: humans are born with an inherent dignity. This is, however, not a natural justification of human rights. Since rights only come into existence via political instruments that specify and protect them, dignity by itself is not the source for rights. Rather, dignity is some contentless human attribute that is the basis of freedom in the world. The second sentence of Article 1 introduces "reason" and "conscience" for the first time. The terms "dignity," "freedom," and "reason" are related as follows: because dignity is contentless, it involves a practical orientation. Reason is the operator of normative human action (because humans "are endowed with reason and conscience," they "should act") that protects and fleshes out dignity by specifying determinate rights via political instruments. Precisely because dignity is contentless, the work of reason is open-ended and interminable, and this links reason to freedom. Freedom is the ideal state of being unconstrained, and reason co-belongs with freedom because it is the persistent ability to question and transform the external situations in which we find ourselves. In other words, human rights are the enterprise by which reason persistently affirms human dignity. We are entitled to them because we are born with dignity but, more important, because we possess the rational capacity needed to reaffirm dignity. The open-ended nature of the human rights enterprise[19] is expressed in the exhortatory nature of the Universal Declaration, which involves a pledge by all signing nations to achieve a nonexhaustive common standard. Apparently, this open-endedness is also reflected in the subsequent increase in human rights instruments and in ongoing debates about different views of human rights.

I have suggested that the normative force of human rights belongs to the realm of political morality rather than morality per se. However, the axioms of political morality are derived from morality. Thus, whether self-consciously or by historical osmosis, the philosophical justification of human rights found in the Universal Declaration is indebted to Kant's canonical definition of the dignity of humans in his second formulation of the categorical imperative. Seeking a law for moral action that would be universally valid for all rational creatures, Kant resorts to the postulate of human dignity as something that is an end in itself. For Kant, inclinations can only have a conditional or relative validity. The object of an inclination merely constitutes a subjective end because it appeals to sensuous desire. By contrast, dignity is an objective end because it is of absolute or intrinsic worth. As such, dignity can serve as a universal law for moral action.

> Now, I say, man, and in general, every rational being exists as an end in himself and not merely as a means to be arbitrarily used by this or that will. . . . All objects of inclinations have only a conditional worth. . . . Therefore the worth of any objects to be obtained by our actions is at all times only conditional. Beings whose existence does not depend on our will but on nature, if they are not rational beings, have only a relative worth as means and are therefore called "things"; on the other hand, rational beings are designated "persons" because their nature indicates that they are ends in themselves. . . . Such an end is one for which no other end can be substituted, to which these beings should merely serve as means. For without them, nothing of absolute worth could be found, and if all worth is conditional and thus contingent, no supreme practical principle for reason could be found anywhere.[20]

What is interesting for us is that Kant proceeds to distinguish between dignity qua end-in-itself and merely subjective ends by means of a mercantile metaphor, even though, technically speaking, what is being discussed—human practical action—is ontologically prior to historical commerce because it is the "rationality" behind historical commerce, trading, or commodification. In the realm of ends constituted by human action, Kant writes, everything has either a *price* or a *dignity.* Whatever has a price can be replaced by something else as its equivalent; on the other hand, whatever is above all price, and therefore admits no equivalent, has a dignity.

That which is related to general human inclinations and needs has a *market price.* . . . But that which constitutes the condition under which alone something can be an end in itself does not have mere relative worth, i.e., a price, but an intrinsic worth, i.e., *dignity.*[21]

Simply put, dignity transcends all relative values, all exchange, all equivalence and has no market price.

Although narrower in scope than Kant's universal moral law, the philosophical justification of the right to human rights inherits these axiomatic oppositions between absolute worth and relative worth, dignity and market price, and the philosophical baggage that goes with them. We will later see that human rights discourse literalizes the quasi-metaphorical opposition between dignity and market price. The important point here is that as a result of this Kantian legacy, "dignity" in the Universal Declaration is not identical to the civil and political liberties invoked by the United States when it accuses Singapore or China of violating human rights. Dignity subtends every specific human right but is not reducible to any specific right because it is its philosophical ground. The concept of dignity refers to nothing less than the peculiar nature of human nature qua rational nature to be free of natural or arbitrary human constraint, the leitmotif of philosophical modernity. This means that all visions of specific human rights are open to contestation if they are found to obstruct the affirmation of dignity.

This separation of dignity from specific rights indicates that the official Asian position on human rights set out in the Bangkok Declaration and the individual statements by Asian ministers at the Vienna Conference do not depart from the normative framework of established human rights discourse. The universality of human rights derives from the shared condition of being human, that is, being endowed with dignity and reason. Dignity and reason make up the ground for both the civil and political liberties associated with Western constitutional democracies as well as the questioning of this vision of human rights by Asian governments as myopic and narrow because it does not live up to the spirit of international cooperation specified in the U.N. Charter and fails to take into consideration the economic problems and cultural specificity of Asian societies. There is thus a tacit agreement by both sides that there is some positive thing called "human dignity" that must be affirmed and protected even if there is disagreement about the best way to protect it. For instance, the official Singapore position is that "poverty makes a mockery of all civil liberties," that "economic growth is the necessary foundation of any system that claims to advance human dignity," that "order and stability are essential for development," and, hence, that "good government is necessary for the realisation of all rights."[22] Even the additional claim to cultural diversity of nations is not, on its face, cultural relativist since Article 29(1) of the Universal Declaration stipulates that "everyone has duties to the community in which alone the free and full development of his personality is possible."

Indeed, the official Asian position or second voice would seem eminently reasonable in its emphasis that "the promotion of human rights should be encouraged by co-operation and consensus, and not through confrontation and the imposition of incompatible values."[23] Not entirely without justification, Asian governments accuse Northern governments of double standards and of using a limited vision of human rights as a power ploy to sabotage the economic success of East Asia. Emphasizing "the interdependence and indivisibility of economic, social, cultural, civil and political rights,"[24] they claim to be the voice of reason. They seek to resist intervention by Northern governments over human rights issues by reaffirming the principles of respect for national sovereignty and territorial integrity.

Asian governments therefore argue that communitarian values and national-territorial integrity are necessary conditions for the concrete maximization of human dignity. Thus, where the first voice is isomorphic with neo-Kantianism, one might see the second voice as more or less expressing a version of Hegel's statist-communitarian critique of Kantian moral politics. For Hegel, morality is merely universal reason in its subjective and abstract form. The nation-state is universal reason in its objective actuality: "The nation state is spirit [*Geist*] in its substantive rationality and immediate actuality and is therefore the absolute power on earth. It follows that every state is sovereign and autonomous against its neighbours. . . . The ethical substance, the state, has its determinate being, i.e., its right, directly embodied in something existent, something not abstract but concrete, and *the principle of its conduct can only be this concrete existent and not one of the many universal thoughts supposed to be moral commands.*"[25] Consequently, Hegel argues that Kant's idea of a world confederation of states, the historical model for the United Nations qua human rights enforcer, could never be fully actualized. Resting "on moral or religious . . . grounds and considerations, . . . [a League of Nations] would always depend ultimately on a particular sovereign will and for that reason would always remain infected with contingency."[26] Likewise, Asian governments counterpose the concrete or actual universality of the national political community against the false abstraction of "humanity" that Northern governments arrogantly deploy. Singapore's statement at the Vienna Convention is entitled "The Real World of Human Rights."

Let us now consider how the third voice circumvents this statist-communitarian argument that the sovereign nation-state alone is the concrete embodiment of universality. In a formal response to the Bangkok Declaration, human rights NGOs in the Asia Pacific region have distanced themselves from both official positions. Like the second voice, the third voice also advocates a holistic and integrated approach to human rights and affirms the right to self-determination of all peoples. However, it deploys these claims against Asian governments that violate human rights. In summary, the third voice stresses that a holistic approach to human rights means that one set of rights cannot be used to bargain for another. It asserts that all governments must observe the right of peoples to freely determine their political status and pursue their economic, social, and cultural development, and it specifically mentions indigenous groups within Asia Pacific nations who are denied the right to self-determination because they have not been recognized by their governments. But what distinguishes the third voice of human rights discourse from the first voice is its attribution of the poor state of human rights to the existing international economic order. These NGOs connect domestic oppression to international exploitation by pointing to the collaboration among local elites, multinationals, and international aid agencies. They reject the capital-intensive and inherently wasteful statist view of development and argue for a more humane, "balanced and sustainable development" that maximizes the social development of the people.[27]

The heterogeneity of this third voice is most evident, of course, in the feminist claim that the international human rights movement reiterates conceptual biases in focusing on the public realm as the primary site of human rights violation.[28] Feminist NGOs have asserted the need to consider all violence against women as human rights issues, regardless of the public or private status of the perpetrator. They have proposed a more flexible theory of culture as an antidote to the abuse of women in patriarchalized national culture.[29] They have also criticized statist development for the additional reason that growth policy–oriented models of development are incompatible with the rights of women in development because the former seeks to integrate women into state-centric plans of economic growth instead of addressing the systemic economic, political, and ideological biases against women.[30] In sum, this third voice envisions a new universalism that is mindful of systemic economic inequality, genuine cultural diversity, and gender. It does not regard the advocacy of human rights as an encroachment upon national sovereignty. Indeed, it claims an entitlement to international solidarity that transcends the national border to protect human rights worldwide.[31]

Notwithstanding the immense doctrinal differences among them, all three voices share the same normative framework. All existing human rights practical discourses are grounded in the Kantian notion of moral respect for dignity as an end in itself and something of absolute worth. Thus, they all exhibit three key characteristics. First, because the point of departure is the concept of human dignity as the supreme value that transcends all material interests or empirical inclinations, each vision of human rights is seen to be separate from the realm of particularistic political or economic interests. Each of the three voices within existing human rights practical discourse discredits its opponent by pointing out that the opponent's vision of human rights is in fact contaminated by its particular site of emergence, that it is an ideological mask for some insidious particularistic interest: Northern domination or global capitalism in the case of the first voice; industrializing Oriental despotism or statist-capitalist development in the case of the second voice. Each of the three voices claims to be the pure voice of reason representing genuine universality in which respect for human dignity can be maximized: the autonomous individual (the first voice); a community of nations that respects cultural differences and the right to development (the second voice); and a polymorphous global community within an equitable international economic order that is genuinely sensitive to sexual difference and cultural diversity (the third voice). Second, this separation of genuine universality from particularistic interests in turn implies a distinction between material reality and rational form. Here, practical primacy is accorded to rational form. It is presumed that a holistic system of rights in which human dignity is respected embodies a total rational form for the ordering of social and collective interaction among individuals and states and interstate relations. Respect for dignity also involves a practical injunction for the persistent rational transformation of existing institutional structures. Through the act of respect, the enjoined agents are elevated beyond their particularistic interests into rational universality, simultaneously (trans)forming themselves and their world according to a moral image prescribed by reason alone.

The third characteristic shared by the three voices is that each believes that through the prescription of rational form critique is able to change institutional structures that oppress or fail to foster human dignity. A lot of faith is placed in both the neutrality and paramount effectivity of the good conscience/reason of various institutional actors, that is, the political morality of states in the act of interpreting the appropriate rights or restrictions necessary in a given situation or international public opinion as the moral conscience keeping state authoritarianism in check and guiding state policy toward sustainable development.[32] As the Kantian scholar Dieter Henrich succinctly notes, such a theory of normativity views the world as a field that is bereft of norms. The world is not itself a source of norms but instead a field to be shaped by norms that only *rational* human agents can bring into play. Any positing of human rights within the existing framework of human rights discourse tacitly presupposes the negotiation between an ideal world image and the existing world situation onto which that rational world image is prescribed and which will accept that world image as universally valid. In other words, what is envisioned is an ideal or rational universality that is anterior to historical human interaction but must be flexible enough to accommodate the diversity and singularity of its global constituent actors in order to be realized as a concrete universality.[33]

This theoretical framework easily leads to a proceduralist account of normativity that models international relations in the image of constitutional-democratic procedures that are accorded quasi-transcendental status. In progressive literature on the topic, many argue for a multilateral international forum in a shrinking world of information command and borderless economies. The third voice of human rights, the international network of human rights NGOs, has been represented and has represented itself as a transnational political morality, or *Sittlichkeit*. Effectively, these claims about the existence of a global civil society or an international public sphere in which peoples' right to self-determination is respected imply that the discrepancy between communitarian and neo-Kantian rational images of the world is in the process of being historically eliminated.

Global Capitalism as a Case of Original Contamination

Human rights NGO networks may dream of living in an undivided but also diverse world. However, the essential problem with the normative framework of human rights practical discourse is that it cannot consider the original contamination of the three voices by virtue of their constitutive inscription within the force field of global capital. In the existing framework, different visions of human rights are explained in terms of a progression toward a more encompassing totality. Each successive voice criticizes the preceding vision for being contaminated by particularistic interests and sees its vision of human rights as subsuming and transcending (*aufheben*—to destroy and preserve at the same time) the preceding vision. This drive toward self-purification—or, which amounts to the same thing, this denial of inscription, of being part of an uncontrollable network of forces—is another manifestation of the notion of pure human dignity that exists outside equivalence, exchange, and market price. To reiterate, because dignity is contentless, it can only be given content by rational action. The open-ended nature of the human rights project is said to reside in the power of reason to take into account changing world contexts in its articulation of a moral world image. In the first and last instance, this rational world image is anterior to politics and economics, although it must subsume them in its concrete realization. This is, of course, a literalization of the Kantian quasi-metaphorical opposition between dignity and market price. Each voice of human rights discourse claims to be the pure voice of reason representing genuine universality and to serve as an external check to particularistic interests and material forces.

But what if the globalization of capital is uncontainable? What if it establishes a de facto and oppressive universality that cannot be transcended by normative action? What if, despite all claims to the contrary, normative institutional action finds itself reinscribed within a weave that includes the very particularistic material forces it seeks to transcend or check precisely because it is generated by this weave of forces? More specifically, if the three voices of human rights are complicit or cannot differentiate/extricate themselves from each other by virtue of their constitutive imbrication in global capital, then their original contamination means that the normativity of human rights can no longer be thought of in terms of an ideal universal form grounded in the co-belonging of pure human dignity and reason. We would then need to rethink normativity otherwise, from the ground up.

The contamination of the first voice by global capital is obvious enough. For instance, when the United States conceptually relates human rights issues to trade negotiations by presupposing that human rights and commercial/industrial growth are causally dependent,[34] this link means that the latter can sometimes override the former as a result of lobbying by relevant business groups. Furthermore, the first voice can also indirectly serve Northern economic hegemony. It can cover up the scandalous open secret that the resource-intensive and inherently wasteful macropolicies of economic development and market economy–led linear models espoused by international development agencies and financial institutions like the World Bank and the International Monetary Fund force some Southern countries deeper and deeper into debt, thereby maintaining an unjust international economic order that is controlled by a handful of elites, corporations, and Northern states. In the current conjuncture, these Bretton Woods institutions are inadequate to prevent the erosion of the technological and economic bases of power of the Group of Seven nations in the face of East Asian economic success. Thus, the General Agreement on Tariffs and Trade (GATT) negotiations from the Uruguay round onward have attempted to reorganize global production and production capacities by enlarging intellectual property protection in other countries. This is a "neo-mercantilist" attempt[35] to destroy the emergence of competition elsewhere. By restricting access to key technologies via multilateral agreements and by pursuing aggressive policies to open up foreign markets in Asian and Latin American newly industrializing economies (NIEs) via export promotion and reciprocal market access, industrialized countries seek to retard industrial development in the South and expand the space and freedom of transnational corporations (TNCs) at the same time. They seek to produce a global division between knowledge-rich and knowledge-poor countries, recolonizing the latter by permanently blocking them from acquiring the knowledge and capacity to accumulate wealth. It is, of course, not nice to steal the ideas of others, especially when these ideas can lead to great profits. But no Northern government is suggesting that the wealth accumulated by Northern countries after centuries of colonial and imperialist theft be returned to Southern countries.

Indeed, the global expansion of intellectual property protection can also be a legalized form of late capitalist theft. As Vandana Shiva points out, international patent and licensing agreements facilitate a new era of bio-imperialism since they are used by pharmaceutical companies and agribusiness in the North to monopolize the genetic resources of biological diversity in the Third World that can be developed into drugs, food, and energy sources.

> The U.S. has accused countries of the Third World as engaging in "unfair trading practice" if they fail to adopt U.S. patent laws which allow monopoly rights in life forms. Yet it is the U.S. which has engaged in unfair practices related to the use of Third World genetic resources. It has freely taken the biological diversity of the Third World to spin millions of dollars of profits, none of which have been shared with Third World countries, the original owners of the germ plasm.[36]

> With worldwide patent protection, agribusiness and the seed trade are trying to achieve truly global reach. While the rhetoric is agricultural development in the Third World, the enforcement of strong patent protection for monopoly ownership of life processes will undermine and underdevelop agriculture in the Third World in a number of ways. . . . Patent protection displaces the farmer as a competitor, transforms him into a supplier of free raw material, and makes him totally dependent on industrial supplies for vital inputs like seeds. Above all, the frantic cry for patent protection in agriculture is for protection from farmers, who are the original breeders and developers of biological resources in agriculture. It is argued that patent protection is essential for innovation— however it is essential only for the innovation that brings profits to corporate businesses.[37]

The negative consequences of globalizing/universalizing intellectual property protection should therefore be seen in a continuum with the curious homology between the first voice's use of human rights universalism to justify encroachments upon the national sovereignty of the developing South and the attempt of industrialized countries to increase the freedom of TNCs from regulation by host governments. Political freedom and the liberalization/freeing of trade go hand in hand. The former secures assent for the globalizing of market mechanisms and the continuing fiscalization of the globe. Needless to say, the global spread of free market mechanisms cannot lead to generalized development. It only exacerbates world polarization and leads, in some cases, to the formation of comprador states that subordinate development to the requirements of transnational capitalism and adjust their economies to global restructuring. The compradorized state is no longer capable of actively shaping its own society and political morality. This handicapping of democratic national projects in the periphery from the start gives the lie to the neoliberal sermon that the global spread of free market mechanisms will lead to global democratization.

Now, the inequality of North-South relations is partly responsible for a seemingly undivided stand by Asian countries on human rights. However, the second voice's catechism on the right to development is just as contaminated by global capitalism. For systemic reasons, the spectacular economic growth of some East Asian states is not evenly distributed to every sector. It is true that many of these governments are no longer comprador regimes in the strict Marxist sense. They are vocal in their policy disagreements with and ideological opposition to the North or the West. Yet their high economic performance, essential to their continued legitimation, depends on their willingness to accommodate transnational capital. These governments acquiesce in the exploitation entailed by profitable foreign investment: poor labor conditions and low pay in free trade zones compared to the countries of origin of TNCs. Indeed, the richer Asian countries are investing in their poorer neighbors and preaching a competing "Asian" model of free trade there. In a visit to Manila in 1992, Lee Kuan Yew urged the Philippines to model itself after the economic policies of Indonesia, Malaysia, and Thailand: "You will have to further liberalise the trade and investment regulations to stimulate activity."[38] Singapore's growing investments in the Philippines[39] (competing with U.S. investment) and the growing economic and diplomatic cooperation between Manila and Singapore form a crucial subtext of the Flor Contemplacion incident occluded by U.S. media coverage.[40] Thus, the real audience of the continuing human rights debate between Asian and Western governments (of which the Contemplacion incident is but one example) is the disfranchised in Asian countries whom their governments are trying to convince about the virtues of their authoritarian path to capitalist development. It is the disfranchised who are caught in the aporetic embrace between a predatory international capitalism and an indigenous capitalism seeking to internationalize.

I come now to the most counterintuitive and politically incorrect part of my argument: the contamination of human rights NGOs. This third voice tries to extract itself from the miasmic complicity between domestic oppression and international exploitation by claiming the normative status of an international public sphere or, which is not quite the same thing, a global civil society. In topographical terms, both "civil society" and "public sphere" refer to zones that exhibit an autonomy vis-à-vis the territorial state and are therefore sites of struggle between dominant and counterhegemonic forces. The normative status of civil society simply comes from this autonomy from the state that allows it to represent society to the state and to alleviate pressures that come from state institutions. By contrast, the concept of the public sphere is formulated by abstracting a universally valid procedural framework for the rational-critical articulation of norms from various historical manifestations of autonomy vis-à-vis the state. The public sphere grows out of civil society but is not reducible to it. Its more exacting normativity comes from the rational universality of the procedures through which social norms are articulated. Thus, in contemporary social theory, "public sphere" is another name for the site where the substantive forms of ethical self-understanding that bind a territorial political community are generated from consensual rational procedures of political decision making and law enactment.

The normative status accorded to civil society and the public sphere has been challenged on various grounds, especially with regard to its claims to autonomy from the state and the rational transcendence of particularistic interests.[41] What is important for us is that the compromised nature of these normative phenomena become even more pronounced when they are generalized on a global scale,[42] for the claims by human rights NGOs to the normative status of a global civil society or an international public sphere are contaminated at various levels. First, the vocabulary of civil society or public sphere presupposes a state versus society topology within a territorially bounded entity, where "civil society" or "public sphere" represents the "nation" side of the nation-state. Ideally, a global civil society or public sphere would transcend nationalist interests because it would be the autonomous site of mediation between "humanity" and a global political order. However, human rights NGOs do not possess the requisite autonomy. In the first place, transnational social movements occur in a decentralized political system where no supranational executive body independent of the compliance of nation-states for the enforcement of its decisions exists and where mass-based loyalty to the world of humanity is insignificant. Thus, civil-society institutions are constrained by and have to rely on the agency of nation-states and are largely defined in terms of national bases.[43] Furthermore, as Martin Shaw points out, social movements have very little leverage on the state and even less impact on interstate relations because they rely more on cultural pressure than on elaborate institutional connections with the political system.[44] At best, social movements with global networks can make national civil societies more globally aware. Indeed, even when NGOs invoke formal international human rights instruments to make their claims on behalf of "humanity," these claims are always channeled through specific national sites, against specific nation-states.

This means that human rights NGOs have to negotiate with shifting interstate relations within an unequal global economic order. As such, their claims are irreducibly susceptible to co-optation by competing states on both sides of the North-South divide at the very moment they are articulated. In fighting against state violations of human rights, NGOs from the South are precariously balanced between, on the one hand, reliance on Northern sources for funding and the risk of co-optation by the international media and the expansionist economic interests of industrialized countries and, on the other hand, criticizing statist models of development in the South without jeopardizing the ambivalent need for the nation-state as an agent of accumulation in defense against transnational capital. Simply put, NGOs are always part of the linkages of global capital as they invest state formations and are only effective by virtue of being so.[45]

I should stress that I am not suggesting that human rights NGOs articulate universal ideals that are subsequently contaminated in their implementation. Rather, I am suggesting that these ideals are always already conditioned by the force field within which they are invoked. These ideals are posited only in their violation. Consequently, the recognizability of these ideals depends on what counts as oppressive in a given historical conjuncture. In other words, we must learn to see that "human dignity" itself is a product-effect. This is obvious enough in the observation that any assertion of right is limited by its positionality. Take, for example, the feminist right to cultural difference. The need to assert the right to cultural self-determination as integral to human dignity is a by-product of unequal North-South relations. It has been contested by feminist groups in the South who seek to assert women's rights as human rights. These groups seek to establish a feminist right to cultural self-determination in opposition to the patriarchal statist model of cultural difference that smothers the possibilities of gender reform. Yet even here it is impossible to locate a pure voice of feminist cultural difference. As Arati Rao observes, much feminist leadership is urban, well educated, middle class, and often government paid. "Since the responsiveness of the state to women's well-being remains debatable, we must remain critical of the relationship between governments and those women's groups permitted to flourish freely."[46] Therefore, "when women's groups or individual women talk about culture, we must remind ourselves that *there can never be a purportedly popular notion of culture that is unmediated by the positionality of the speaker;* we must look at claims for exemption [from human rights issues] on cultural grounds in relation to the axes of class, ethnicity, race, sexuality and age, and so on."[47]

I believe that the argument about the contamination of the subject of rights should be made at an even more fundamental level, going beyond a critical analysis of positionality. The politics of positionality or location implies a distinction between an inauthentic or dominant institutional position and a repressed but residual authentic voice that is retrievable by an exhaustively universal vision of human rights. My point is that an irreducible-because-systemic contamination occurs in the very court of claims in which the voice of the oppressed can be heard, although it is in this court alone that justice can be done and we cannot *not* want this justice-in-violation. The impossibility of locating a pure voice of the subject of oppression or a genuinely popular voice, and therefore of any vision of human rights claiming an all-encompassing universal validity, is especially salient in the assertion of aboriginal rights by "tribals" in Southeast Asia. As Benedict Anderson observes, "in most cases their humble wish is to be left alone." But they are compelled to defend against the encroachment of nation-states and the forces of global capital on their lifestyles by staging a collective identity and demanding rights in the name of that identity.

> Their very isolation leaves them unacquainted with the ceremonies of private property, the techniques of coalition politics and even the organizational methods needed for modern self-defense. The irony is that typically, they are not ethnic groups; to survive they may have to learn to think and act as such. . . . Yet, the costs of going ethnic, that is, participating in ethnic majority politics and economics within the nation-state, are not to be underestimated. . . . These [ethnic] identities . . . occlude and submerge non-ethnic local identities in the very process of attempting to defend them. Such identities, may, under ill-starred circumstances, invite conscious oppression rather than malign neglect, but they also open the way to developing a necessary political and economic bargaining power.[48]

The dilemma of "going ethnic" illustrates that rights only accrue when the subject claiming them is a collective subject endowed with institutional or epistemic recognition. Put another way, rights claims are contingent upon the performative positing of a subject of rights within and by a given conjuncture, although this performative is then necessarily taken to be a constative declaration about and by a preexisting subject. Jacques Derrida makes the same point in a different context when he observes that "this obscurity, undecidability between . . . a performative structure and a constative structure. . . . is essential to the very positing or position of a right as such."[49] Human rights NGOs often make the observation that "one of the major issues is how to overcome the barrier of ignorance on the part of the rural poor about their rights, including the right to organize [because] to make matters worse, the poor do not know they are poor."[50] Without dismissing the necessity and importance of the project of the political education of "the rural poor," it is nevertheless important to note that what we are witnessing is a performative-constative ruse by which the rural poor begin to think of themselves as such, in terms of a collective identity capable of articulating "their human rights." They are being taught to make cognitive sense of their exploitation by global capital even as the project of consciousness-raising is necessarily part of the same systemic violation. They are constituted as an institutionally recognizable collective, which they were previously not, so that they can have leverage as the subjects/objects of institutional decision making. Yet this fabulation also reduces them to the accountable data of sustainable-development policies that may disrupt their old ways of life even further. This is the crisis. No easy claims of historical relativism or nihilism here but the sobering acknowledgment that in global capitalism this is the only way to help them and the only way for them to help themselves.

Normativity in Original Contamination: Global Capitalism Is a Text and Not a Totality

It may be fruitful at this point to briefly situate the performance of human rights practical discourse in contemporary global capitalism in relation to the two main competing theories of international society in intellectual history: cosmopolitanism and realism. We have already encountered cosmopolitanism in the concepts of international public sphere and global civil society. Clearly, the contaminated normativity of international human rights claims can no longer be explained in terms of the Kantian idea of cosmopolitan right asserted by an institutionalized world community of "individuals and states, co-existing in an external relationship of mutual influences, [who] may be regarded as citizens of a universal state of mankind."[51] As I have suggested, no international public sphere or global civil society in the full sense has come into existence in the contemporary interstate system. None of the three voices of human rights can represent universal humanity. Although they can be complicit with one another, the hegemonic North, the weak neocolonial states in the South, the high economic performing Asian NIEs, and the human rights NGOs in both the North and South clearly do not share identical interests.

In international relations theory, the alternative to a cosmopolitanist conception of international society is realism. Hedley Bull represents a more moderate example. As one commentator observes, "[Bull has cautioned that] 'cosmopolitanist ideas can determine our attitudes and policies in international relations only to a limited extent' since states were 'notoriously self-serving in their policies.' Having suggested that a commitment to basic human rights should underpin any cosmopolitanist world culture, he pointed again to the continuing lack of agreement among states as to what is meant by human rights, and the dangers of subverting co-existence by pursuing partial conceptions of justice."[52] Hegel offers an even stronger philosophical articulation of the realist position. He argues that the normativity of international society would "never go beyond an ought to be." Resting "on moral or religious . . . grounds and considerations," Kant's world confederation of states, one philosophical model for the U.N. qua human rights enforcer, "would always depend ultimately on a particular sovereign will and for that reason would always remain infected with contingency."[53] Hence, for Hegel, international relations "are on the largest scale a maelstrom of external contingency and the inner particularity of passions, private interests and selfish ends, abilities and virtues, vices, force, and wrong. All these whirl together, and in their vortex the ethical whole itself, the autonomy of the state, is exposed to contingency."[54]

We can thus see that in its most cynical version a realist account of international society is a relativism that emphasizes the historical contingency of state action toward other states. In the face of the ineluctable historicity (*Geschichtlichkeit*) of moral-political norms, Hegel asserts the rational-universal normativity of state action by resorting to a teleology of world history. He argues that the institutionalization of certain norms coincided with the direction of world historical progress and that these norms retained their universal validity in later stages of development. Such world historical norms cannot be revoked even though they can be modified.[55] The nation-state that embodied the world spirit of a certain epoch would lead all other states, and its actions would have universal normative force. Thus,

> out of [the dialectic of the finitude of national spirits] arises the universal spirit, the spirit of the world, free from all restriction, producing itself as that which exercises its right—and its right is the highest right of all—over these finite spirits in the "history of the world which is the world's court of judgement." . . . History is spirit clothing itself with the form of events. . . . The nation to which is ascribed a moment of the Idea . . . is entrusted with giving complete effect to it in the advance of the self-developing self-consciousness of the world spirit. This nation is dominant in world history during this one epoch. . . . In contrast with this its absolute right of being the vehicle of this present stage in the world spirit's development, the spirits of the other nations are without rights, and they . . . count no longer in world history.[56]

We clearly cannot follow Hegel's rationalist impregnation of the contingency of historical events with teleological significance. The neocolonial ideology of development deployed by the International Monetary Fund and the World Bank under the leadership of the Group of Seven nations is world history in its misdestination, or *destinerrance*. Indeed, both the United States, in its self-staging as the champion and defender of human rights, and the authoritarian governments of the South that justify human rights violations in the name of the right to development try to endow their actions with normative force by exploiting weaker variations of the same teleological argument. The question is whether, in the face of the irreducible contamination of human rights in global capitalism (a case of ineluctable historicity), we must give up their normativity and reluctantly embrace cynical realism if we reject a teleological solution to historical contingency.

The situation is not as bleak as it seems, for if idealist universalism is unrealistic, cynical realism is equally unrealistic given the very real normative power that human rights exert on various types of actors, notwithstanding the fact that their normative basis cannot clearly be separated from global-systemic imperatives and particularistic tendencies. To be a concrete agent in history is, after all, to be contaminated in turn by historically existing ideals and norms, no matter how contaminated these ideals and norms are. Rather, the task is to rethink the normativity of human rights claims within the original contamination and violence of global capitalism, that is, within ineluctable historicity. It is to accept that our principles of rational action are irreducibly conditioned by what they seek to alleviate and transform even as we cannot *not* invoke these principles because they in turn condition us. But this will require a radical break with the theory of normativity behind human rights practical discourse that, in claiming exhaustive universal rationality, has always taken as axiomatic the coextensivity of ethicopolitical change with the prescription of a total rational form by the human agent to historico-material forces.

Indeed, all existing theories of normativity regard normative force as something that issues from and expresses self-present reason, and these theories define rational normative activity as the elimination, regulation, or transcendence of historical contingency. The struggle of normative reason to transcend historicity can take different forms. As is the case with neo-Kantian human rights discourse, it can involve the prescription of an ideal total form—for example, a holistic system of rights maximizing respect for human dignity—that is distinct from and even transcendent to historical reality but that functions as a regulative or asymptotic horizon of the Kantian type, a guiding thread for the transformation of reality. Or, as with Hegel, normative reason can be reconciled with historical contingency: that is, normative reason can transcend the contingent by actualizing itself in history through autonomous action that affirms the ethical institutions of the nation said to embody the spirit of world history. The struggle of reason to transcend historical contingency can even take the form of Fredric Jameson's neo-Marxist argument that human rights, like the ideals of other progressive social movements, are necessarily compromised as long as they are articulated in global capitalism. The full realization of human rights would then be premised on the transcendence of the capitalist world system, and the first step toward transcendence is said to involve an aesthetic of cognitive mapping that enables us to imaginatively outline global capital into the form of an oppressive social totality in urgent need of transformation.[57]

But we can no longer rely on these rationalist accounts of normativity if we want to make cognitive sense of the normative force that human rights can exert in their very contamination by global capital. This is because the normativity of human rights is coextensive with their historical contingency. I have already suggested that the irreducible contamination of the subject of human rights indicates that we can no longer theorize the normativity of rights claims in terms of the rational universality of a pure, atemporal, and context-independent human dignity that is ultimately separated from economics or politics. But more important, however hard it may be for leftist critics to accept, this irreducible contamination also indicates that we may never be able to transcend global capital, for the very constitution of a subject entitled to rights involves the violent capture of the disfranchised by an institutional discourse that inseverably weaves them into the textile of global capitalism. Our interconnectedness in global capitalism generates a real and unequal universality that caricatures the ideal universality at the basis of conventional human rights discourse. Rights are thus not, in the original instance, entitlements of intersubjectively constituted rational social agents but violent gifts, the necessary nexi within immanent global force relations that produce the identities of its claimants. Yet rights are the only way for the disfranchised to mobilize.

From the above, we can see that the normative force of human rights issues from the material linkages that make up the global capitalist system without either being reduced to these forces (historicist relativism) or being able to transcend them (varieties of neo-Hegelianism and neo-Marxism). In his recent reflections on the aporias of justice and the gift, Jacques Derrida articulates an account of normativity that is explicitly distinguished from the Kantian and Hegelian accounts of normativity underpinning cosmopolitan and realist accounts of international relations. I want to suggest that Derrida's idea of justice can help us better understand the contaminated normativity of human rights in their ineluctable historicity.[58]

As we have seen, Hegel's critique that Kant's idea of a world confederation of states remains a mere ought-to-be culminates in his own argument that the political morality of the state constitutes an "ought" that already "is," a sphere in which normativity and actuality are reconciled and historical contingency is transcended. In this sphere of normative facticity, justice is immanent to the present. Contra Hegel, Derrida suggests that it is unjust to regard justice as being exhausted by or reduced to present historical determinations. This is because justice must remain fundamentally open to unpredictable future circumstances: "The deconstruction of all presumption of a determinant certitude of a present justice itself operates on an infinite 'idea of justice,' . . . [which] seems to me to be irreducible in its affirmative character, in its demand of gift . . . without economic circularity, without calculation and without rules, without reason and without rationality."[59] But, unlike Kant's idea of cosmopolitan right, this infinite idea of justice is not a projected ideal form that bears no effective relation to present actuality. Justice is not a transcendent exteriority that can only function as an ideal horizon. It demands an immediate intervention into and transformation of the present: "I would hesitate to assimilate too quickly this 'idea of justice' to a regulative idea (in the Kantian sense) . . . or to other horizons of the same type . . . (. . . eschato-teleology of the neo-Hegelian, Marxist or post-Marxist type). . . . As its Greek name suggests, a horizon is both the opening and the limit that defines an infinite progress or period of waiting. But justice, however unpresentable it may be, doesn't wait. It is that which must not wait."[60]

In other words, to be just, justice must not be either simply immanent or transcendent to the historical present. Paradoxically, justice must be immanent and transcendent at the same time. To be just, justice must give itself to the historical present and, in the same instance, withdraw itself or be effaced from the present. Thus, justice must give itself in its own violation, contaminate itself by appearing in the present. What is important here is that Derrida argues that the source of infinite justice or normativity—its condition of possibility—can only be the absolute surprise or chance of the event that reopens and keeps history going. Justice ought not to be exhausted by rational action in the present. But at the same time, it must have an effect on the present through rational action. This persistent, sheer possibility of the transformation of historical actuality must therefore issue from a contingency original to and constitutive of historical actuality, namely, the historicity of history.

Normative reason is born in an unconditional response to this original contingency, but since historicity is constitutive of finite reason, reason cannot cognitively master, eradicate, or transcend it. The "historicity" or "finitude" of reason thus refers to reason's constitutive inscription within a shifting field of historical forces that it cannot control or transcend. But at the same time, this moving base also holds the ineradicable promise of ethical transformation because it exceeds and cannot be captured by the hegemonic forces of any given historical present. In this sense, normativity is both unconditional and coextensive with historicity, which is precisely why normativity cannot be reduced to existing norms or their historical conditions.[61]

> Justice remains, is yet, to come, à venir, it has an, it is à venir, the very dimension of events irreducibly to come. . . . Perhaps it is for this reason that justice, insofar as it is not only a juridical or political concept, opens up for l'avenir the transformation, the recasting or refounding of law and politics. "Perhaps," one must always say perhaps for justice. There is . . . no justice except to the degree that some event is possible which, as event, exceeds calculation, rules, programs, anticipations and so forth. Justice as the experience of absolute alterity is unpresentable, but it is the chance of the event and the condition of history. No doubt an unrecognizable history . . . for those who believe they know what they're talking about when they use this word, whether it's a matter of social, ideological, political, juridical or some other history.[62]

This is precisely the structure of justice-in-violation that characterizes the unconditional but contaminated normativity of human rights in their ineluctable historicity, for as we have seen, human rights are double-edged but absolutely necessary weapons that are given to the disfranchised by the global force relations in which they find themselves mired at a given historical conjuncture. On the one hand, we should be able to account for the historical conditions that determine and impose limits on any invocation of human rights so that we can calculate the effectiveness of human rights claims in a given situation. On the other hand, because they are in history, these contextual conditions are subject to radical mutability. A mutation in historical conditions will cause a corresponding change in the effectiveness of human rights. At the same time, the contaminated normativity of human rights can be a factor in bringing about and inflecting a mutation in historical conditions.

This normativity in historical contingency is not a historicist relativism that reduces normativity to a ruse of hegemonic power. First, conjunctures have an immense stability. Second, no collective institutional actor can predict when and how a given conjuncture will mutate. Thus, although some actors may be invested with hegemony by the existing state of affairs, no single actor can be said to have exhaustive mastery over it.

By the same token, human rights are also not inevitably strategic or ideological instruments available for progressive or reactionary use. The normative force and effectivity that human rights have are given by the force relations that make up the global capitalist system. They are not *our* instruments as rational actors, for we are their product-effects rather than their originators. Neither we nor capitalism can choose to either embrace or repudiate human rights, for they are given to us as finite historical actors by existing historical forces and they constitute us. What we *can* do is calculate their effectiveness in situations we can envision and act accordingly. Derrida puts it this way: "It is a matter . . . of responding faithfully but also as rigorously as possible both to the injunction or the order of the *gift* . . . as well as to the injunction or the order of meaning (presence, science, knowledge): *Know* still what giving *wants to say, know how to give* . . . know how the gift annuls itself, commit yourself [*engage-toi*] even if commitment is the destruction of the gift by the gift, give economy its chance. For finally, the overrunning of the circle [of economy] by the gift, if there is any, does not lead to a simple, ineffable exteriority that would be transcendent and without relation. . . . it is this exteriority which puts the economy in motion."[63] Thus, as we have seen, although the three voices of human rights discourse can be complicit, the line of force that joins them together and in the service of the global capitalist economy can also mutate to separate their interests and pit them against each other and against capitalism. In the shifting global force field, nothing is etched in stone, and we must learn to tap this motility.

It follows that human rights are not just part of an ideological structure that needs to be reembedded within the systemic totality of global capital by immanent critique. Neo-Marxist understandings of human rights follow rationalist theories of normativity that prescribe an ideal totality or world image onto material reality. Undoubtedly, global capitalism has brought about material interconnectedness on a world scale. But contra Jameson, the contaminated normativity of human rights practical discourse suggests that global capitalism is not a totality but a textual network, a sheaf of differential processes, for the conditioning power of human rights on our rational actions and their ambivalent effects indicate that the global relationality that enables each agent to act and to affect others is marked by a randomness that cannot be entirely harnessed by either hegemonic or emancipatory interests, that is, the randomness of the shifting linkages that sustain global capital. This chance of economy means that although global capitalism is an overarching "structure," this "structure" cannot be enclosed as a cognizable totality because there are points of weakness "it" generates but cannot account for. This radical alterity immanent to the "structure" of global capitalism makes totality impossible because it opens up the structure to a general textuality at the very moment that totalization occurs.[64] The positive effects of human rights arise from these unpredictable points. But by the same token, these neuralgic points are not spatially exterior to the structure. They are part of it, conditioned by its historical determinations, and do not present a visible historical or imaginary limit to it. They do not make up an external present site from which we can (imagine and) transcend capitalism as a totality. This is why human rights are originally contaminated, pulled back into the particularistic forces they seek to transcend or check in their very movement of transcendence.

Let me be more concrete: the globalization of market mechanisms and production requires the creation of a technologically educated laboring and administrative class in the South. But the requisite globalization of education also leads to the formation of a strata of activists. These human rights NGOs, in response to the proliferation of new needs, make claims that are provisionally against the interests of global capitalism. Yet, as I have suggested, these provisional points of resistance are also reinscribed into the text of global capitalism: witness the co-optation of "sustainable development," "environmentalism," and "international civil society" by the International Monetary Fund and World Bank. Thus, what gives a particular vision of human rights more normative validity and historical effectivity depends on the constellation of forces at a given conjuncture rather than an ideal or imagined horizon of all-inclusive universality that vision has managed to grasp.

I have argued that the unconditional normativity in original contamination of human rights arises from their inscription within the text of global capitalism and not from a self-present exteriority grasped by enlightened reason or neo-Marxist cognitive mapping. Such an approach deprives human rights claims of absolute rational justification since, by viewing normativity as arising out of the radical alterity of the global force field, it sunders the co-belonging of normativity with reason and presence. But then, what are the theoretical alternatives? A dogmatic idealism of human rights is disproved by "the real world of human rights." At the same time, an outright realist dismissal of human rights denies their very real enabling force in the current conjuncture. Given that the transcendence of global capitalism is not in imaginary sight, we have no choice but to take the risk of conjuring with and against the inhuman force field of global capitalism as it induces changing forms of human dignity.

Notes

An earlier version of this essay appeared in *Public Culture* 9:2 (Winter 1997): 233–66. © 1997. Used here by permission of Duke University Press. A paper on which this essay is based was read at the Modern Language Association meeting in Chicago, December 1995, in a session entitled "Cultures of Human Rights." A subsequent version was presented at the Department of General Philosophy, University of Sydney, and at the School of Law, University of Melbourne, in March 1996. My thanks to the participants of these seminars for their questions and to the Department of General Philosophy for its hospitality when I was a visiting fellow in the first half of 1996. I am grateful to György Markus, who patiently corrected my speed readings of Hegel, and to Benedict Anderson, for teaching me the complexity and importance of empirical evidence and saving me from incomprehensible theoretical abstraction. Although the Asian financial crisis that occurred after the initial publication of this essay has erased many of the gains of East and Southeast Asian NIEs and altered the post–cold war world, it does not affect my general argument about the normativity of human rights.

1. See, for instance, Karl Marx, "On the Jewish Question," in *Early Writings* (Harmondsworth, U.K.: Penguin, 1975), 211–41. For an incisive discussion of Marx's critique of rights, see Claude Lefort, "Politics and Human Rights," in *The Political Forms of Modern Society: Bureaucracy, Democracy, Totalitarianism* (Cambridge: Polity Press, 1986), 239–72.

2. Adamantia Pollis and Peter Schwab, "Human Rights: A Western Construct with Limited Applicability," in *Human Rights: Cultural and Ideological Perspectives*, ed. Adamantia Pollis and Peter Schwab (New York: Praeger, 1979), 1–18 (quote on 17).

3. Marnia Lazreg, "Human Rights, State, and Ideology: An Historical Perspective," in Pollis and Schwab, *Human Rights*, 32–43 (quote on 34).

4. Statement by Wong Kan Seng, minister of foreign affairs of the Republic of Singapore, Vienna, 16 June 1993, reprinted in *Human Rights and International Relations in the Asia Pacific*, ed. James Tang (London: Pinter, 1995), 242–47 (quote on 243).

5. First-generation rights refer primarily to civil and political rights. They are basically negative rights that protect the individual from arbitrary state action and are associated with Western liberal democracies. They are said to have their roots in the French and American revolutions and are articulated in the Universal Declaration and the International Covenant on Civil and Political Rights. Second-generation rights refer to social, economic, and cultural rights. They are positive rights associated with socialist states and are said to have their roots in the socialist revolutions of the early twentieth century. They are specifically articulated in the International Covenant on Social, Economic, and Cul-

tural Rights. The Covenants were ratified by the General Assembly only in 1966. Third-generation rights are summed up under the right to development and are rooted in the anticolonialist revolutions that began after World War II and culminated in independence in the 1960s. The right to development is implicit in Articles 55 and 56 of the U.N. Charter and Articles 22 and 27 of the Universal Declaration. In June 1979, the U.N. Commission on Human Rights resolved that the right to development is a human right. Most developed countries (Denmark, Finland, Germany, Iceland, Israel, Japan, Sweden, and the United Kingdom) abstained from voting on the Declaration on the Right to Development. Canada and Australia adopted a compromise position and voted in favor. The United States voted against it. For an overview of the politics involved in the ratification of these rights and their pertinence in a cold war and post–cold war scenario, see Brenda Cossman, "Reform, Revolution or Retrenchment? International Human Rights in the Post–Cold War Era," *Harvard International Law Journal* 32:2 (Spring 1991): 339–52. For a discussion on how the right to development relates to the other two types of rights, whether the right to development is an instrumental or third-generation right or a resultant or consequential right, and whether it refers to the development of the individual or the state, see R. N. Treverdi, "Overview of International Human Rights Law in Theory and Practice: Its Linkages to Access to Justice at the Domestic Level" in *Access to Justice: The Struggle for Human Rights in South-East Asia,* ed. Harry Scoble and Laurie Weisberg (London: Zed Books, 1985), 22–30, esp. 27–30.

6. On contemporary Asian capitalism, see *Southeast Asian Capitalists,* ed. Ruth McVey (Ithaca, N.Y.: Cornell Southeast Asia Program, 1992); and "Asia's Competing Capitalisms," *The Economist,* 24 June 1995, 16–17.

7. See Edward Gargan, "An Asian Giant Spreads Roots," *New York Times,* 14 November 1995, D1, D4; and Edward Gargan, "Asia Guide Calls Local Partners Key to Success," *New York Times,* 14 November 1995, D4.

8. Edward Gargan, quoting James Rohwer, author of *Asia Rising: Why America Will Prosper as Asia's Economies Boom,* in *New York Times,* 14 November 1995, D4.

9. David Sanger, "Real Politics: Why Suharto Is In and Castro Is Out," *New York Times,* 31 October 1995, A3.

10. James Tang notes that "the post–Cold War confrontation between East Asia and the West over human rights . . . has to be understood in the context of the spectacular economic development in the Asia-Pacific region." He observes that "some East Asian states seem to have drawn the conclusion that the East Asian model of development has proved to be more successful than the Western model" and have asserted "that their political systems and economic policies are better than the Western political models, and can offer an alternative vision of the values needed for a better world." See "Human Rights in the Asia-Pacific Region: Competing Perspectives, International Discord, and the Way Ahead," in Tang, *Human Rights,* 2.

11. See H. L. A. Hart, *The Concept of Law* (Oxford: Clarendon Press, 1961). Hart calls this set of standards "the rule of recognition": "To say that a given rule is [legally] valid is to recognize it as passing all the tests provided by the rule of recognition and so as a rule of the system. . . . There are therefore two minimum conditions necessary and sufficient for the existence of a legal system. On the one hand those rules of behaviour which are valid according to the system's ultimate criteria of validity must be generally obeyed, and, on the other hand, its rules of recognition specifying the criteria of legal validity and its rules of change and adjudication must be effectively accepted as common public standards of official behaviour by its officials" (100, 113).

12. On the relation between law and morals in legal positivism, see ibid., chap. 9.

13. For elaborations of political morality and public sphere, see, respectively, Ronald Dworkin, *Law's Empire* (London: Fontana, 1986), chap. 6, and Jürgen Habermas, *The Structural Transformation of the Public Sphere* (Cambridge, Mass.: MIT Press, 1989).

14. "Public" in "public international law" is a sociological term designating the realm of state activity as opposed to the private realm of the actions of individuals. The sociological use of the term should not be confused with the normative notion of the public sphere (*Öffentlichkeit*), which lies resolutely within the private realm since it is the public sphere *of* civil society.

15. For an analogous justification of basic human rights from the standpoint of liberal political philosophy, see John Rawls, "The Law of Peoples," in *On Human Rights,* ed. Stephen Shute and Susan Hurley (New York: Basic Books, 1993), 41–82.

16. G. W. F. Hegel, *The Philosophy of Right,* trans. T. M. Knox (Oxford: Oxford University Press, 1967), § 330, 212.

17. "All men are created equal, that they are endowed by their Creator, with certain inalienable Rights."

18. "Constitutionalism and Human Rights," in *Constitutionalism and Rights: The Influence of the United States Constitution Abroad,* ed. Louis Henkin and Albert J. Rosenthal (New York: Columbia University Press, 1990), 383–95 (quote on 388).

19. See also Etienne Balibar, "'Rights of Man' and 'Rights of Citizen': The Modern Dialectic of Equality and Freedom" and "What Is a Politics of the Rights of Man?" in *Masses, Classes, and Ideas: Studies on Politics and Philosophy before and after Marx* (New York: Routledge, 1994), 39–59 and 205–25, respectively, for a similar argument about the risky, open-ended, and non-natural nature of human rights based on a reading of the 1789 Declaration of the Rights of Man and of the Citizen.

20. Immanuel Kant, *Foundations of the Metaphysics of Morals* (New York: Macmillan, 1987), 46–47, 428–29.

21. Ibid., 53, 435.

22. Wong Kan Seng, "The Real World of Human Rights," in Tang, *Human Rights,* 245.

23. Bangkok Declaration, 29 March 1993, reprinted in Tang, *Human Rights,* 204–7 (quote on 204).

24. Ibid., 205.

25. Hegel, *Philosophy of Right,* § 331, 212 and § 337, remark, 215, emphasis added. Throughout, I translate *Geist* as "spirit" instead of "mind," as in the Knox translation.

26. Ibid., § 333, remark, 214.

27. Bangkok NGO Declaration and Response to the Bangkok Declaration, 29 March and 3 April 1993, reprinted in Tang, *Human Rights,* 208–12 (quote on 209).

28. See the contributions to *Women's Rights, Human Rights: International Feminist Perspectives,* ed. Julie Peters and Andrea Wolper (New York: Routledge, 1995).

29. See Arati Rao, "The Politics of Gender and Culture in International Human Rights Discourse," in Peters and Wolper, *Women's Rights,* 167–75.

30. See Rhoda E. Howard, "Women's Rights and the Right to Development," in Peters and Wolper, *Women's Rights,* 301–13.

31. "We are entitled to join hands in solidarity to protect human rights world-wide. International solidarity transcends the national border, to refute claims of State sovereignity and of non-interference in the internal affairs of the State" (209).

32. For instance, in his analytical account of an alternative ("Asian") normative theory of human rights which respects cultural diversity, Joseph Chan makes repeated appeals to the good faith of rational collective actors at various levels. See "The Asian Challenge to Universal Human Rights: A Philosophical Appraisal," in Tang, *Human Rights,* 25–38.

33. See Dieter Henrich, "The Contexts of Autonomy: Some Presuppositions of the Comprehensibility of Human Rights," in *Aesthetic Judgment and the Moral Image of the World* (Stanford, Calif.: Stanford University Press, 1992), 59–84: "If one advocates rights generally, it must be because of their universal validity. But then, it must be possible to clarify rights within the context of other cultures and traditions—which again implies that we acknowledge their incompatibility with some forms of life and self-image. Nevertheless, it

would have to be shown that real possibilities of life are opened up within their context—and not just those from which the political institutions of the West arose" (84).

34. This causal dependence exists even though human rights considerations are not technically part of trade negotiations, as in the case of China's preferential trade status or its admission into the World Trade Organization. See David E. Sanger, "U.S. Again Tries a Trade Issue as a Carrot and Stick for Beijing," *New York Times*, 15 December 1995, A7: "'But we are now sending them the message that while human rights is not explicitly part of the negotiations, it is part of the atmosphere, and they are ignoring that at their peril.'"

35. See Chakravarthi Raghavan, *Recolonization: GATT, the Uruguay Round, and the Third World* (Penang: Third World Network, 1990), 38–40. The rest of this paragraph is a summary of the argument of Raghavan's book.

36. Vandana Shiva, "Biodiversity: A Third World Perspective," *Monocultures of the Mind: Biodiversity, Biotechnology, and the Third World* (Penang: Third World Network, 1993), 65–93 (quote on 80).

37. Vandana Shiva, "Biotechnology and the Environment," in *Monocultures of the Mind,* 95–131 (quote on 122–23).

38. See Reginald Chua, "Take Proven Path to Growth, SM Urges Manila," *Straits Times,* 18 November 1992, 2.

39. Singapore is the sixth largest investor in the Philippines. See, for instance, Reginald Chua, "Ramos to Woo S'pore Industries to Relocate in Philippines," *Straits Times,* 11 February 1993, 13, and "Ramos Happy with S'pore Investments," *Straits Times,* 16 February 1995, 18.

40. Flor Contemplacion was a Filipino maid who was convicted of killing another Filipino maid and a four-year-old Singaporean boy. She was sentenced to death and was hanged by the Singapore government on 18 March 1995. The case provoked great public outcry in the Philippines and led to severe strains in diplomatic relations between Singapore and the Philippines. In the wake of the Michael Fay incident, the U.S. media portrayed the hanging as another example of the authoritarianism of the Singaporean state. The Contemplacion incident is thus a libidinal site for the articulation of U.S. relations with both Singapore (a competing model of capitalism that provides a destination for exploitative labor practices) and its former colony. The U.S. media coverage represses the previous history of U.S. colonial exploitation, which created the oppressive conditions that make domestic labor migration necessary to sustain the Philippines economy.

41. I have discussed the limits of the normative concept of the public sphere in "Violent Light: The Idea of Publicness in Modern Philosophy and in Global Neocolonialism," *Social Text* 43 (Fall 1995): 163–90.

42. For "global civil society" and the limitations of the concept, see Martin Shaw, "Civil Society and Global Politics: Beyond a Social Movements Approach," *Millennium: Journal of International Studies* 23:3 (1994): 647–67: "Civil society can be said to have become globalised to the extent that society increasingly represents itself globally, across nation-state boundaries, through the formation of global institutions. . . . The emergence of global civil society can be seen both as a response to the globalisation of state power and as a source of pressure for it" (650).

43. Cf. M. J. Peterson, "Transnational Activity, International Society, and World Politics," *Millennium: Journal of International Studies* 21:3 (1992): 371–88: "Societal actors need states. Though political philosophers and visionaries have looked for alternate institutions, a state or something like it appears necessary to provide minimal security, guarantee property rights and help enforce contracts—all three of which are necessary to the good functioning of civil society and the activities of its members" (386).

44. Shaw, "Civil Society," 655.

45. To give two examples, Vandana Shiva points out that "sustainable development" and "the Green Revolution" have been co-opted by TNCs and the World Bank in their

drive toward biodiversity-destroying agricultural modernization. In his discussion of the precariousness of people's diplomacy in the Philippines, Francisco Nemenzo points to the paradox of the current conjuncture where the appeals of people's diplomacy to world public opinion to place pressure on the government to respect human rights are less effective as a result of the benign image of the Ramos/Aquino regime in the international media and the decline in U.S. interest in the Philippines because of the loss of its military bases. See "People's Diplomacy and Human Rights: The Philippines Experience" in Tang, *Human Rights,* 112–24.

46. Arati Rao, "The Politics of Gender and Culture in International Human Rights Discourse," in Peters and Wolper, *Women's Rights,* 171.

47. Ibid., emphasis added.

48. "Introduction," *Southeast Asian Tribal Groups and Ethnic Minorites,* Report No. 22 (Cambridge, Mass.: Cultural Survival, 1987), 1–15 (quote on 11).

49. Jacques Derrida, "Declarations of Independence," *New Political Science* 15 (Summer 1986): 7–15 (quote on 9–10).

50. *Rural Development and Human Rights in South East Asia* (Penang: International Commission of Jurists and Consumer Association of Penang, 1982), 173–74.

51. "Perpetual Peace: A Philosophical Sketch" in Immanuel Kant, *Political Writings,* ed. Hans Reiss (Cambridge: Cambridge University Press, 1991), 98–99n. Cf. Kant's discussion of cosmopolitan right (*ius cosmopoliticum*), §62, in *The Doctrine of Right, the Metaphysics of Morals* (Cambridge: Cambridge University Press, 1991), 158–59.

52. Nicholas J. Wheeler, "Pluralist or Solidarist Conceptions of International Society: Bull and Vincent on Humanitarian Intervention," *Millennium: Journal of International Studies* 21:3 (1992): 463–87 (quote on 476).

53. Hegel, *Philosophy of Right,* § 333, remark, 214.

54. Ibid. § 340, 215.

55. As the Budapest School philosopher György Markus points out, this is an aestheticizing conception of normativity "since it resolves the seeming contradiction between the historicity of origin and the universal validity of norms on the analogy of the historical situatedness and atemporal significance of 'classical' works of art." See "Political Philosophy as Phenomenology: On the Method of Hegel's *Philosophy of Right,*" *Thesis Eleven* 68 (1997): 1–19.

56. Hegel, *Philosophy of Right,* §§ 340, 346–47, 216–18.

57. See Fredric Jameson, "Cognitive Mapping," in *Marxism and the Interpretation of Culture,* ed. Cary Nelson and Lawrence Grossberg (Urbana: University of Illinois Press, 1988), 347–60, and, more generally, *Postmodernism; or, The Cultural Logic of Late Capitalism* (Durham, N.C.: Duke University Press, 1991).

58. Derrida has developed this infinite idea of justice into an account of a New International based on the notion of a global democracy to come. See *Spectres of Marx: The State of the Debt, the Work of Mourning, and the New International* (New York: Routledge, 1994). In my view, his New International is rather feeble because it is not institutionally grounded. In contradistinction, I use Derrida's notion of justice-in-violation to flesh out an account of the normativity of existing human rights practical discourse.

59. Jacques Derrida, "Force of Law: 'The Mystical Foundation of Authority,'" *Cardozo Law Review* 11 (1990): 919–1045 (quote on 965).

60. Ibid., 965, 967.

61. Cf. Geoffrey Bennington, *Jacques Derrida* (Chicago: University of Chicago Press, 1993), 279–82: "This movement, which would traditionally be represented as a movement upward . . . is . . . at the same time, a movement 'downward' for it is the empirical and the contingent, themselves necessarily displaced . . . toward the singular event and the case of chance, which are found higher than the high . . . in height's falling. . . . the quasi-transcendental . . . is not to be taken as a historicizing or cultural relativizing of the transcendental. . . . any attempt to explain transcendental effects by invoking history must

presuppose the historicity of that same history as the very transcendental which this system of explanation will never be able to comprehend."

62. Derrida, "Force of Law," 969, 971.

63. Derrida, *Given Time: I. Counterfeit Money* (Chicago: University of Chicago Press, 1992), 30.

64. For the methodological presupposition of the general text, see Jacques Derrida, "Politics and Friendship," in *The Althusserian Legacy,* ed. E. Ann Kaplan and Michael Sprinker (New York: Verso, 1993), 183–231: "Precisely for the reason that through *differance,* the necessary reference to the other, the impossibility for a presence to gather itself in a self-identity or substantiality, compels one to inscribe the reality effect in a general textuality or differential process which, again, is not limited to language" (223).

2. Bodies, Letters, Catalogs: Filipinas in Transnational Space

Rolando B. Tolentino

> Constructs of identity serve as the points of epistemic depar-
> ture from which theory emerges and politics itself is shaped.
> —Judith Butler, *Gender Trouble*, 128

> Migrant labour is women['s] labor.
> —Kanlungan Centre Foundation, "Overseas Filipina Domestic
> Helpers," 26

TRANSNATIONAL SPACE KEEPS the Philippine economy afloat. The top three exports—electronics, garments, and contract labor—have consistently been reliable sources of foreign exchange that sustain the economy, especially in times of crisis. The Filipina and her body prefigure this space, moving from work in the home to home-work outside the home. Filipinas have been integrated into the circuits of transnationalism in various ways: as sweatshop factory workers in multinational corporations within the national space; and as entertainers, domestic helpers, nurses, and mail-order brides in international spaces. These spatial locations, after all, are artifacts of power relations. The analysis of these various locations remaps the discursive circuits in the oblique enforcement of power that places bodies and nations in a transnational juncture. This chapter examines the geopolitics of Filipina bodies inscribed in the transnational space, specifically focusing on the problematics of the mail-order bride phenomenon as a social and political practice.

Advertised mostly for middle-class, elderly white men, mail-order brides em*body* hyperreal shopping for the first-world male and the hyperreal commodification of women and the Third World. From 1983–93, 50,000 Filipinas came into the United States as mail-order brides.[1] Each year, some 19,000 Filipinas leave the Philippines to unite with husbands and fiancés of other nationalities, the majority of whom are in the United States.[2] This chapter provides a cognitive map of the discourse of mail-order brides, analyzing the marketing mode (catalogs in particular) at the cultural level (representations of race, sexuality, etc.) as well as at the sociopolitical level (economics, development, geopolitics, immigration). The discourse of mail-order brides in transnational space posits women and femininity as sites of critique and complicity. At the same time, however, the discourse also allows for recuperating modes of activity that are a conduit for and circumvention of the mail-order bride businesses and their male clientele.

The discourse of mail-order brides is situated in the historical positioning of Filipina bodies into the transnational space, inscribed in colonial, militarist, and capitalist histories. The discourse is also connected to the practices of shopping, especially as these practices are placed in the network of the postal and mail-ordering systems. The various circuits of postmodern "love connections"—for example, television dating shows, phone sex, phone dating, and Internet sex—further link the discourse to American popular culture. My analysis of the packaging of brides relates the marketing strategies used to two kinds of nostalgia: a nuclear family fantasy that supports gender and sexual reinforcement of loss and recuperation; and a colonialist fantasy that brings racial conquest and rescue into consideration.

The term "mail-order bride," while signifying the basic operations of the exchange of bodies and currency over a more or less efficient postal network, also connotes a whole regime of pejorative associations for the woman (re)situated in this position. This regime has prevented me from working ethnographically with these women, whose positions as exchange brides remain, for the most part, an individually kept secret. While there is a general knowledge of the existence and operations of mail-order brides, the network is poised to conceal this aspect of the women's past, thus making ethnography difficult to undertake. Since there is no body willingly constitutable as subject, the body can only be located in geopolitical terms. The dominant position undertaken by leftist women's groups on the issue is to define mail-order brides as exported victims in a neocolonial trade. Ethnographic studies of the domestic scene have suggested that, within this space, women make sense of their lives and thus pose resistant and subversive pleasure. In contrast, the mail-order bride has been confined in a commodity trade apparently devoid of pleasure for this body. However, while literal violence does exist as a constant threat to mail-order brides, various forms of pleasure and mobility as seen in ethnographic domestic studies can also be said to underwrite the exchange.

My own subject position and stake in this chapter needs to be foregrounded. As a Filipino exchange scholar in the United States, my critical intention is to initiate a discussion of issues that continue to be linked to the colonial and neocolonial histories and institutions (primarily) between the Philippines and the United States. The discourse of mail-order brides certainly is symptomatic of the Philippine-U.S. relationship. At the very least, I hope this study raises consciousness about the discourse, one whose conditions are inequitably more detrimental to the mail-order bride than to the first-world groom. I do not intend to construct a rescue narrative or a victimage paradigm for the mail-order bride; both inevitably position Filipino women as oppressed, therefore providing for liberation as key to the question, What is to be done? By examining the conditions in which the mail-order bride discourse is constructed, I attempt to call into focus some of the issues and stakes in this discourse, its relation to other power/knowledge networks, and the implicit and explicit struggles entailed in these discourses and networks. I hope for other interventions to occur that, in turn, may lead toward some theoretical and practical empowerment tactics for the actual marginalized bodies/voices experiencing these effects of colonial and neocolonial histories in their daily struggles.

Multinational and Transnational Bodies

> Bodies are maps of power and identity.
> —Donna Haraway, *Simians, Cyborgs, and Women,* 180

> [T]he body becomes a useful force only if it is both a productive body and a subjected body.
> —Michel Foucault, *Discipline and Punish,* 26

Donna Haraway's feminist-socialist myth of the cyborg exposes some possible openings for resituating pleasure and responsibility in the bodies of women in transnational space. As transnational space is set into place by information technology, the cyborg becomes "a hybrid of machine and organism, a creature of social reality as well as fiction," able to breach boundaries between human and animal, organism and machine, and so on.[3] Haraway refers to third-world women in transnational space as "real life cyborgs [who] are actively rewriting the texts of their bodies" and claims, therefore, that "survival is the stakes in this play of readings."[4] However, the myth's radical potentials have yet to yield to a practice of affinity and networking, a practice Haraway situates as the collective manifestation of the politics of the cyborg. To a large extent and though problematic even in the first-world context, Haraway's myth addresses a first-world audience able to realize, in some individualizing form, the body's pleasure in technology. I do not know how this pleasure corresponds to any Philippine practice in a way that can recuperate some progressive strains for marginalized groups. In patriarchal and racialized labor-capital situations in the Third World, technology remains an apparatus that foregrounds power relations, an apparatus utilized by political and cultural authority (as in "technologies of power") toward the production of a hegemonic moment, a mode of disciplining (in Foucauldian terms) the body.

By being circulated in the transnational space, the Filipina's body becomes a symptom of these debates. On the one hand, the body becomes a tool for (limited) economic empowerment, placing the Filipina in the nontraditional role of "wage earner" or "head of the family." On the other hand, the Filipina's body becomes the very requisite for being positioned in this "new" economic situation: her supposedly nimble fingers and perfect eyesight, her youth, and her unmarried status all add up to a stereotypical performative body in transnational circuits. Her traditional role as homemaker allows her body to perform similar work outside the home. The body is integrated into the circuits of multinationalism and transnationalism, generating a political economy marked by a highly sexualized division of labor. Third-world governments are only too eager to provide this habitat, which, as in most of the Third World, is imbued with the feminization of poverty: women bear the burden of the impact of changes in transnational circuits (debt servicing, debt rescheduling, value-added taxation schemes, structural adjustments, etc.) while at the same time functioning as homemakers. After their own wage work, women are still expected to do the marketing, cooking, household chores, and child rearing. As first-world women vacate the domestic sphere, the demand for international labor has shifted focus to third-world women's domestic labor. At the same time, men are forced to adopt nontraditional roles and attitudes: as women work, men accept the idea of wage-earning couples as a necessity for economic survival, and they learn traditionally female professions—nursing, midwifery, and so on—to better their chances of working abroad.

These have been the gendered effects of multinationalism and transnationalism. Neocolonialism, the postindependence condition(s) arising from the shift from colonialism to postcolonialism in the era of late capitalism, is translated through multinationalism, militarism, and transnationalism. While multinationalism and transnationalism present seemingly divergent patterns of economic development and capital movement, for the purposes of this chapter "multinationalism" refers to the operations occuring in the national spaces, while "transnationalism" refers to those occuring in the international spaces. However, the areas differentiating the two processes inevitably collapse in practice. Both are examples of attempts to master and command space as a means of controlling class struggle. Among the tactics employed by multinationalism and transnationalism are geographical mobility and decentralization, deindustrialization and industrialization, and capital investment and flight.

Beginning with multinationalism, export processing zones (EPZs) were established by the International Monetary Fund and World Bank (IMF-WB) prescription for third-world industrialization that sought to induce foreign investments. Through the EPZs, the IMF-WB has positioned the Third World and third-world women in their places, perpetuating its function to oversee their "development" by marking off the Third World and third-world women in terms of cost-benefit analyses of natural and labor resources. Cost-benefit analysis foregrounds the direction of multinational capital that collapses national boundaries and homogenizes women's bodies. Multinational corporations are guaranteed maximum profits for their investments with incentives including cheap labor; the absence of customs duties, import quotas, and foreign exchange controls; an assurance of unlimited profits, repatriation, long tax holidays, cheap loans, and subsidized utilities; and tolerance for 100 percent foreign ownership. As more stringent policies are activated to systematize and ensure smooth-flowing operations, the absence of restrictions for multinational business is eventually borne by the bodies of workers. Originally intended as sites for the free flow of technological exchange, EPZs have become conduits of global assembly lines and virtual sweatshops. By 1983 electronic products produced in these EPZs had already become the number one export of the Philippines.

In this sexual division of labor, heavy industries such as mining, petroleum refining, and machinery and equipment manufacturing generally utilize male labor while light industries such as food processing and the manufacture of textiles, garments, footwear, tobacco, and pharmaceuticals utilize mostly female labor. Women's body parts are idealized, "synergizing" nimble fingers, 20/20 eyesight, and hardy bodies in the performance of multinational work. In short, women are preferred for all the stereotypical reasons: lower labor costs, traditional feminine skills, manual dexterity, more productivity, greater tolerance of and better performance in repetitive and monotonous tasks, reliability, patience, low expectations, lack of employment alternatives, a willingness to put up with dead-end jobs, higher voluntary quitting rates, and so on.[5] As multinationalism has provided women with work space, it has done so without radical departure from women's traditional social roles and functions. Women's marginality becomes the essence of multinationalism and transnationalism, which, premised upon women's oppression, reconstitute these traditional modes of oppression for their own economic and cultural prerogatives. This reconstitution amounts to the exploitation of women and the Third World in global, transnational terms.

Third-world women are further stratified within the hierarchy of the multinational paradigm: young, single, childless women are preferable (in fact, to be thirty years old is to be old in the trade, and 88 percent of Filipina workers engaged in multinational work are under the age of twenty-nine).[6] Most employers prefer younger women for the following reasons: employers are often reluctant to pay generous maternity benefits; single women are considered more flexible and reliable workers than married women—freer to work shift hours and with lower rates of absenteeism caused by child-care problems; young, unmarried women are more efficient, since they are seen on average to have better health, eyesight, and physical reflexes than older women, and they are less likely to be fatigued from the burden of combining factory work with unpaid domestic work at home; employers themselves are reluctant to disrupt family life, believing that married women belong in the home; employing young single women ensures a rate of natural or voluntary turnover when the women leave to marry or raise children.[7]

Furthermore, between the spaces of wage work, the female body is also reconstituted in the respites from actual multinational work. Management exploits the femininity of women workers by promoting soft-sell conspicuous consumption in its "extraoccupational" activities. Cosmetic and Western-style clothing bazaars are organized periodically; beauty contests are also staged in which women within the firms compete for the title of beauty queen; and bonuses and incentives take the form of gift checks from department stores. In another instance, "raffles are held to determine the lucky employee who will be given the use of a Timex watch for nine months" (if the watch is lost, the worker is made to pay its full value).[8] Such insidious promotion of consumption offers a crucial clue for understanding the extent of the sexualization of labor. The production of desire for consumer goods foregrounds the way such desire becomes the undercurrent in the exportation of brides. When multinational work has maximized its utilization of the still-young female body, the body remains anchored in dreams of modernity, making it refurbishable as a bride transportable to first-world sites. The preparation of the female body for female work in multinational operations incipiently also prepares the body for transnational work as a mail-order bride.

Multinational work is precarious work, to say the least, as work given can easily be taken back. Multinational corporations close shops at the slightest suggestion of labor unrest or at the promise of cheaper labor and better incentives elsewhere. Multinationalism is characterized by its mobility as it resets boundaries, selling its operations to the host nation that offers the highest benefits for the lowest costs. This, in turn, results in another shift in the circuits of labor and bodies: women from closed sites are displaced, while women from new sites are integrated into the transnational grid. In the global economy, each site in foreign countries (each body of laborers) is condensed to worker status, to be hailed and dismissed in the expanse of the reserve army of available global labor sites and bodies.

Militarism provides another mode of translating neocolonialism. The twentieth-century rise of the United States as a global power escalated the need to expand and secure its interests worldwide. Its military bases mushroomed in sites where its interests were directly and contingently at stake. These sites acted as magnets, producing a layer of entertainment establishments servicing the needs of servicemen. In these sites, women perform sexual labor. "Hospitality girls" have an affinity with the work done by Filipino women in multinational operations. "Hospitality girls" work in the hub of other transnational nodes in the Third World; in the Philippines, these sites are in the urban centers that used to host the American military bases and in cities vigorously projected and exoticized by the tourism circuit. The International Labor Organization reported in 1982 that some 200,000 sex workers operated in the Philippines.[9] Some 12,000 to 18,000 of the women worked in the American military hubs in the cities of Angeles and Olongapo.[10] Most of these women were migrants from the depressed regions in the country. The military bases served as magnets, attracting surplus bodies from the depressed areas. Performing tasks that provided the servicemen's "R and R" (rest and recreation), these women were labeled by sailors as "LBFMs" (little brown fucking machines). The cyborg reappears here as a sexual machine that occupies a highly problematic position in the confusion of body and machine boundaries. Where men's leisure is translated to female work, the issue of pleasure and pain is not so much obscured as clarified in the sexual economy at play. Women's sexual body parts are instrumentalized for male leisure and female work. The "pleasure in the confusion of boundaries" in the cyborg myth is but a transnational reterritorialization of bodies in the service of capital's movement.

The experience of interracial, crosscultural relations foregrounds "hospitality women" as precursors to the mail-order bride discourse and economy that began in the mid-1970s and erupted in the 1980s. With the last of the American bases closed in 1992, some women continued their trade as the former base sites were converted to investment and tourism destinations. It is estimated that there are still 500,000 women and children engaged in sexual work in the Philippines.[11] Implicated in this work are children's bodies, now activated into the circuits. Fifty thousand interracial children, known as Amerasians, are the living legacy of these closed bases.[12] Japan's growing dominance in Philippine economics, as it has overtaken the United States as the primary donor of foreign aid, creditor of foreign loans, and investor of multinational business, has brought another crop of children. As more Filipinas move into this Asian first-world site (working as "cultural dancers/ entertainers"), marrying a Japanese man is regarded as offering social mobility. The Japanese Embassy in the Philippines reported in 1991 that there were 20,000 Filipina-Japanese marriages. Only 10 percent of such marriages are considered to be successful or to have endured beyond the period expected of such relationships. One consequence of these relationships is a growing number of Filipino-Japanese children called Japinos.

The third mode of translating neocolonialism is through transnationalism, which circulates the bodies of women and men in international spaces.
The travails of modern development place the Philippines in a recurring
juxtaposition of crisis and progress. In the dysfunctional national space, one
of ten Filipinos is seriously seeking employment abroad.[13] With 775,699 college graduates annually, there is no place else to go but overseas; 56 percent
of the 428,121 Filipinos who join the international work force annually are
women.[14] The lack of employment opportunities within the Philippines is
the primary cause for the migration of Filipinos overseas. There are more
than two million overseas contract workers in some 125 countries.[15] Some
600,000 families have a family member working abroad; an estimated nine-
teen million Filipinos are directly and indirectly benefiting from migrant
labor.[16] Migrant labor earns some $3 billion annually for the Philippine econ-
omy, capable of sustaining a quarter of the entire population.[17] The worldwide annual figure, however, jumps to an estimated $6 billion (about the
same amount as the Philippine national budget) when remittances by nationalities of Filipino descent are considered, $1 billion of which comes from
remittances by more than two million Filipinos in the United States.[18]

Historically, labor migration from the Philippines has come in waves: the
first as agricultural workers in the United States beginning in 1903; the second from 1945 to the late 1960s when thousands of professionals in the medical field left for the United States and Canada; and the third under Marcos's
martial law regime, which was more massive than the first two and which
continues into the present. The men were concentrated mostly in the Middle East, doing work in the spending spree of the oil boom. Women were
mostly in the centers of established and emerging first-world formations—
chambermaids in Europe; domestic helpers in Saudi Arabia, Hong Kong, and
Singapore; entertainers in Japan; nurses in the United States; and mail-order
brides in the First World. Women leave the domestic sphere of the national
space only to reenter that sphere by performing home-related work in international spaces. That is, unpaid home labor in the domestic sphere becomes paid labor in international spaces. Thus, because they can earn more
for home-related work in international spaces than for the work they were
trained to do in the national space, half a million women are leaving the
Philippines, whether legally or illegally, every year to work primarily in international domesticated professions.

For most Filipinas, to be an overseas contract worker is to be in a triple bind:
first, as a foreigner; second, as a woman in patriarchal society; and third, as a
woman working in professions regarded as menial and even socially undesirable. In migrating to find work overseas, Filipinas have supported a layer of
businesses in the Philippines and abroad, such as promotion and recruiting
agencies, airlines, and banks. Filipina domestic overseas contract workers are

mostly single women (80 percent) and in the prime age range of twenty-one to thirty years (67 percent).[19] Most of these women are educated and skilled, yet they do menial work abroad for higher salaries than they would receive for the professional jobs they are capable of doing in the Philippines. This work outside the home presents a dilemma, as Ruby Palma-Beltran observes: "On the one hand, we want our women to grow out of their traditional functions of child rearing and housekeeping and to realize other potentials which are more highly valued and compensated. On the other hand, market demands overseas show an increasing trend for domestic jobs."[20]

Paradoxically, it is in these domestic spheres that Filipinas are allocated to transnational space. Domestic work is an invisible space in that it is done in the private sphere, yet the live-in arrangement places workers at the "beck and call of the employer 24 hours a day."[21] Ninety-eight percent of Filipina workers in Hong Kong are domestic helpers.[22] In Singapore, of the 40,000 foreign household workers employed in the country, almost 60 percent are Filipinas.[23] About 90 percent of Filipina workers in Spain are domestic helpers, chambermaids, or waitresses.[24] There are some 100,000 Filipinos in Italy, most of whom are Filipinas working as domestic helpers; only 35,000 have legal status.[25] The international space accords other possibilities for the migrant worker; working in Italy, for example, is considered only as a transient stop toward a permanent residence in the United States, Canada, or Australia. After getting their new citizenship, they are able to petition family members to come to the first-world site as immigrants. Within the Philippines, they are also able to provide the financial support for their family's social mobility, providing anything and everything from used appliances and clothing to education, rent, and vehicles.

The postcolonial geobody moves on: in specific locations—as nurses in the United States and as entertainers in Japan—and in various first-world sites as mail-order brides. Nursing is traditionally positioned as domestic and feminized labor. Half of all Filipino nurses are already practicing their profession abroad, and 25,0000 more are deployed annually.[26] Fifty thousand Filipino nurses in the United States remit some $100 million annually to the Philippines.[27] The Alliance of Health Workers, a Philippine-based nongovernmental organization, attributes the exodus to three structural factors, all of which make the graduates marketable in foreign countries: the government's labor export policy, aggressive recruitment strategies by local and international agencies, and the Western orientation of Philippine nursing education.[28] The educational system honed during the American colonial period continues to produce graduates more attuned to the needs of overseas markets than those of the local setting. Gender shifts are tolerated in consideration of economic gains. In recent years, male enrollment in nursing programs has been on the rise as men accept their own feminization in exchange for the promise of dollar earnings abroad. This feminization of labor has been on the rise, but paradoxically it has also resulted in a masculinization of the nursing profession. With the lack of breadwinner opportunities on the home front, men territorialize traditional feminine positions that provide better economic rewards abroad. Income earned abroad eventually reconstitutes the men's place in the private and public spheres of the nation space.

Filipinas have also come to Japan as entertainers. *Japayuki-san* is the pejorative term used to describe Filipinas and other Asian women entertainers working in Japan. The term is derived from *karayuki-san,* referring to Japanese prostitutes who serviced the sexual needs of Japanese soldiers all over Asia prior to and during the World War II.[29] In the 1970s a huge volume of Japanese tourists to Thailand, the Philippines, Taiwan, and Korea enjoyed company-paid holidays that later were exposed as sex tours. In more recent years, entertainers were exported/ferreted to Japan to meet the sex market demand. In 1991, there were already 45,899 Filipina (and Filipino) entertainers in Japan.[30] By January 1992, 65.28 percent of foreign entertainers in Japan were Filipinas.[31]

Control over women's bodies is located in the organizational layers of businesses. To prevent the mobility of women, their passports are confiscated upon arrival. The body is depersonalized, delegitimized, and denationalized. As the most important transnational identification paper, the passport bears the markers of individual and national identity. Without the passport, the individual does not exist as a legitimate entity outside the nation space. With the confiscation of the passport, the body is also criminalized in a move to fixate women in the proper border between male work and leisure. A customer quota is enforced, and the entertainer is fined if the quota is not met. Furthermore, because she can only work legally for six months, the promise of savings is precluded: she cannot generate enough income to pay her debts or to send money back home. This time limit also means that the entertainer's body, like that of her counterpart in multinational work, is continuously recycled, subject to periodic replacement by other bodies.

Despite these precarious conditions, Filipinas still pursue, for lack of better options, the promise of making concrete the cultural standards of middle-class living. In the Philippines, these standards are represented by Betamax, television, cassette recorders, oversized stuffed toys, gold jewelry, and so on. The body is resignified by being commodified in exchange for the signs of material affluence. This exchange is also the logic behind mail-order brides and is, in a more general schema, the reason why women and men allow themselves to be circulated in transnational space in the first place. As the nation space has yet to yield progress from economic subsistence to material affluence, that fulfillment is sought elsewhere. In turn, the desire for consumer goods has become hegemonic, and an explosion of consumerist signs penetrates the body in national and international spaces. The motivation for withstanding pain and anguish relies on the promise of deliverance via the acquisition of these goods or markers of affluence. The deliverance is made more significant because the signs are available in the Filipino's place of origin. In transposing these markers back to the national space, a leverage for the community's acceptance of the family's economic ascent is created. The body that allows itself to be mobile, to be exchanged, to be commodified, and to be marked becomes the precondition for social mobility in the transnational space.

The discourse of mail-order brides is premised along a similar promise of deliverance. Both bride and groom bind themselves into a contract of marriage without physically seeing each other. The first-world groom and third-world bride will most likely meet for the first time a few days before their marriage. The phenomenon has been on the rise. In 1970, only 34 women were issued K-1 (fiancée) visas in the United States; in 1986, visas were issued for 3,867 Asians, 2,276 of whom were Filipinos.[32] By 1990, the Dallas regional office of the U.S. Immigration and Naturalization Service alone had received some 15,000 "fiancée petitions."[33] In 1985, immediate visas through marriage were granted for 124,093 people.[34] It is estimated that between 50 and 60 percent of mail-order brides are Filipinas.[35] Two-thirds of the 81 percent of Filipinas in the former West Germany are married to German man, with some 10,000 more undocumented women residing in the country.[36] Of the 47,692 Filipinas residing in Australia in 1991, 70 percent were sponsored by male residents.[37] There are now some 50,000 Filipina mail-order brides in the United States.[38] Despite the cases of abuse, death, and forced prostitution, applications for international marriage continue for the promise of a better life.

The body moves along this promise. As the letter is premised on a promise to be "properly" delivered—in the "proper" time to the "proper" person in the "proper" place—the letter then prefigures the body's movement.

Letters and Obsolescent Technology

Letters mark exchanges and the fulfillment of the promise. Letters conquer distance and at the same time maintain it. Letters (mis)introduce, (mis)inform, (in)formalize, (un)plan, accept, and reject; they hail and interpellate. But most of all, letters promise. As letters promise the delivery of mail-order brides— and mail-order brides themselves promise to be "promising"—the letters become crucial in the fulfillment of the promise.

Gary B.'s letter to his agent attests to the "mail-order bride" narrative:

Dear Friends,

    Just thought I would drop this letter in the mail. I wanted to let you know that through your pen pal club, I was able to meet and marry my beautiful wife, Marietta. Enclosed you will find a photo of my wife and two adorable children. We started writing in 1986, met in Manila in 1988 and got married in 1989. We will be celebrating our anniversary this January. Our story is truly a romantic one.

Sincerely,
[Gary's full name][39]

The characters, setting, and plot are encapsulated in the testimonial attesting to the deliverance and realization of the promise. Gary's testimonial as another satisfied customer evokes both a capitalist orientation (a union of desire and capital realized) and a patriarchal/racialized imperative of speaking for and on behalf of the third-world woman (represented again in writing the other and in the photograph). The letter becomes a condensed signifier for the "mail-order bride" narrative in particular and for shopping in general.

Shopping has also been psychically and historically imbued with the promise of acquiring an object that represents desire. Capitalist culture is driven by consumerist desire and channeled through the purchase of an object that materializes desire. The mail-order bride becomes part of the shopping circuit through the mail-order system: purchasing something the shopper has not seen in the hope that this object fulfills his desire. Though the shopper has not physically inspected the object, the drive is powerful enough to convince him to instigate the purchase.

The confluence of the postal and shopping systems has worked toward greater efficiency. The postal system has generated some circuits to network this confluence. The struggle to establish a postal system in colonial America was characterized by the ability to territorialize within and between colonies in order to service and link these areas. It was only upon Benjamin Franklin's coappointment as postmaster general in 1753 that the postal system became a viable enterprise. In utilizing the system to further the interest of his publication, Franklin refurbished the production and dissemination of news and public opinion by admitting all newspapers to the mail at a reasonable rate.

Ideologically, the postal system also privileges individualism and individual rights. The ideology of mail sanctity interjects notions of individualism and humanism, public trust and liberalism, democracy and capitalism. Capitalist imperatives transformed the postal system into a public enterprise that eventually became a bureaucracy. With 740,000 workers, the Post Office was the third largest employer in the United States in 1970, topped only by AT&T

and General Motors. Its income of $6 billion has made it one of the biggest businesses, larger than such industrial giants as Texaco and IBM. In 1970, the Postal Reorganization Act formalized the bureaucracy into a government corporation.

As an enterprise that rode on the growing success and efficiency of the postal system, mail-ordering was successfully transformed by Sears Roebuck into an equally viable enterprise. Early catalogs already emphasized efficient and affordable delivery, banking on such mythology as the Pony Express. The other factor that made mail-ordering successful was that it allowed for a variety of choices. Testimonials from customers attested to their satisfaction with the service, the quality of the goods, and the availability of a range of choices, all of which turned skeptics into patrons. The right to choose embodied the workings of liberal democracy, while the efficient supply and delivery of the goods embodied the workings of capitalist transformation during the late 1800s, the era of imperialism.

The 1897 Sears Roebuck catalog advertised products from all over the world (e.g., Java coffee, India tea, Jamaican ginger, "watches made by poor peasants in Switzerland," beauty products from colonized countries). U.S. supremacy as a juncture for global products—in Sears Roebuck's words, "the cheapest supply house on earth"—was a recurring theme in the catalog. It was also symptomatic of the period of transformation from colonialism to imperialism, selling the colony and its products, colonialism and its ethos to the imperial countries and its citizens/shoppers. The cover page, featuring the agricultural icon Ceres (the corn and earth goddess), celebrated agricultural abundance and the desire for markers of middle-class life, foregrounding new technologies and privatized modes of experiencing industrialization. The catalogs were embarking on a private colonial project that circulated the colonies' products to the homes and farms in the United States.

The United States would also embark on its colonial project with the Philippines as its first experiment in colony building. One of the initial communication institutions established upon conquest was the postal system. Dean C. Worcester, secretary of the interior of the Philippine Islands (1901–13) and Franklin's counterpart as quintessential enlightened colonizer, took pains to report on the innovations undertaken in the Philippine postal system: the expansion of postal routes, pay increases to letter carriers, and the establishment of innovative delivery services. Losses of articles were conscientiously investigated: "Now, even the most trivial complaint is painstakingly investigated, and only in rare cases is there failure to recover the value of lost or stolen articles from the postal employee."[40] As such, a new ethos of individualism as evoked in the sanctity of the letter was introduced with the conquest of the Philippines, seeking to assimilate the conquered land and people to the ideology and practices of democracy and capitalism.

U.S. euphoria surrounding the Philippine conquest was only topped by the trauma of defeat in the Vietnam War. By the 1970s, the loss in the Vietnam War marked the United States's own decline in global hegemony. The postal system's ability to deliver was also on a decline. The system has not made innovations in deciphering the words that direct delivery. Approximately one billion pieces of domestic mail annually are never delivered because of incorrect or unreadable addresses.[41] The future of mail-ordering was also implicated. (Sears's profits declined, resulting in closures of a significant number of retail outlets in the early 1990s.) The promise of the letter arriving at its destination was materializing elsewhere. New technologies, with innovations like interactivity, fulfilled the promise of unlimited choices and instantaneous satisfaction of desire. Not only is desire mediated through technology, it is also transmitted through technology.

Television shopping offers consumers expanded visibility of products. Figures of authority become fixtures to explain product innovations. Phone testimonials provide audible expressions of satisfaction and trust based not only on the customer's experience with a purchased product but, more significantly, on the experience of television shopping. Television becomes more than just a department store's display window. It marks a domestic cycle that eventually returns to the domestic space: one orders an item from the domestic space to utilize the purchased item in the confines of that space. Technology's alleviation of physical work in the domestic sphere has also generated new work. Television shopping provides for new technological products that operate differently in order to accomplish this new work.

Television shopping is also limited in the scope of items available for purchase. Sexual items that fulfill sexual desires are located somewhere else. Bodies are called upon in this fold to be (dis)played and (dis)placed elsewhere. "Love Connection," a televised dating show, allows for the condensation of body spaces within the television frame. The show displays the ideological features of liberalism and capitalism. Democratic participation is practiced by audience members as they lock in their choice of a date for the contestant. The final decision, however, is made by the player, who is allowed to interject, depending on the participant's class origin, his/her working- or middle-class views on heterosexual relationships. It is only at the point when a decision is made that the full body of the choice date is called onto the stage. Formerly displaced, the body is shown in full view for a face-to-face exchange, for final inspection.

Television as public communication also integrates the categories of permissible and forbidden to determine what will be included and excluded. The fulfillment of overt sexual desire is thus derived elsewhere, altering sex practices significantly. Phone and Internet sex allow the initiation and consummation of words and bodies entangled. Words—whether printed, spoken, or heard—prefigure the body. The body is inscribed in words; pleasure is implicated through words. Sex is consummated through words that perform the body that performs the words. Not seen, the body is entangled in words that recount not a historical body but a nostalgic body imbued in electronic desire and pleasure. The absent body, inscribed in words, signifies the loss of the organic body. The nostalgic body, inscribed in technology, is made to stand in as the image of the absent organic body. The cessation of words marks the reappearance of the historical body. Electronic mail (e-mail) has shifted the function of words; the promise is transformed from being physically delivered to being electronically generated.

Yet much of the shopping for mail-order brides takes place in cyberspace. The nostalgia for old technology and colonialism inscribed in women's bodies in printed catalogs now shifts to one directed more toward the organic body in cyberspace catalogs. Unlike cybersex, where climax is initiated and realized through cyberspace, the Filipina's narrative experiences closure only through the delivery of the material body to the male shopper through the circuit of marriage. The Filipina's body signifies both the temporal loss of her material body and the massive reproduction of her virtual body. She is commandeered to the first-world sites through telecommunications technology, much like capital and information are transferred at present. Through cyberspace, she is electronically generated for the promise of reinvented materiality in the first-world domestic spheres. In the course of the transfer—or, at the very least, its possibility—the Filipina body is disciplined, regimented for use and transformation in first-world sites.

These new innovations of technology call for greater interactivity. Interactivity allows the body to move through various spheres, shopping for another body that represents desire and pleasure. The bodies turn to images; sex becomes simulated. The information superhighway is only too eager to celebrate shopping in the living room with choices no one has ever imagined before. Surveillance figures in all these technologies of power. The use of the courier in the earliest years of the postal system also functioned as surveillance, to report deserting soldiers and runaway slaves; the sanctity of the letter, as in all rights, is not absolute (during times of war, letters may be opened); new technologies often are produced initially for military purposes. Activated within the circuits of desire, these technologies are also fragmenting, simulating the body.

The mail-order bride remains largely "outside *in*" this grid.[42] Despite the increasing use of the Internet, letters and catalogs still prefigure and circumscribe the exchange. The third-world woman as commodity is made to embody this nostalgia for previous technology. As Michael Taussig writes, "obsolescence is where the future meets the past in the dying body of the commodity."[43] That the third-world woman is aligned with the previous technology of the postal system serves to position her with the primitive, placing her in the realm of "second nature," which separates her from her own historical and cultural positionality. She functions in relation to modernity's fascination with obsolescence in the way she is made to represent its ethos of a copy of the First World's past. This means that the third-world woman is made to embody the novelty of imagining and concretizing forms of first-world nostalgia for its past: "The Third World and its objects are in a global perspective generally seen as permanently 'recently outdated,' a reservoir of First World hand-me-downs and sleepy-eyed memories of its earlier consumer items."[44]

Catalogs, Nostalgia, and Multiculturalism

> Mar 205 Virginia (31) Philippines/ 5'3; 98; Toy company employee
> (former seamstress; highschool grad). "Seek a penpal 30 to 35 of
> age and have a stable job, not that much ugly and not that much
> handsome, and fair in everything."
> —ad by Filipina[45]

> I appreciate their kindness when they write long letters, telling
> me about himself, his job, his family and the American way of
> life.
> —testimony by a Filipina applicant[46]

The mail-order bride functions as a commodity embodying the outdated first-world narratives of the nuclear family and coloniality. On the one hand, in the exchange of marriage proposals and bodies through the previous technology of the postal system, the third-world woman assumes the domestic and sexual tasks vacated by emancipated white women. On the other hand, the third-world woman is rescued from oppressors in her native land—native men and poverty. The nuclear family and colonialist fantasies are entwined in the operation of the catalogs. While allowing the male clientele to make a variety of choices, from the potential bride's point of view the catalogs work in a different mode. For the men, catalogs provide a listing of available mail-order brides, itemized descriptions of these women, agency services, and procedures for establishing correspondence and arranging marriage. From the women's perspective, however, catalogs package women's bodies, representing them through certain conventions. Through the women's photographs, their bodies are imbued with casualness rather than formality; the face is privileged above other bodily parts. The smile is the rhetorical gesture. It is very rare to find full-body shots of women. Women's bodies are never complete, constructing a lack in their desire to enter subjectivity via the public sphere allowed in the catalog pages. Subjectivity becomes similarly segmented as the mail-order bride's body in the catalog. The desire for

subjectivity is a lack needing liberal fulfillment. Like the subsequent exposure of the organic body at the end of the "Love Connection," the mail-order
bride's subjectivity can only be realized as a desirable end to the fulfillment
of her metanarrative. She anticipates fulfillment through the heralding of her
bodily parts into an organic liberal being. Once she is rescued from the printed and into the literal material conditions, she becomes closer to the promise of liberal subjectivity. In her spousal status, she maintains her quest for
subjectivity—ironically, by hiding her mail-order origin.

The nostalgia for a national family has been historically and racially activated by photographs. When male Chinese and Japanese immigrants were
finally allowed to bring family members to the United States, pictures connected prospective couples for marriage. Fearing the demise of family and
race, picture brides were imported to increase the population, thereby re-
signifying national/ethnic and familial presence against American racism's
operations of marginalization and absence.

The brief texts accompanying the photographs provide for the coding of
identities of the women according to cultural categories and structures of
taste. Each woman's picture is introduced with information in this order: her
numerical code, her first name only, age, and nation of origin. What follows
are her physical, professional, and personal background: height, weight, birth-
date, profession, interests. In *Cherry Blossoms,* a bride correspondence catalog, a woman's marital status and information on children (sex, number, age)
are also mentioned. The last item in the description is her concept of a worthy man/penpal/husband, usually articulated along the lines of acceptable
race, religion, age brackets, and other gauges she herself has chosen. For the
user, the description provides sufficient information on women's bodies and
lives to pass judgment. The functional third-world woman's body is made
symptomatic of the ideal first-world male nuclear family narrative.

The text brings into perspective the desire to situate women in an American space and time when women were idealized schoolgirls and perfect house-
wives. The family romance is, after all, "a way of 'inventing history' that allows
us not only to exchange but to *improve* upon the received and socially sanc-
tioned versions of our beginnings."[47] A refurbished national and familiar origin is continuously generated, always better than the actual story. In maintaining the nuclear family fantasy, nostalgia becomes a libidinal investment in
recuperating liberal American women's bodies in the (post)feminist age. The
layout of spaces with photographs and brief descriptions recalls a body of related texts: high school or college yearbooks. Casual shots, group photos, and
childhood and teen pictures in yearbooks articulate the graduating high school
student's presence. The graduate is allowed to memorialize people—from
parents, friends, sweethearts, and faculty members to quotes from Nietzsche,
Walt Whitman, Bob Dylan, and other cultural icons. By association, graduates

memorialize themselves and their historical moment (which encompasses fash-ion, hairstyle, aspiration, gaze, and so on). The page marks off an age of inno-cence, an idealized moment of juvenile triumph when compared to the busi-ness of adulthood, income generation, marriage and family, relationships, and so on. These relational texts emphasize an ideal femininity that has its domes-tic roots in the ideal family of the American 1950s—one that never really ex-isted. Then, in the 1970s, many white women liberated themselves from the domestic space. Women of color and third-world women are filling this void in the domestic spheres, whether as hotel employees and maids or as brides within the American national space. In the case of the mail-order bride, both domestic and sexual functions are inscribed on the bride's body.

As the mail-order bride's discursive body is technologized in the catalogs (and also in video), her body becomes inscribed in a robotic function. On the one hand, the cottage technology used to produce the catalog (e.g., mim-eograph, dated quality of production and layout, mostly black-and-white photos) remains underdeveloped and, to a large extent, intentional: it rep-resents the women and their national origins as inferior to the user's own. On the other hand, the discourse of bodies is retechnologized for the first-world home, in which technology is required in the efficient management of the domestic sphere. The bride becomes a robotic technology that opera-tionalizes the functions of appliances. In maintaining the technology of the domestic sphere, the bride's body is also technologized. The slave of the co-lonial era is transformed into a post-Fordist robot.

Another historical narrative regenerated through third-world women's bodies is the U.S. experience in overseas colonial building. Colonialism pre-sents another nostalgia in various ways. Women's bodies encapsulate the desire for conquest and rescue. Within the sphere of popular culture, even science fiction films—such as those in the Alien and Terminator series—present mothering as both an issue of conquest and rescue of the nation. The fantasy of conquest is also fed by sex tours: sites become "every single man's paradise," where the main activity is "chasing and conquering the fairer sex." In a sex tour catalog for Southeast Asia, the erect breasts of Thai women are emphasized in the colored collage cover. First-world men aim to regain the pleasure of authority of the lost phallus through a conquest of third-world women categorized either as lustful en masse ("thousands upon thousands") or as a virginal rarity ("your virgin bride"). The catalog aims to make clear the distinction between hookers and virgins, promising men that they will "always have the upper hand in dealings with Asian women." The clarity of this advantage then enables the men to separate the grain from the chaff, thereby choosing those worthy of redemption in the First World.[48]

Tourism also works in a similarly familiar mode: conquest is triggered in glossy pictures in travel magazines and materializes in actual visits to and photographs taken of the tourist sites. As geography is imbued with passivity, activity then is generated through the bodies of people. The travel catalogs hinge on these bodies as generic signifiers of exoticism, whether of single models posed in some natural tourist attraction or masses of people sweating through a religious procession. The native bodies are exoticized, denied their particularities. In the sexual economy, the body is eroticized but nevertheless also denied its specificity to engender anything but the desire to be conquered. In this sense, the body is made generic and anonymous, collapsed of its specific identities in order to signify the collective exotic. As such, a body is made substitutable for another in the fulfillment of the desire to conquer and to know. Women's bodies, however, are doubly functional in providing the distress signal from which conquest and rescue become modes of racialized imperatives. In a national allegorical reading, women's bodies become the trope from which to measure the alarming gauge that preconditions the desire to liberate the marginal(ized) race in general. The feminized national space awaits rescue by the penetration of foreign capital, loans, aids, and investment as the objective path to modernization and, consequently, the alleviation of poverty. This resonates with opportunities for transnational exploitation for both foreign investors and their local compradors whereby resources and relations of production, especially labor, are feminized.

Another fascination with third-world women arises from the fantasy of rescuing the women from their own kind. In the catalogs, this point is emphasized in the women's comparison of men from their own countries with the idealized image of the American male. The women in the photographs all gaze at the male user. In their best smiles and poses, these women project themselves to draw the user's gaze. The user, confronted by pictures of hundreds of women, becomes aware of their collective presence and perhaps their collective condition. In an effort to save at least one among the hundreds, the user activates a process of multiple penpal correspondence, until the most worthy is chosen for marriage and rescued to the First World.

Nostalgia is spoken through the language of philanthropy. Catalogs reconstruct the postcolonial geobody in their represention of the third-world woman through gender and racial stereotypes that operate as surveillance mechanisms on the third-world woman's body. The 1897 Sears Roebuck catalog is imbued with such a philanthrophic worldview: "It is safe to say that we are doing more for the farmer and the laborer than all the political demagogues in the country. The economy of any man's life revolves itself into a judicious expenditure of what money he has, whether the amount is large or small." *Cherry Blossoms* equally boasts of its own commitment to its Western, male audience: "Whether looking for a woman around the world or in your own backyard, we are committed to your success. That is what has made us successful."

Testimonials from satisfied Western customers perpetuate this imperative. The philanthropic, as reinforced by the users, demarcates the bodies of the worthy and unworthy. First-world benevolence and patriotism are attached to this mode. Not surprisingly, the newest wave of mail-order bride applicants come from Eastern Europe, from which new rescue narratives are generated to ensure that if democracy remains slow to develop in these nation spaces, the transposition of bodies to first-world sites promises to make democracy perform.

Gender and racial stereotypings become the direct ramifications of philanthropy. Sunshine International's cover letter to prospective clients reads: "Asian women are renowned for their beauty, femininity, traditional values and loving dispositions. They are sincere, faithful, devoted and believe in a lasting marriage and a happy home." The mail-order bride business depends, after all, on this characterization of passive women, the very antithesis perceived of the supposedly liberated first-world woman. The answer to the item, "Do you believe in women's liberation?" in the questionnaire filled out by prospective male clients to American-Asian Worldwide Service, a correspondence club, is a "100% no."[49] Furthermore, the liberated first-world woman unknowingly serves as conduit to the philanthropy project. By moving on to higher positions, she vacates her domestic duties, leaving ample space for occupancy by the third-world woman. Within liberal feminism, a hierarchy of positions is also contingently emplaced through the discourse of philanthropy.

In all these catalogs, there is also a disdain for white space. Pages condense as many images and life stories as possible. The dominance of pictures and texts signifies the seemingly unlimited variety and availability of choices. This plenitude pressures the user to make a choice, thereby providing a praxis to his individualism. More directly, the choice is made to emanate from within the selections of the page, as there is nothing outside the page. Desire is hinged within the page, only to be unhinged from its referent when the choice is made.

In the mail-order bride catalogs, the photographs implicate the user. In a study on multicultural relationships, most of the men who engage in the practice of obtaining mail-order brides seem to be "attempting to avoid repeating mistakes that undermined previous marriages."[50] The few younger men who engage in brokerage relationships "confess feeling ill at ease in encounters with Western women. . . . most blame the women's liberation movement for their plight."[51] In this respect, the catalogs simultaneously imply a crisis of masculinity in the First World and function as a self-help kit that enables men to reassume that masculinity via the conquest and rescue of a third-world woman. The catalogs are supported in their self-help function by booklets such as *How to Meet Exciting Ladies from All Over the*

World, which provides a step-by-step guide to correspondence with women for marriage and offers chapters devoted to topics such as "choosing your correspondents," "making your letter stand out," "sending gifts and money," and "what if you change your mind about her?"[52] It also includes an appendix on such items as prenuptial agreements, immigration, sample letters, and foreign phrases. These booklets and catalogs are the emasculated man's guides to redeeming his self-worth, which has been weakened in first-world women's challenge to patriarchal social structures.

The crisis comes from the male sense of lack in the face of the absence of a stable white female figure in the home, the domain of the private, the spiritual, and the pure. Men seek to preserve the ideals of purity in the postmodern, thereby preventing their own destabilization by envisioning a past, present, and future that align women, domesticity, and spirituality, on the one hand, and men, work, and materiality, on the other hand. Masculinity's domain over the public requires maintaining femininity in the realm of the private. With the perceived loss of gender dominance, race dominance is positioned as a surrogate ideal, a concession of in-betweens. On the one hand, first-world women are demonized, pitted against third-world women; on the other hand, this positions the third-world woman as merely accessory and concessionary. The family, masculinity, and individual self-worth rely on this positioning of the third-world woman.

Catalogs list and package bodies. Like dossiers, these are technologies of surveillance. They position women within the confines of racial and sexual criteria that act as modes of identification and differentiation between the consumer's subjectivity and the applicant's identity. In the psychic drive of the user, nostalgia places the bodies of women within organic fantasy narratives of family and colonial glories. Like the mail-order bride's body, the narratives move on in other contexts and present histories that continue to implicate the circuits of the mail-order bride discourse.

A special fall 1993 issue of *Time* magazine on immigration is symptomatic of the positioning of race and women of color in the United States.[53] The cover is a computer-generated image of a woman based on photographs of fourteen models of diverse ethnicities. Labeled the "image of our new Eve" and a "symbol of the future, multiethnic face of America," the woman's face reinscribes representative democracy (she is 15 percent Anglo-Saxon, 17.5 percent Middle Eastern, 17 percent African, 7.5 percent Asian, 35 percent southern European, and 7.5 percent Hispanic). As she does not exist, she also heralds the fictionality of liberalism.

In *Time*'s project, the desire is toward an incorporable multiculturalism that synthesizes rather than differentiates cultures. The technology of morphing produced this synthesis, using quantitative characteristics to achieve multiethnic representation. However, it has also produced a face that merely reflects the existing state of races and ethnicities sutured in the body of woman. The project is Frankenstein's creature or Frankenstein's bride, a perpetuation of the constructed *self* of multiculturalism, always torn between notions of discipline and benevolence.[54] *Time* framed the issue between the hysterics of immigration and the euphoria of globalism. The first article is based on the results of a *Time* poll of people's perceptions of immigration: Should the United States keep its doors open to or strictly limit immigration? Toward which groups of recent immigrants do people feel most favorably and least favorably? What stereotypical perceptions of immigrants do people have (i.e., do they add to the crime problem, are they basically good/honest people)? The last article heralds the ("final") arrival of the global village and the transformation of Americans into "transnational subjects."

Other representations, however, view transnational bodies in less sanguine ways. The highly praised film on cross-dressing and performance, *The Adventures of Priscilla, Queen of the Desert* (1994), portrays a Filipina mail-order bride in Australia. Cynthia (Julia Cortez) is depicted as the conniving sex worker who tricked an elderly Australian man into marriage, providing her with a means to immigrate to the groom's country. She is made to serve as catalyst to the development of affection between her husband and the elderly transgendered character who often refers to himself as "a true gentleman." Cynthia abandons her husband because he has a small "ding-a-ling" and is too old for her passions. Depicted as scheming, loud-mouthed, alcoholic, and neurotic, Cynthia is made to perform the fantastic act of popping ping-pong balls from her vagina. This encore recalls her supposed Philippine profession; in doing so, she is linked to a generic exotic/erotic bodily and national entity enmeshed in the liminal space of the white man's fantasy and loss. Everything negatively imagined of the concept of the "Filipina" in Australia is embodied in the mail-order bride character. Cynthia is reduced to a geobody, a body made allegorical for a sexualized and gendered, nationalized and racialized body of people. Together with the provincial woman, Cynthia becomes one of two demonized and alien(ated) female figures in this road narrative. In reconstituting these stereotypes, the historically oppressed figure of the Filipina is doubly disempowered: not only is she demonized, she is further alienated from her *real* situation, which is more advantageous for the man than it is for her.

As represented by Western cinema, then, the figure of the third-world female subject acts to slow down the political agenda of new social movements in the West; while queer issues were being foregrounded, the third-world woman's issue was being sidetracked. In positing the third-world woman in the unenviable role of oppressor in film narrative and of Western interlocutor in discourse, *Priscilla* also presents the Western bind. In the project of instantaneously liberating various marginal sites, the issue that succeeds the most is that which is discursively fashionable at the time the project is launched. What gets trampled are issues that question the one or two most privileged issues in a project that purports to have multiple political agendas, especially in terms of the most privileged issue's definition in relation to the more marginalized issues. In other words, the lack of concern for multicultural issues prevails even as the film and text purport otherwise in selecting and privileging a marginal group. Marginal groups are made to compete for limited visibility. In the hailing of a representative marginal group, other groups are further obscured; more bodies are concealed.

The issue of liberalism is also at work in allowing for a multiplicity of emergent positions to appear, only to herald the most populist one. In *Priscilla*, the issue of race relations is sidetracked in order to highlight the empathy for queer relations. While sexuality is presented as a civil rights issue, race, already a civil rights issue, is obfuscated from the discourse of liberalism. Furthermore, what is not said in the film's race relations is that the third-world woman's experience remains disparate compared to other first-world subjects. Her experience, though allowed to appear, is marginalized by a related marginal position of queer politics. In liberalism, marginal positions are made to compete for limited dominant space. This competition often reproduces the ethos of liberalism. It foregrounds signs of coalition building, but in the end the competition reinstalls a further hierarchy among the margins.

As transnationalism provides more kineticism to bodies already in motion, the maneuver of making the mail-order bride network more overt in popular culture inevitably produces further sedimentation in the concealment of life stories of the women. The secrets remain, only to be ripped open in their deaths, as in the 1995 gunning down by a Seattle man of his Filipina wife, whom he had met through a mail-order service. He had filed for an annulment, which would preempt her green-card application; she had filed for divorce, claiming battery. Since 1980, sixteen Filipina brides have died at the hands of their husbands in Australia. "Death becomes her," or only in death is her story as a bride told. Even as popular representation has taunted her to expose herself, the mail-order bride rests between silence, sedimentation, and death.

What can be gathered from a discourse on transnationalism and women is a geopolitics of place and location: how and why women are here or there instead of elsewhere; what they implicate in their space; why place and placelessness are vital issues for women who choose to be relocated outside the national space. The imperialist fascination with mail-order brides is constitutive of a mechanism to imagine its past as a coherent family and nation. However, the continuing diasporic movement of bodies in transnational space attests to the flexibility, versatility, resilience, and endurance of their owners' stories. These narratives of emplacement and location are significant in mapping the bodies of Filipinas and their making-do processes as they are circulated and as they navigate the transnational space.

Notes

For their comments, criticisms, and support, I thank Delia Aguilar, Ellen Berry, Luisa Aguilar-Cariño, Laura Holliday, Shirley Geok-lin Lim, Randy Martin, and especially Lynn Spigel. An earlier version of this essay was read in the panel "Personal/Political: Filipino/ a Bodies in Postcolonial and Neocolonial Space" at the conference "The Politics and Poetics of the Body: Pacific Rim Triangulations," University of California at Santa Barbara, 1994. An earlier version of this essay was also published in *Social Text* 48 (Fall 1996): 49–76. This essay is dedicated to the memory of Angela Serra (1963–95), a fellow Filipina traveler.

1. Ninotchka Rosca, quoted in "The Many Faces of Feminism," *Ms.* 5:1 (July–August 1994): 43.

2. Ninotchka Rosca, "Mrs. Contemplacion's Shameful Sisters: The Philippines' Shameful Export," *The Nation* 260:15 (17 April 1995): 524.

3. Donna Haraway, "A Cyborg Manifesto: Science, Technology, and Socialist-Feminism in the Late Twentieth Century," in *Simians, Cyborgs, and Women: The Reinvention of Nature* (New York: Routledge, 1991), 149.

4. Ibid., 177.

5. International Labour Organization, *Women Workers in Multinational Enterprises in Developing Countries* (Geneva: ILO, 1985).

6. Rosca, "Mrs. Contemplacion," 526.

7. Rosario del Rosario, *Life on the Assembly Line: An Alternative Philippine Report on Women Industrial Workers* (Quezon City: Philippine Women's Collective, 1986).

8. Sr. Mary Soledad Perpinan, "Philippine Women and Transnational Corporations," in *Philippines Reader: A History of Colonialism, Neocolonialism, Dictatorship, and Resistance*, ed. Daniel B. Schirmer and Stephen Rosskamm Shalom (Quezon City: Ken, 1987), 237.

9. Quoted in Jill Gay, "The 'Patriotic' Prostitute," *The Progressive* 49:2 (February 1985): 34.

10. Charmayne Denlinger Brubaker, "U.S. Bases Spread AIDS Virus," *The Progressive*, February 1987, 14.

11. GABRIELA, *Statement for International Women's Day Celebration*, 8 March 1998.

12. Sheila Coronel and Ninotchka Rosca, "For the Boys," *Ms.* 4:3 (November–December 1993): 15.

13. For an overview of Philippine migrant work and particularities of Filipinas in overseas employment, refer to Mary Ruby Palma-Beltran and Aurora Javate de Dios, eds., *Filipino Women Overseas Contract Workers: At What Cost?* (Manila: Goodwill, 1992).

14. John Batara, "Imperialism, APEC, and Migration of Filipinos," Migrante Papers No. 2, Quezon City, 1996, 5.

15. KAIBIGAN Briefing Paper (1989), quoted in Aurora Javate De Dios, "Japayuki-san: Filipinas at Risk," in Palma-Bertran and de Dios, *Filipino Women*, 40.

16. Ibid.

17. Mary Ruby Palma-Beltran, "Towards a More Purposive and Responsive Overseas Labor Strategy: A View from the NGO Sector," in Palma-Bertran and de Dios, *Filipino Women*, xv.

18. "Editorial," *Philippines-USA News Tribune* 5:22 (28 July–3 August 1994): 4.

19. Ruby Palma-Beltran, "Filipino Women Domestic Workers Overseas: Profile and Implications for Policy," in Palma-Bertran and de Dios, *Filipino Women*, 4.

20. Ibid., 7.

21. Kanlungan Centre Foundation, Inc., "Overseas Filipina Domestic Helpers Issues and Problems," in Palma-Bertran and de Dios, *Filipino Women,* 29.

22. Ibid., 30.

23. Ibid., 32.

24. Ibid., 34.

25. Graziano Battistella, C.S., "Filipina Domestic Workers in Italy," in Palma-Bertran and de Dios, *Filipino Women,* 15.

26. Philippine Overseas Employment Agency, quoted in Anesia Dionisio, "Filipino Nurses Overseas: At What Cost?" in Palma-Bertran and de Dios, *Filipino Women,* 60.

27. Quoted in E. San Juan, Jr., "Where Are You From? When Are You Going Back?: The Predicament of Filipinos in the United States," *Kultura* 5:2 (1992): 6.

28. Quoted in Dionisio, "Filipino Nurses Overseas," 61.

29. De Dios, "Japayuki-san," 39.

30. Palma-Beltran, "Towards a More Purposive and Responsive Overseas Labor Strategy," xiv.

31. De Dios, "Japayuki-san," 43.

32. David McQuay, "Filipino Women Touted as Top Mail-Order Brides," *Denver Post,* 20 December 1987, A-12.

33. Steven Long, "Mail-Order Brides," *Houston Chronicle,* 29 July 1990, G-1.

34. Gary Libman, "Lonely American Males Looking to the Orient for Mail-Order Brides," *Los Angeles Times,* 16 September 1986, pt. 4, 16.

35. Andrew Low, "Mail Order Bride Business Continues to Grow," *Pan Asia News* 9:2 (June 1987): 1.

36. German Federal Statistical Office, quoted in "Filipinas in West Germany: Some Background Information" (Frankfurt: Association against International and Sexual Racist Exploitation, 1987), 1.

37. Bureau of Population and Migration Research, quoted in Chris Cunneen and July Stubbs, *Gender, Race, and International Relations* (Sydney: Institute of Criminology, 1997), 13.

38. Rosca, "Many Faces of Feminism," 43.

39. Quoted in *Cherry Blossoms* 21:3–4 (March–April 1994): 16.

40. Dean C. Worcester, *The Philippines Past and Present* (New York: Macmillan, 1930), 612.

41. U.S. Postal Service, quoted in Rainbow Ridge, *How to Meet Exciting Ladies from All Over the World* (Kapaau, Hawaii: Rainbow Ridge, 1988), 3.

42. Gayatri Chakravorty Spivak, *Outside in the Teaching Machine* (New York: Routledge, 1993). In her foreword, Spivak's position ("outside *in*") foregrounds "the margin or 'outside' [as it] enters an institution" and the "kind of [institution] it enters [that] determine[s] its contours" (ix).

43. Michael Taussig, *Mimesis and Alterity: A Particular History of the Senses* (New York: Routledge, 1993), 232–34.

44. Ibid., 232.

45. *Cherry Blossoms* 21:3–4 (March–April 1994): 13.

46. Rainbow Ridge, *How to Meet Exciting Ladies,* 53.

47. Meaghan Morris, "On the Beach," in *Cultural Studies,* ed. Lawrence Grossberg, Cary Nelson, and Paula Treichler (New York: Routledge, 1992), 455. As a male fantasy, the family romance is a conservative as well as a nostalgic genre because it allows the child "to mature while refusing to progress."

48. Gay tours, especially to third-world countries, are implicated along these same circuits. Extending the scene of the cruise to these third-world sites, the tours also hinge on pleasure as inscribed on the bodies of third-world peoples and the conditions in which these peoples are located. These tours yield a highly problematic correlation between

pleasure and poverty, on the one hand, and the distinction and similarity between exploitation and benevolence, on the other. Men's catalogs (especially those intended for a gay clientele) reconstruct the enclaves of homoerotic colonialist fantasy. Utilizing hypermasculine models to suggest strength, bulk, the phallus, and homosexual pleasure, *International Male* and *Undergear,* men's activewear catalogs, feature thematic photo fashion spreads (Arabian nights, lifeguards, gyms, World Cup, etc.) as enclaves of homosocial fantasy that reinscribe power through nostalgic conquest and (cultural) cross-dressing, death and rescue, narcissism and performance, global unity, and so on. The models' bodies implicitly construct an absent other as the bodies of third-world men become the junctures to reconstruct these homosocial fantasy enclaves. Situated in exotic homosocial locations, the models' bodies make clear the absence of the native other, those bodies that are "natural" to the colonial environment. Not only do the dominant mass and strength of the models' bodies declare, "I have conquered these lands," they also declare, "I have conquered the men of these lands" in the absence of local bodies. Local male bodies are erased to construct their enclave as the sole geography of prototypical first-world homoerotic bodies and desires.

49. Louis Florence, quoted in Raymond A. Joseph, "The American Men Find Asian Brides Fill the Unliberated Bill," *Wall Street Journal,* 25 January 1984, 22.

50. I am specifically referring to a study by the sociologist Davor Jedlicka, of the University of Texas at Tyler, in which he surveyed 265 men seeking partners from Southeast Asia. The survey excluded women from the data gathering, emphasizing instead the competition between first- and third-world women and the middle- and upper-class backgrounds of both the men and third-world women. See Joseph, "American Men," 1; Libman, "Lonely American Males," 1; and Long, "Mail-Order Brides," G-1.

51. Quoted in Joseph, "American Men," 1.

52. Rainbow Ridge, *How to Meet Exciting Ladies.*

53. *Time* magazine special issue on "The New Face of America: How Immigrants Are Shaping the World's First Multicultural Society," 22 November 1993.

54. This idea of love and discipline is discussed in Vicente L. Rafael, "White Love: Surveillance and Nationalist Resistance in the U.S. Colonization of the Philippines," in *Cultures of United States Imperialism,* ed. Amy Kaplan and Donald Pease (Durham, N.C.: Duke University Press, 1993). Rafael's project suggests "that the link between benevolence and discipline was constructed through the practice of surveillance" with respect to census, popular representation, and so forth (187).

3. The West's "Comfort Women" and the Discourses of Seduction

Lynn Thiesmeyer

Silence and Deafness

> The line between rape and purchase is as thin as a fine membrane.
> —Saundra Pollock Sturdevant and Brenda Stoltzfus, "Disparate Threads of the Whole," in *Let the Good Times Roll,* 325

In this chapter I attempt to juggle talk of actual exploitations with talk of the discursive exploitations that occur in a place nowadays called "the West."[1] In the discourse of this west toward Asia, verbal and imagistic suggestions about a generalized Asian woman are linked to the particular, frequent, and ugly fact of the now-rampant exploitation of her sexuality within western nations and by westerners located elsewhere. What I describe below results from the political and discursive avoidance of the actual, abused body and the privileging of the discursive or represented Asian body, that of seduction.

Since the mid-1990s, media attention has sensationalized the problem of western sex tours to Asia, western trafficking of Asians to brothels in the west, sexual abuses at western military bases, and the escalating rate of western abuse of small children. To say that such treatments are sensational, however, simply allows us to ignore them. Yet even the most superficial media attention has revealed the tip of an iceberg that cannot be ignored without increasingly greater discursive efforts: not only the recorded millions who go each year to Asia from the west and may buy indentured prostitutes, but the innumerable brothels and "massage parlors" that are "suspected of offering indentured or enslaved women for prostitution" in major U.S. cities that have brought women and children from developing regions of Asia and elsewhere for American consumers.[2] The dilemma, of course, is how to begin to articulate this situation within a discourse that has long maintained that the sexual and gender abusiveness of Asia has no parallel in the kinder, gentler west.

The political and discursive basis of western exploitation of Asians certainly has a long and complex history, but its operation can be summed up quickly: assure the western audience through academic, mass media, and travel discourses that Asians politically, financially, and sexually seduce; that is, they offer their own exploitation.[3] Seduction is a symbology used to implicate the victim in her own abuse by removing her from her own body and voice into the realm of another's discursive images and text. A major effect of the transference of the actual Asian body into a symbology of seduction is the convenient silencing of the woman herself, because she is seen by the other culture as speaking in an actuality that is untranslatable to them. Jean Baudrillard has described our manufacture of such seduction, its strength greater than that of desire: "Out of desire we have made a force or irreversible energy. . . . [But s]eduction is stronger. . . . It is a circular and reversible process of challenge, one-upmanship, and death."[4] Unlike desire, the discourse of seduction is the murder of the body, not its production or reproduction. Where Gayatri Chakravorty Spivak can speak of "sexual-reproduction" and "subject-production" in the western manufacture of other women,[5] we must, but cannot seem to, speak of their sexual destruction or of "other subjects . . . the living members of the . . . culture, who provide the [specialist] with a means of externalizing his loss and directing his blame."[6] The silencing of the used body also ensures the silence of the user.

The silencing of discourses of the actual woman takes several forms, among them censorship, distortion, displacement, disinterest, and death. It is a fortunate coerced prostitute who lives beyond the age of twenty-five: the physical abuse by her captors and customers can kill her faster than AIDS. The market for Asian women in the west also results in death in other ways: Asian women desirous of emigrating may find themselves in picture-bride marriages to American males who can abuse or kill them because the woman's visa depends on the continuation of the marriage.[7] They may also end in the legal limbo of the United Kingdom's special Immigration Rules Concession, serving the host British family both domestically and sexually without the means to escape.[8]

Though I discuss mainly the human trafficking of Asian women and children into the United States and U.S.-controlled regions of Asia, the situation of prostituted Asians in many western nations is similar. However, this chapter is not simply about the problem of abuse around military bases and sex-tour venues; rather, it is about the systematic discourse of Asia in relation to the west and its actualization in the "insatiable demand" for underage Asian sex objects who can be kept silent about the demand. As Cynthia Enloe has stated, sex tourism to developing countries "requires men from affluent societies to imagine certain women, usually women of color, to be more available and submissive than the women in their own countries."[9]

From the time when Alexander the Great referred to "wanton, luxurious . . . Asiatics," westerners have seen the Asian people they wished to conquer as the purveyors of the lusts projected upon them.[10] Critics of Orientalism have remarked on this tendency in works of western history, literature, and travel. Lisa Lowe traces the writing of such desires from eighteenth-century Europe, where a French traveler's assumption of sexual slavery in a Middle Eastern harem "suggests that the theme of female enslavement is a male fantasy that emerges from the context of European sexual relations."[11] Yet, until recently, few works available to academic or popular readers in the west have dealt with the exploitation and death that accompany the sexualizing of images of Asians. Rita Nakashima Brock and Susan Thistlethwaite's *Casting Stones: Prostitution and Liberation in Asia and the U.S.* includes analyses of the systematic western cultural values that encourage millions of men to seek out purchased sex and underage partners rather than stereotyping this as merely an Asian cultural practice. However, the actualities of the bodies involved are more usually denied expression in several middle-class forms of western discourse ranging from scholarly Euro-American works that claim "different" Asian sexual values to the mass-market travel publications and the wire and broadcast services that circulate in a homogenized form throughout the global media. Various forms of discourse have long been the chief voices of the gratified rather than of the gratifier. Yet because in postmodern culture discourse is also the chief instrument for gratification, in practice this means both the marketing as well as the justification of various forms of Asian sexual slavery, including the west's participation in the forcible trafficking in, abusive sex with, rape of, and child prostitution of individuals from the Pacific, South Asian, and Southeast Asian regions.

* * *

Thousands of Asians work in locked, airless brothels throughout the world in the colossal industry of sex tours and sex services marketed by American and European firms. They work in the jurisdictions covering U.N. and U.S. military bases where thousands of sexual assaults have been reported by local authorities within recent decades. It is important to emphasize here that this is sexual slavery. Women in a highly commercialized sex trade and children in prison brothels, whether in Los Angeles or Chiang Mai, do not have what a western academic would call a real choice in their prostitution. Furthermore, thanks to the global indenture system of debt bondage, in most cases they do not receive real or adequate wages.[12] If, while in a western country, they escape and report their abuse to the authorities, it is quite possible that they will not be taken seriously. Even though in the 1990s the U.S. Department of Justice has been investigating the numerous claims by Asian women forcibly prostituted in American cities, the outcome of earlier claims is a matter of "no comment" by local law authorities.[13] Moreover, many western legal systems, including those of the United States and Germany, see prostitution and illegal immigration, even when forcible, as a disqualification or drawback to criminal testimony against those who have prostituted the witness.[14]

A major concern here is to delineate ways in which discourse is a practice and also leads to practice. That is, discourse can enjoin and lead to actions and interactions within one society and also among societies. Some of the following examples are thus from discourses that affect individuals' behavior toward others and are produced and read in order to so affect behavior. Generalizations about western sexual consumption of Asians are beyond the scope of this essay. The popularity of western discourse about Southeast Asian sex destinations and partners provides much of the focus and most of the examples.

One consistent rhetoric on Southeast Asia may be found in upmarket travel books and in development studies publications for audiences of nongovernmental organization (NGO) workers, policymakers, and on-site development workers. That is, this rhetoric is intended for and in fact reaches a wide audience, one that expects academic expertise and can do something about what it reads. An example is provided by one NGO director, attempting to combat child prostitution in Thailand, who came to the following conclusion in his book on tourism and pedophilia in Asia: "The force which drives parents to sell their children is not just poverty but an erosion of values. There is a consumerist motivation behind a rural family exchanging their daughter for a black and white television set. An educational programme which stresses communal and social values is needed in rural communities of many countries."[15] The second example comes from the annual report of the United States Agency for International Development (USAID). In its HIV/AIDS policy for the developing world, USAID's specialists, medical and academic, make frequent reference to the patronage of commercial sex in a given country as an indicator of the AIDS risk potential. Here we must bear in mind that the HIV transmission rate through sex is higher in North America than in many areas of Southeast Asia that are considered epidemic regions and apparently for some of the same reasons: multiple partners with unsafe sex practices (refusal or unwillingness to use condoms). USAID, however, in 1995 described its cross-border strategy (encompassing several contiguous nations in Southeast Asia) as one that targets such regional problems as a "highly mobile population," "recreational centers [with] hotels, nightclubs and commercial sex establishments [that] draw local and international tourists," and the situation where "casual sexual relationships with multiple partners are tolerated."[16] How these three might differ from the modes of HIV transmission in developed nations—for example, the highly mobile population of the United States, where casual sexual relationships are tolerated—is difficult to assess given the decontextualization and the assumptions about regional characteristics.

These discursive features can also be seen in widely read books such as Lonely Planet's *Thailand*, a prize-winning guide to Thailand that offers historical and cultural background along with descriptions of tourist sites. *Thailand* won the American Travel Writers Journalism Awards gold medal; its main author is Joe Cummings, an American academic with a master's degree in Asian studies from the University of California at Berkeley. *Thailand* offers readers a detailed section in which it conflates prostitution with several other practices: "concubinage," the keeping of mistresses, the courtesan system, and polygamy. Modern Thai prostitution is traced to these traditional Thai customs, leading one to wonder to what tradition prostitution and the keeping of mistresses and "second families" in the United States could be traced. The Lonely Planet's claim that Thai businessmen and politicians "entertain in private brothels and member clubs" almost pales in comparison to some of the well-publicized rendezvous of leading entertainment and political figures in the United States.[17]

This rhetoric is to the effect that Asian ideas of family or an Asian cultural psychology has led to the large-scale commercialization of the sex trade. There is no disputing the primary claim that there has been a large-scale commercialization of the sex trade in Asia. The secondary claim, that Asian cultures possess certain traits as a whole that allow sexual exploitation, is not only reductive and imprecise but, like the primary claim, decontextualized. There is no Asian country in which the entire population and all social classes engage in or approve of a sex trade; nor is there an Asian country so homogeneous that generalized values are accepted and implemented by the whole population. Indeed, Southeast Asian countries have women's government and nongovernmental agencies as well as community groups to protect children, educate against sexual exploitation, and mobilize individuals and groups to resist prevailing ideologies (including ideologies considered "inappropriate" to modernizing gender and family structures as well as certain ideas of modernized development itself, also a government-promoted ideology in some states).

Furthermore, the decontextualized nature of claims about Southeast Asia ignores the crises in the United States and elsewhere of child abuse, child prostitution, and patronage of adult prostitution and "men's clubs" that offer strippers and lap dancing during business meetings. The discursive question here is that if we label the long tradition of prostitution in Asia an "Asian cultural value," what are we to label the long tradition of prostitution patronage in the west, including the importation to the United States of Asians to serve in American brothels? Western nations, including the United States, are complicit in the patronage of and the trade in Asian sexual exploitation (the importation of Asians to western countries for sexual use). Patronage by westerners in Thailand—for example, in the brothels of Bangkok's tourist-oriented Patpong district—was rated by one Thai women's studies researcher as high as 80 percent.[18]

There is also the issue of the sexual use of Asians within the United States and other countries. First, in the United States and Canada there are an unknown number of patrons of brothels that offer Asians; given the large number of such brothels, the demand can be estimated as high. The "World Sex Guide," available on the Internet, directs customers who prefer Asians to brothels throughout the United States that operate under shop names such as "Oriental Massage." The guide offers such information for each state, with locations and in some cases telephone numbers. It also provides directions for drivers and lists prices along with descriptions of the prostitutes' looks, estimated ages, and proficiency at meeting specified sexual demands. Obviously not all of this demand results in coercion. However, police raids since 1995 have unearthed Asians forcibly prostituted in locked brothels throughout major cities in the United States and Canada.[19]

Finally, there are the mail-order marriages of American men to Asian women and the use of au pairs and other domestics from Asia as household workers in the United States, Canada, the United Kingdom, and other advanced nations. Saundra Pollock Sturdevant and Brenda Stoltzfus state it directly: "The international exchange of Third World women as prostitutes, domestic servants, and wives is another aspect of the power relationship between industrialized countries and the Third World."[20] Detailed study is required to reveal the number of these cases involving deception, coercion, or injury and their relation to attitudes toward Asians generally, a project that is outside the scope of this essay. My concern here is with the rhetoric of advanced nations where there is treatment of Asians according to standards different from those of the advanced nation itself. The question is how certain rhetorics support such treatment.

Sturdevant and Stoltzfus emphasize the hierarchical nature of the "exchange" of women in positions serving people in industrialized nations. This aspect of global relations also helps keep the "third world" side of this exchange relatively silent. It is much easier to find information on sexploitation of Asians by Asians—as with the newsworthy issues of child prostitution and child labor in Asia and the Japanese military's "comfort women"—than to find information on sexploitation of Asians by westerners. The difficulty of access to such information is increased by another rhetoric, that of the silent, uncomplaining Asian, where a perceived (not necessarily real) silence is taken to mean the absence of suffering or lack of need for redress. My analysis points instead to the "first world's" silence on, or deafness to, the existence of its own prostitution culture and its use of forcible and child sex.

The American silence on contemporary Asian exploitation by westerners rests partly on the difficulty of acknowledging it, especially when it occurs on American soil, as in the case of Asians in American brothels. One difficulty in acknowledging this comes from the fact that so many contemporary Americans (and Australians and New Zealanders, who also use imported Asians for prostitution) are "hyphenates" whose ancestors also immigrated or were brought to America under circumstances of poverty, persecution, or servitude. In realizing this connection, however, we may find something we fear to acknowledge: the link between our ancestral immigrants, slaves or bonded servants, and the contemporary American situation for those from other countries now forcibly or voluntarily at our service. The historical link is that existing exploitees may be in similar positions to those occupied by our immigrant ancestors. The contemporary link is that we may be of the same ethnic origin as people bound to our sweatshops and massage parlors, leading Americans to remember that we still have cousins in those other countries—and not only in Asia—whose sex trade we patronize.

Yet we practice a historical and a spatial distancing that constructs a discursive boundary between us and those we exploit, a belief that their current and our former problems originated with the less-enlightened cultures from which they/we came. It is this discursive boundary, however, that helps keep the exploitation operative. It supports the notion that those who are exploited are less enlightened and therefore have been socialized to exploitation; it also supports the appearance that information from the exploited is unavailable, an absence that can be presumed to mean they have nothing to say or nothing about which to complain.

This kind of contemporary western discourse, from popular culture to the mass media to congressional and parliamentary discussions on human trafficking, allows the construction of sites outside the public and territorial discourse of the west where the stereotypes of exploitable sexuality can be applied. These are sites where the discourse of Asians is hidden from actual view. They include the locked brothels for sex slaves that exist in the west, on military bases, and in sex-tour destinations in Asia. What I call actual, not discursive, sites are the location for the bodily victimization and exploitation of the Asian women and of children of either gender, and these actualities are precisely what is not put into public discourse. In fact, in the international community it is much more common, and overtly encouraged, to discuss Asian male victimization of women, as with the serious discussion on both sides of the Pacific about comfort women. Yet as the surviving comfort women themselves point out, it is more than fifty years too late, raising the question of whether it will also be fifty years too late for existing sex slaves. It is this partial disclosure—about Asians but not about westerners—that reveals the gap in our own discourse. We do not ordinarily allow such discussion of the victimization of women into public speech if the discussion involves western males. When, in late 1996, a California sex-tour agent said on the CBS television program "60 Minutes" that he bore no responsibility for the acts committed by men he sent to brothels in Southeast Asia, he was doing the expected thing: using a western discourse (that of individual responsibility) to conceal or silence the representation of western male values and behavior. This silencing, however, is more clever than simple silence: it covers its tracks, replacing the voice of the desired with the voice of the desirer who speaks for her.

The narrator of Theresa Hak Kyung Cha's *Dictée* attempts to explain her own silencing, doubly colonized as she is and provided with several languages, none of which articulates her actual self. She feels precisely "the others each occupying her . . . until in all cavities she is flesh . . . caught in their threading, anonymously in their thick motion in the weight of their utterance. . . . The wait from pain to say. To not to. Say."[21] At a further remove, in our own discourse of such a figure, "signifiers work insofar as they gesture toward another place (the lack in discourse-construction) . . . that cannot be admitted into the circuit of exchange," as Chow points out.[22] Our public language, in fact, uses signifiers for the Asian woman in Asia and in the west that type her as a set of problems, whether of poverty, minority, or gender inequality, that is an essential part of her national or ethnic identity. Simultaneously, the other's language, and in this essay the other is the west, deprives both her and the language about her of expressiveness in the economy of verbal exchange. As with Cha's narrator and with the Asian women who serve western men, the body or the persona who actually transcends such national and linguistic boundaries—the immigrant, the transnational, literally, the translated person—is further marginalized when confronting the culture that dominates not only within her community but within the global hierarchy of nations. One example is the 1996 Washington reception of Naha City councillor Takazato Suzuyo's group of Okinawan women appealing for the removal of U.S. bases for the reasons detailed above. Though well-armed with years of police reports on the continued violations of the human rights of women and children by the U.S. military in Okinawa, Takazato was confronted with American responses of "You need to take a more balanced approach" and the suggestion that the Okinawan women were being stereotypically "emotional."[23]

This phenomenon forces the Asian woman into a situation where "the 'native' cannot simply 'speak' but must also provide the justice/justification for her speech,"[24] a justification that further demonizes the culture and gender she is seen to embody. My next examples come from two divergent but widely circulated media about forced prostitution of Thai women and children: the *New York Times* report on Asians trafficked into the United States and Andrew Vachss's Web site and Dark Horse comic book about exploited Thai children that started the "Don't! Buy! Thai!" boycott campaign in 1995.[25] Both used the same adjective to describe what they saw as the nature of the problem: "evil" Thais. In five articles published throughout 1995, the *New York Times* only twice—and only briefly—mentioned an American male on trial as part of an alleged conspiracy to kidnap Thai women and children and bring them to New York for prostitution. The suggestion of American involvement was absent from other articles, leaving the supposition that the alleged "thousands of indentured Asian prostitutes" in the United States could have been brought in without the involvement of any U.S. immigration officials, police, local housing authorities, or brothel customers. The article that mentioned the American male, a "former corrections officer," was followed by two others that proclaimed the arrest of several Thai men and featured a photograph of a Chinese-American policeman who had taken bribes and his Japanese-American attorney that was large enough to leave no doubt about the ethnicity of those who ought to take blame.[26]

A related case in 1996 presented more obvious contradictions: a Nobel Prize–winning Caucasian scientist working at the National Institutes of Health in the United States had been allowed to bring fifty-four different Papua New Guinean children to live with him as his sexual partners by listing them with the immigration department as his "family." This was characterized in the *Washington Post* as the misfortune of a man who was trying to help children and who had written scientific pieces claiming Papuan children have a "sexuality" leading them to seduce adults.[27] By early 1997, some U.S. officials were quoted in the *San Francisco Examiner* as insisting that "the multimillion-dollar sex-slave trafficking stretches from Thailand to San Francisco, from Russia to New York City" in "massage parlors suspected of offering indentured or enslaved women for prostitution."[28] The article itself cites only Thai and Chinese names among the traffickers. Yet a quick search on the World Wide Web reveals hundreds of Web sites for Caucasian males promoting what is quaintly termed "Oriental Massage" in every state and city of the United States, including which sexual services are available for what price and the names of local newspapers and directories where Asian sex is openly marketed. The "insatiable demand" for sex from Asians is a color-blind phenomenon. But as with the captive Thai prostitutes in the United States described in East and West Coast newspapers, the Papuan children's sexual abuse by an American, as well as the obvious negligence or complicity of the Immigration Service, members of the community, and co-workers who knew about the situation, was acquitted by the silence the articles maintained on these points. Trinh T. Minh-

hà has said that stories are a means of keeping oneself alive;[29] part of what
is killing sexploited Asian women and children are the mainstream stories
that silence theirs.

Containment and Censorship

> [E]very story one chooses to tell is a kind of censorship,
> it prevents the telling of other tales.
> —Salman Rushie, *Shame*, 72–73

Many examples of the containment and distortion of information relating to the western prostitution of Asia occur in the mass media, as in the *New
York Times* articles, weekly newsmagazines, Web sites, and adult comics cited above. Yet these sources also quote scholars who specialize in fields related to Asian studies. The fact that more accurate and direct information is
available from the same sources used by both media and scholars alike is what
constitutes censorship and distortion. The "Don't! Buy! Thai!" campaign,
originating with a comic book in 1995 and a Web site in 1996, claiming that
the largest and worst of the world's child prostitution industry is due to Thais,
is a salient example. It misquotes and fragments information from Thailand
presented in documents by the international organization ECPAT (End Child
Prostitution in Asian Tourism). The "Don't! Buy! Thai!" campaign falsely
claims support from ECPAT and the U.S.-based Human Rights Watch, yet it
omits information from both sources on the westerners involved in child
trafficking and forced prostitution of Southeast Asians to western countries,
and it ignores those parts of Human Rights Watch publications about the
demand for a Thai sex industry to service U.S. troops on "R and R" from
Vietnam and about the purchase and abuse of a Myanmarese girl by a westerner.[30] A March 1996 article in the *Economist* quite explicitly blames Cam-
bodians for the large trade in children frequented by what the writer calls "a
few foreign paedophiles."[31] At the same time the writer acknowledges that
Phnom Penh "is becoming a foreign paedophile tourist destination" and that
there are advertisements for Phnom Penh in English on the Internet, which
is already a male- and English-language-dominated medium that offers to
other male speakers of English hundreds of such promotions for Asian sex.

The acrobatics that western discourse must perform to characterize sexual abuses as Asian rather than western are at times quite contorted. A *New
York Times* article on child prostitution in Cambodia and the Philippines
followed the lead of the *Economist* with interviews with Japanese, Chinese,
and Southeast Asians, but only one resident Briton about their participation
in child sex. It also claimed that sex tours had originated in Japan. It mentioned only in a short paragraph that the U.S. military may have "helped

build" child prostitution and that westerners seeking or advertising prostitutes are now in "partnership" with "local people."[32] As a balance to such assertions in the press, it is well to adduce the results of Enloe's research on militarized and commercialized prostitution in Asia:

> This is not, of course, to argue that local men are the root of the commercialized and militarized sex that has become so rife, especially in countries allied to the United States. Without local governments willing to pay the price for the lucrative R and R business, without the U.S. military's strategies for keeping male soldiers content, without local and foreign entrepreneurs willing to make their profits off the sexuality of poor women—without each of these conditions, even an abusive, economically irresponsible husband would not have driven his wife into work as an Olongapo bar girl.[33]

A female member of the Liberal Democratic party in Japan, attending an April 1997 ECPAT meeting in Tokyo to discuss child prostitution and stricter legislation against child pornography, made the surprising claim that in western countries there is no pornography or nudity available where children can see it, including on prime-time television. She stated that among advanced countries only Japan allowed such displays, and she made a similar statement to the *Christian Science Monitor,* which repeated it without correction.[34]

The two incidents most involving discursive constructions and contradictions in the 1990s about U.S. sex crimes against Asian women have been the reported rape of a twelve-year-old by American military personnel on Okinawa and the "Don't! Buy! Thai!" campaign. After the comment by U.S. Admiral Richard Macke following the Okinawa rape, to the effect that there was no need for rape when there were women to buy, a female *Washington Post* reporter visited and wrote about the prostitutes' area near the U.S. base. The headline of her article, whether her own or the editors', used sex-tour phraseology: "On Okinawa, GIs Find Prostitutes Cheap and Plentiful."[35] Takazato Suzuyo and Carolyn Francis, with whom the reporter met on Okinawa and who traveled to the United States in February 1996 to speak on the military base problem, have provided Japanese- and English-language documentation on the dozens of unreported or unprosecuted rapes and assaults of Okinawans by the U.S. military, facts that have never found their way into U.S. public discourse.[36] The question now looms even larger: Why are there no western discussions of comfort women appeals against the west?

When Okinawa was first occupied by the United States, the U.S. Government Jurisidiction Office was established to oversee life on Okinawa. Local authorities were ordered to set up a prostitutes' health inspection center specifically for the prostitutes that were generally considered as "belonging" to the U.S. bases. A similar situation prevailed in the area around the U.S.

naval base at Olongapo in the Philippines until that base was closed in 1991.[37] U.S. authorities thus admitted by their actions that women of territories hegemonized by the United States are the sexual property of the United States. Such actualities give the lie to reports in the national and international press that the Japanese authorities established prostitution for the U.S. military occupation, to the surprise of the U.S. officers.[38] The World Health Organization conducted its own study of Filipina women working as "bar girls" throughout the Pacific region whose brokers contract them for sex with U.S. military personnel. Some Filipina women also find themselves trafficked to American possessions in the Pacific where, like the earlier comfort women and their present-day counterparts in U.S. brothels, they are locked in tiny cubicles or barracks to which only their employers and customers have access.[39]

While the military base system of forced prostitution is widespread, it is not the only sexual use of women and children in Asia and the Pacific. Rey Chow is correct in indicating the sort of racial and sexual hegemony fostered not only through direct enemy conquest but also by the establishment of U.S. bases in the Far East during peacetime.[40] But these bases do not exist only in East Asia; rather, they can be found throughout Southeast Asia and other developing regions—and, not coincidentally, in the areas that have been advertised as sex-tour destinations for civilians. For U.S. troops in Vietnam, it was a short hop to Thailand, where the terms of the 1967 "R and R treaty" between that country and the United States meant that sex tourism was available to U.S. military personnel. As earlier as 1959, before U.S. involvement in Vietnam had escalated, the CIA had established its own areas in Thailand, ostensibly as a bulwark against possible communist insurgency in the region.[41] Thereafter, the yearly "Cobra Gold" U.S. military exercises in the Bay of Thailand and use of the nearby Sataheep airfield made the once-quiet beach town of Pattaya into the sex resort that is now touted on the Internet and in none-too-discreet travel books for foreigners on holiday.

The promotion of child prostitution is another type of discourse that makes use of justification in academic as well as travel discourses. Even self-justifying rhetoric by child-sex travel promoters rarely denies the enslaving aspect of the sexual encounter, and it sometimes emphasizes it as part of the fun for the buyer, displacing the blame for enslavement onto the child's "culture" or "family," frequently characterized as a people and nation who sell their own children. Yet taboos against sex with children prevail throughout the world and do lead to prosecution outside the west. ECPAT puts the figure for westerners arrested as sex offenders in Asia at over 50 percent, most from the United Kingdom, northern Europe, Australia, and the United States. More interesting are figures on child prostitution worldwide compiled by the World Congress Against Commercial Sexual Exploitation of Children that put the number of child prostitutes in the United States at 300,000, a figure that a single glance at police reports will show to be low, not high. The number of child prostitutes in New York City alone was estimated to be 20,000 by the mid-1980s.[42] Western discourse is now attempting to explain what nonexploitative western cultural values have to do with this western situation.

In regions that either have been or still are under direct U.S. control, such as the Philippines, Vietnam, and the Marianas (especially Guam and Saipan), the situation for purchased women and their children (i.e., children of American fathers) is represented as one that benefits both those being exploited and those back home who know nothing about the exploitation. In the Philippines, for example, American men can enjoy cheap sex their own way, while the further commercialization of any resulting pregnancy can be justified in "humanitarian" terms as benefiting both the United States and those initially exploited: "Middlemen in the Philippines search out pregnant women in the night clubs and honky-tonk bars near USA military bases in order to buy mixed-blood babies and then resell them to Western couples."[43] The profit motive results in a situation where, though a verbal champion of human rights, the United States is economically benefiting from the abuse of those outside the United States. Vietnamese women in brothels, until recently commercialized by U.N. troops, are still forced to serve visiting Americans and may also be taken to U.S. possessions elsewhere in the Pacific to continue making money for the investors in the U.S. sex trade there. This development is not surprising given that the involvement with U.S.-style comfort women in Vietnam began during the war in which "they raped the girl, and then, the last man to make love to her shot her in the head."[44]

What is fueling this drive to the East? The western image of the Asian female, the Asian body, and Asian sexuality has been reproduced yet scarcely updated for centuries. As a late twentieth-century representative body of cultural feudalism and exoticism, the Asian/Asian-American woman has no parallel in the fantasies of the west. Wendy Chapkis points out that "advertisements using Asian women, for example, are evocative not only of the sexual mystery but also the docility and subservience supposedly 'natural to the oriental female.' . . . These women thus become metaphors for adventure, cultural difference and sexual subservience."[45]

As we have seen, the United States itself is a region where Asian/Asian-American women, often underage, are kidnapped and forced into prostitution. There are two problems that hamper any attempt to take measures against this slave trade. First, unlike the military sex slavery of World War II, contemporary sex slavery is now carried out for much greater investment profit, hence global economic forces apply. Current policies and reports emphasize the Asian supply side of this sex-slave trade, but that leaves half the transaction unexamined. As the Worldwatch Institute points out,

"the explosion of the . . . sex trade comes down to two basic market forces: supply and demand." Though many reports attempt to humanize the
exploitation of increasingly younger prostitutes as a way of seeking to avoid
AIDS, the historical actuality is that "men have used their positions of
power to elevate the status of their sexual gratification, to make the debasement of young girls socially acceptable."[46]

The fact is that not only "men" but entire societies utilize a discourse of
contradiction in which sexual gratification is signified as that which is un-
speakable. It is therefore debased and always belonging to another culture,
never to oneself. This contradiction makes societies like the United States
not only silent exploiters of Asian women but also the most vocal propo-
nent of their human rights. Enslavement and abuse of Asians by U.S. citizens is the last bastion of information denial in a media and policy climate
that openly addresses sexual slavery elsewhere. In Sweden, the Netherlands,
and Australia, media attention as well as legal penalties are directed at sex
abusers among their citizens who commit offenses in Asia or with Asians
at home. By comparison, the United States and Britain have often suppressed such information about their own citizens. Though the debate has
since been reopened, in 1995 the British government tabled a resolution
calling for the inland prosecution of British sex offenders abroad at the
recommendation of Home Secretary Michael Howard, even though such
laws obtain in other parts of the European Union. ECPAT's office in Australia receives government funding; ECPAT Japan oversees grants from two
ministries in the Japanese government to provide assistance to Southeast
Asian organizations;[47] ECPAT Taiwan works with the government to pass
legislation. By contrast, ECPAT U.S.A.'s office in New York was closed during part of 1996 because it received no public funding. At times it has not
had sufficient private funding to afford Internet access and thus has had
more limited options for gathering and communicating information about
trafficking involving U.S. citizens.[48] Whereas the embassy of the Netherlands in Thailand includes information on how to reach women's shelters
and assistance groups in their visas for Thai women, and a Japanese wom-
en's NGO provides help and shelter phone numbers to organizations in
Thailand that counsel women going to Japan, no official U.S. entity has yet
provided such information for women entering the United States. On the
contrary, the various forms of U.S. media in Asia, such as universally available newswire services, popular television programs dubbed into local languages, and Hollywood films, create the opposite impression for many
young Southeast Asians: that the United States still promises an escape from
the poverty, discrimination, and prostitution they might face at home.[49] As
a consequence, it is not uncommon for disadvantaged Asian women and
youth to believe that being taken to the United States by a broker means

they will escape the fate perceived to await them in other Asian countries. Such U.S.-inculcated beliefs are what makes them easy prey for procurers for U.S. brothels and sweatshops.[50]

In May 1995, members of the U.S. House and Senate proposed resolutions against Thailand that mimicked the implications of the "Don't! Buy! Thai!" campaign without checking the facts available through the campaign's own sources in Human Rights Watch, ECPAT, or in the English-language news stories about Thailand that are available on the Internet. But the facts or sources available to the U.S. Congress go far beyond those provided by human rights organizations and investigative journalism. Histories and autobiographies of Asian immigrants to the United States are fraught with descriptions of the trade in Japanese, Chinese, and other Asian prostitutes from the time of the Gold Rush. Yet the tradition of vilifying the Asian country from which the prostitutes come in order to idealize the America in which they are enslaved goes back as far as the history of their prostitution itself. One Japanese historian, describing the importation of Japanese prostitutes along with the first Chinese and Japanese labor in the west, only apologetically mentions that "American officials aided [prostitute brokers]. . . . Caucasians had gotten entangled in this problem."[51] The passive discourse of "getting entangled" is an exact displacement of blame: Asians actively procure and seduce, westerners get seduced.

Prostitution in American cities has long thrived on white men buying women of color. The ideology of this transaction, involving the commodification of women, the justification of class and racial inequality, and the reinforcement of notions of gender and ethnic superiority, has been discussed at length elsewhere. In many cases, however, the discussion of gender and racial issues involving prostitution has focused on prostituted individuals in the United States who are African-American and Latina. Yet the historical importation of Asian prostitutes and the treatment of Asian-American women according to stereotypes of their sexual availability are just as deeply archived as other ethnic biases. And like those other biases, they are still difficult to enunciate.

The Liberators

> Why should sexual exploitation be so obvious and
> so soundless?
> —Bruce Cumings, "Silent but Deadly," in
> *Let the Good Times Roll*, 171

The reasons for the simultaneous convenience and inconvenience of our constructions of the Asian/Asian-American female are several. Spivak has pointed out the ways in which western assumptions of moral superiority result in the ironic contradiction of "the white man trying to save the brown

woman from the brown man."[52] As Cha also muses in *Dictée*, "We are sev-
ered in Two by an abstract enemy an invisible enemy under the title of liber-
ators."[53] Chapkis refers to the "split images" of "third world" countries used
in various popular media, images that provoke lust even as they moralize
about the debasement of its object: "The exotic is marketed as a holiday fan-
tasyland while 'the underdeveloped world' is used in the West as shorthand
for poverty, hunger, political corruption."[54] This is borne out by the bulletin
board service on the World Wide Web for American men seeking Asian prostitutes: "I just came back from Bangkok and Pattaya in mid-Jan, and, well,
things are a little different from my last trip. . . . Basically, the little goddess-
es have options now other than f—ing and s—ing."

The signifier of the west, particularly the United States, as savior and
moral arbiter, how does the experience of the Asian woman become thus
suppressed, denatured, and distorted in the language of the west? Like Cha's
narrator, the woman forced into prostitution at a very young age must adopt
the language of the colonist or invader in order to use it in the brothel where
her sexual services can only be articulated in fragments of that language, just
as fragments of her body are the only version of her the customer wants. Yet
the larger problem is the more public and righteous language that western
media and politics have adopted to deracinate their own otherness, what
Homi Bhabha calls "the racist language with its own alterity, its foreign-
ness."[55] What is seen as the problem of the language, or lack of it, of the colonized body is more properly a displacement of the current western problem of language about the exploited, or the lack thereof.

The rhetoric of offered help or liberation can also displace and silence the
testimony of the victims themselves.[56] Chow points out that for the Asian
female subject to gain international attention, she often must be portrayed
only in her "victim status."[57] This victimization itself is further extrapolat-
ed as a chosen one because it is part of the western definition of her essential culture. Various empirical proofs are adduced to show that the Asian family and culture traditionally expect children and women to sacrifice their
bodies, along with suggestions that forced prostitutes are really "sex workers" who choose such lives and deaths.[58] In turn, the indignant rhetoric of
official bodies from the nations that provide abusers also characterizes the
destination and its victims in typological ways that perpetuate the images of
sexuality for sale.

In fact, the specialized travel discourses that invite the abuser to the "adventure" in Asia or the Asian prostituted in the United States spin out a political dialectic of desire and righteous disgust. Here there is no need to cloak
the misery of a raped child or sex slave in euphemisms about chosen and
willing partnership; both reality and euphemism can openly coexist. Nor is
there a sop to western virtue suggesting that because westerners are appalled

at the economic conditions just outside the attractive Asian resort, we are ameliorating the prostitute's standard of living through contact with ourselves. On the contrary, the pathos of the prostitute is attractively advertised, as is the adventure of surviving a dirty and poor, hence challenging, set of circumstances. The repressed information is not any suffering by the prostitute (and not all prostitutes suffer all the time); rather, in some cases it is the selling point. Nor is it the descriptions of the apparent poverty of the lower classes of the prostitutes' nation, which is what we have to thank for making the prostitutes available; rather, the absent information is that such circumstances exist in any western city as well and that the tally of victims of sexual violence is peaking not only in non-western countries but in western ones as well. Furthermore, in the United States the number of violent crimes of bias and hostility against Asians generally has climbed in the past decade.[59]

The content of this information is a true late twentieth-century discourse: namely, the eroticization of victimhood, the sexualization of abuse, that drives the contemporary cultural production and sale of abuse and violence within and without the practitioner's own community. This discourse coexists with another kind of boundary between within and without, namely, the fear that the marketing of prostitutes or children is an attempt to lull. A purchased or prepubescent partner is not supposed to be susceptible to pregnancy, thus repressing the fear of actually allying oneself with the other race through the production of "degenerate" offspring.[60] However, in repressing such fear on the part of the practititoner/consumer, the contemporary sex trade actually realizes it. Commodified sex results in the most strictly tabooed violence of both a social and physical nature toward the commodified sex object: when the practitioner goes to the community outside for both adult and child sex commodities . . . well, the child you molest in Thailand may be your own.[61]

* * *

Shame, dear reader, is not the exclusive property of the East.
—Salman Rushie, *Shame*, 23

Scholars as different as Rey Chow and Shi-xu point out that the mystification of "cultural difference" leads to the conflation of nationality with personal identity.[62] All personal identities in the "different" area become homogenized with each other. Consequently, that all people in the other nation are homogeneous produces misunderstanding or ignorance of their language, which becomes homophonous, all syllables leading to the one desired message, namely, the invitation to the heart of a supposed darkness.

Similarly, the homogenizing of blame for an "evil" that is seen as simultaneously inviting and repelling the westerner means a certain censorship.

What is censored is the cross-cultural sameness, not difference, of the wrong, the participation in it of west and East across imprecise cultural boundaries. Instead, blame is centralized on a single other agent, Asia itself: people exploit women there "because" they are Asians. In turn, this serves to homogenize the west into the liberator and standard-bearer for a human rights ethic that it also transgresses, and the transgression can only be kept out of our own discourse by being displaced onto the other's. This displacement is one practical function of our ideology about the East as passive, the receptacle not only of our abuse but of our entire construction of its supposed relationship to us. In relation to female victimization, what Mohanty calls "feminist interests as they have been articulated in the U.S. and Europe" to some extent help codify and limit the knowledge those in the west possess about a seemingly unitary Asian woman.[63]

I am arguing, however, that the most direct consequence is not the distorted knowledge we think we have about an other but the distorted knowledge we have about ourselves, knowledge that opposes the construction of others to an idealized construction of ourselves that we then deploy on them. For example, as a result of the East being cast as passive and the west as active, the sex-and-evil-Thailand debate on the Internet, on CBS, and on NBC has easily found its way into the proactive, enactive rhetoric of the U.S. government. One of the ironies of this discourse is that the Thai police mentioned in the Senate resolution below have been trained and equipped by a United States that nevertheless seems to have nothing to do with their corruption, and one of the missing parts is that some traffickers in and brothel owners for forced Asian prostitution are U.S. citizens. Yet the resolution contradictorily presents the United States as a passive, innocent bystander in the face of the exploitations it shares.

SENATE CONCURRENT RESOLUTION 12

Whereas the United States Government conducts training programs for the Thai police and United States arms and equipment are sold to the Thai police . . .

Whereas Assistant Secretary of State for Human Rights and Humanitarian Affairs John Shattuck has testified that the United States "urgently needs to encourage countries in which trafficking of women and children goes on with impunity to enact new laws, and to enforce existing laws. A particular target of this stepped-up law enforcement should be government officials who participate in or condone trafficking, as well as brothel owners and traffickers";

The United States State Department should continue to press the Thai Government to strictly enforce all laws that can lead to the prosecution of those involved in trafficking and forced prostitution, including procurers, traffickers, pimps, brothel owners, and members of the Thai police who may be complicit.[64]

This is the very active discourse of international law and diplomacy that re-verberates directly onto lives and bodies by enacting the realities it decides. As such, it evinces the hierarchy of nations. The problem of the exploitation of the female body is not only one of sexism within and without a culture but of national rankings that allow a contemporary world order to issue commands and apply pressures to nations that cannot equally reciprocate such demands. The fact that such discourse is in English, just like the Inter-net ads for Southeast Asian bodies, makes it the language of the consumer and not of the consumed. It reconfirms English as the supposedly highest or most politically powerful discursive entity among national discourses. It is also one of the primary reasons for the silencing of Asian/Asian-American women themselves.

The gap between what the body, in this case the exploited body, strives to say and what it appears to be saying in the other, more dominant language sphere is a manufactured one. Yet even the interrogation of this gap is fraught with danger: the anger of the west, which is a heavily armed and moneyed anger, and the silencing of the issue in media whose investors, both finan-cial and readerly, have something to lose in an exposure of their complicity.

Chow notes that "in the confusion of contending notions of visuality and the media, real bodies are slaughtered and sacrificed."[65] It is precisely the dis-appearances of media and disappearances performed by media, their silenc-ing of other discourses, that sacrifice real bodies. The contemporary notions of an evil Orient pimping for its own young ("Don't! Buy! Thai!") and of the western righteousness of helping them are the halves of a double-edged silenc-ing that can ignore the voices from actual bodies and denature their discourse into one of our own that condemns their ethos and sanctifies ours.

It is also a mistake to think that this happens only in the popular media. What Chow calls "the native as silent object," one that is "turned into an absolute entity in the form of an image,"[66] is the image that is sold not only in western magazines and travel brochures but also in academic discourse. Traditional as well as postcolonial scholarship is subject to the distortions of Asian women inherent in the situation of such figures within the absolute and blanket terms "Asian" and "woman," along with the situating of that whole discourse within western class and academic contexts. Hence, the dis-course, or discursive gaps, we can and must accurately examine are really our own. As westerners have a responsibility toward the exercise of power, the first power in our own work to reexamine is its system of silencing.

Notes

This essay is based on an earlier version that appeared in *Hitting Critical Mass* 3:2 (Spring 1997): 44–67. I lowercase the terms "west" and "western" throughout to indicate their constructed quality.

1. The focus of this essay is on the western, chiefly American, discursive construction of Asians as sexual commodities, especially as linked to circumstances of forcible prostitution by westerners or occurring on western soil. I concentrate on ordinary sex-consumer notions, with less attention to the already well documented problems of militarized prostitution. The primary theme here is not sex work or sex worker. Conclusions drawn from sex-work research done in Asia in Asian languages (see notes below) helped contribute to the conceptual framework of this essay.

The reader may also find recent American research on sex work to be of interest, including Rita Nakashima Brock and Susan Brooks Thistlewaite, *Casting Stones: Prostitution and Liberation in Asia and the United States* (Minneapolis: Fortress Press, 1996); Cynthia Enloe, *Bananas, Beaches, and Bases: Making Feminist Sense of International Politics* (Berkeley: University of California Press, 1989); idem, *The Morning After: Sexual Politics at the End of the Cold War* (Berkeley: University of California Press, 1992); Wendy Chapkis, *Live Sex Acts: Women Performing Erotic Labor* (London: Routledge, 1997); Ryan Bishop and Lillian Robinson, *Night Market: Sexual Cultures and the Thai Economic Miracle* (London: Routledge, 1998).

2. Seth Rosenfeld, "Global Sex Slavery," *San Francisco Examiner*, 6 April 1997, A1+.

3. Three writers on the western academic treatment of Asian issues, Edward Said, Rey Chow, and Chandra Talpade Mohanty, describe at length the kinds of scholarship that configure Asians in reductive and sexualized terms as well as ignoring writing and research by Asians themselves. In Said's *Orientalism* (New York: Pantheon, 1978), the chapter "Orientalism Now" suggests ways in which twentieth-century academic and policy research discourses on Asia depend on nineteenth-century stereotypes, including those that make sexuality a western consumer issue. An "association between the Orient and Sex . . . [has been] a remarkably persistent motif in Western attitudes to the Orient. . . . the Orient seems still to suggest not only fecundity but sexual promise (and threat), untiring sexuality, unlimited desire" (188). The influence on the general reading public of this academic or specialist writing about sex in the Orient is that "in time 'Oriental sex' was as standard a commodity as any other available in mass culture, with the result that readers and writers could have it if they wished without necessarily going to the Orient" (190). The use of academic science to back up racial-cultural claims, including those about sexuality, may be seen in the example of the NIH scientist and his child sex partners described in this essay. As Said points out, "typing [of Oriental attributes] was naturally reinforced by sciences" (231).

Rey Chow, in *Writing Diaspora: Tactics of Intervention in Contemporary Cultural Studies* (Bloomington: Indiana University Press, 1993) and in "Violence in the Other Country: China as Crisis, Spectacle, and Woman" (in *Third World Women and the Politics of Feminism,* ed. Chandra Mohanty, Ann Russo, and Lourdes Torres [Bloomington: Indiana University Press, 1991], 81–100), critiques certain norms of East Asian scholarship that situate discussions of women in a larger context of endemic problems in developing countries. Chow points out that these assumptions portray Chinese women, for example, in a "victim status" ("Violence," 93) that then relates their victimization to long-standing conditions at home, ignoring the nonvictimized life events of women as well as the victimization that occurs not in the developing but in the developed world.

Mohanty's essay "Under Western Eyes: Feminist Scholarship and Colonial Discourse" (in Mohanty et al., *Third World Women and the Politics of Feminism,* 51–80) describes the ways in which some western research that is feminist or deals with women in developing countries has used a generalized "third world woman" to homogenize and distort the possibilities of knowledge about actual women in those countries. Her examples come from a publication series by Zed Books in London and from U.N. and other conferences on women and/or development.

4. Jean Baudrillard, *Forget Foucault* (New York: Semiotext[e], 1987), 47–48.

5. Gayatri Chakravorty Spivak, "Three Women's Texts and a Critique of Imperialism," in *"Race," Writing, and Difference,* ed. Henry Louis Gates (Chicago: University of Chicago Press, 1986), 262–80 (quotes on 263, 273).

6. Chow, *Writing Diaspora,* 4.

7. Timothy Egan, "Mail-Order Marriage, Immigrant Dreams, and Death: Murder Trial in Washington State Brings Scrutiny to Vigorous Market for Foreign Brides," *New York Times,* 26 May 1996, 12.

8. Bridget Anderson, in *Britain's Secret Slaves: An Investigation into the Plight of Overseas Domestic Workers in the United Kingdom* (London: Anti-Slavery International, 1993), details this special immigration category that allows British citizens to import young people from developing regions to live with them under unknown and unsupervised conditions.

9. The term "insatiable demand" is Kathleen Barry's, quoted in Rosenfeld, "Global Sex Slavery." For Enloe's assessment, see *Bananas, Beaches, and Bases,* 36.

10. Arrian's *History of the Expedition of Alexander the Great, and Conquest of Persia* is quoted in Gary Okihiro, *Margins and Mainstreams: Asians in American History and Culture* (Seattle: University of Washington Press, 1994), 9.

11. Lisa Lowe, *Critical Terrains: French and British Orientalisms* (Ithaca, N.Y.: Cornell University Press, 1991), 39. See also, among others, Said, *Orientalism,* chap. 2, pt. 4; Joseph Boone, "Vacation Cruises; or, The Homoerotics of Orientalism," *PMLA* 110 (Jan. 1995): 89–107; Mary Louise Pratt, *Imperial Eyes: Travel Writing and Transculturation* (New York: Routledge, 1992), chap. 5; Rana Kabbani, *Europe's Myths of Orient* (London: Pandora Press, 1986).

12. Kathleen Barry, in *The Prostitution of Sexuality* (New York: New York University Press, 1995), provides definitions and describes the circumstances of global sexual slavery in the contemporary era.

13. Rosenfeld, "Global Sex Slavery," A1+.

14. See [Siriporn Skrobanek], *The Diary of Prang,* trans. Pikul Thanapornpun (Bangkok: Women Press/Foundation for Women, 1994).

15. Ron O'Grady, *The Child and the Tourist: The Story behind the Escalation of Child Prostitution in Asia* (Bangkok: ECPAT, 1992), 127.

16. "USAID's Cross-Border Strategy: Reaching Mobile Populations in Asia," in *USAID Responds to HIV/AIDS* (Washington, D.C.: U.S Agency for International Development, 1995), 12–13.

17. Joe Cummings and Richard Nebesky, *Thailand* (Hawthorn, Vic.: Lonely Planet Publications, 1995), 146–47.

18. Interview with Dr. Amara Pongsapich, director of the Social Research Centre, Chulalongkorn University, advisor to the National Commission for Women's Affairs, and a member of the Foundation for Women, Bangkok, 13 March 1996.

19. Rosenfield, "Global Sex Slavery"; Carey Goldberg, "Sex Slavery, Thailand to New York: Thousands of Indentured Asian Prostitutes May Be in U.S.," *New York Times,* 11 September 1995, B1+. See also the *Christian Science Monitor* series during and after the World Congress in Stockholm on child sexual exploitation. The *Monitor* ran several articles in August and September 1996 on the extent of child prostitution in the United States and Canada. On 13 September 1997, the *Bangkok Post* ran an article about the trafficking of women to the United States and Canada. The article, entitled "Thai, Malaysian Women Sold as Sex Slaves," had been picked up from Reuters in Toronto and described the monetary value of part of "North America's sex circuit" as "between two to three million Canadian dollars a year in Canada alone" (6).

20. Sandra Pollock Sturdevant and Brenda Stoltzfus, "Disparate Threads of the Whole: An Interpretive Essay," in *Let the Good Times Roll: Prostitution and the U.S. Military in Asia,* ed. Sturdevant and Stoltzfus (New York: New Press, 1992), 300–334 (quote on 315).

21. Theresa Hak Kyung Cha, *Dictée* (Berkeley, Calif.: Third Woman Press, 1995), 3–4.

22. Chow, *Writing Diaspora*, 118.

23. Takazato Suzuyo, "Heiryoku sakugen wo motomeru josei houbeidan ni sanka shite" (Participating in the women's group visit to the U.S. to ask for the reduction of military forces), *Yui News* 2 (20 March 1997): 4.

24. Chow, *Writing Diaspora*, 38.

25. Andrew Vachss, "Don't! Buy! Thai!" Web site (http://members.aol.com/dbtlori/dbt1.html). In June and July 1996, Vachss also gave two broadcast interviews in which he described Thailand as a nation that promotes and participates in child prostitution for financial gain. The June interview was with KCNR Talk Radio, Salt Lake City, Utah. Vachss subsequently gave an interview to CBS Television on Friday, 12 July 1996, stating his views on the topic.

26. See Goldberg, "Sex Slavery, Thailand to New York," for the estimated numbers in the "thousands." The four other *New York Times* articles about the proceedings are N. R. Kleinfeld, "Five Charged with Holding Thai Women Captive for Prostitution" (5 January 1995, B1); idem, "More Suspects in Smuggling of Prostitutes" (24 May 1995, B4); idem, "Former Officer in Chinatown Admits That He Took Bribes" (14 June 1995, B2); James C. McKinley Jr., "Woman Testifies on Weeks Held against Her Will in a Brothel" (6 June 1995, B2). The articles with accompanying photographs are those by McKinley on 6 June and Kleinfeld on 14 June.

27. Justin Gillis and Philip Pan, "NIH Scientist's Diaries Described Child Sexuality," *Washington Post*, 6 April 1996, A1+.

28. Rosenfeld, "Global Sex Slavery."

29. Trinh T. Minh-hà, *Woman Native Other: Writing Postcoloniality and Feminism* (Bloomington: Indiana University Press, 1989), 123.

30. *Asia Watch and the Women's Rights Project: A Modern Form of Slavery* (New York: Human Rights Watch, 1993), 24, 65.

31. George Moore, "Virgin Territory," *The Economist*, 2 March 1996, 67. A subsequent, longer article in *The Economist* a few months later gives details on child slavery and bonded labor, including prostitution, in the "International" section of the magazine. However, its examples come almost exclusively from South Asia, "some areas of Peru and Brazil," "the brothels of South-East Asia," the Sudan, Mauritania, China, and Japan. There is one sentence devoted to the "Thai workers who were found locked into their clothing factory in Los Angeles," where the writer mentions that they too "could plausibly be called slaves" ("The Flourishing Business of Slavery," *The Economist*, 21 September 1996, 49–50).

32. Nicholas Kristof, "Asian Childhoods Sacrificed to Prosperity's Lusts," *New York Times*, 14 April 1996, 1+.

33. Enloe, *Morning After*, 153.

34. Representative Noda Seiko, Lower House (LDP-Gifu), quoted in Cameron Barr, "Why Japan Plays Host to the World's Largest Child Pornography Industry," *The Christian Science Monitor*, 2 April 1997, 1+; speech at Tokyo ECPAT meeting, 7 April 1997.

35. Mary Jordan, "On Okinawa, GIs Find Prostitutes Cheap and Plentiful," *The Washington Post*, 23 November 1995, A31+.

36. For accounts of some of these assaults, see Takazato Suzuyo, *Okinawa no onnatachi: josei no jinken to kichi guntai* (Women of Okinawa: Women's rights, bases, and the military) (Tokyo: Akashi Shoten, 1996), 237–46. (An English-language chronology of the assaults is available on request from Lynn Thiesmeyer.) Takazato's sources are the *Okinawa Times*, the *Naha-shi shi* (Naha city history) 3:8, the *Uruma Shinpou* newspaper, and the following books: Higa Choushin, *Okinawa gojuunen hanzai shi* (The fifty-year history of crimes in Okinawa) (Fudoukisha, n.d); Fukuchi Hiroaki, *Okinawa ni okeru beigun no hanzai* (U.S. military crimes in Okinawa) (Doujidaisha, 1995); idem, *Beigun Kichi Hanzai* (U.S. military base crimes) (Roudou Kyouiku Center, 1993); Takazato Etsu, ed.,

Okinawa Josei tachi no Sengou (Okinawan women in the postwar period) (Okinawa Fujin Undou shi Kenkyuu kai, n.d.); Kaisouroku henshuu iinkai (The editorial committee for the memoirs of Shima Masu), ed., *Shima Masu no ganbari jinsei* (The life and efforts of Shima Masu); the Japanese public television (NHK) documentary *Okinawa wa nani wo okotta no ka—guntai to seibouryoku wo tou josei tachi* (Why is Okinawa angry? Women look at the military and sexual violence); and personal testimony by citizens who formed patrols in 1945 when the number of rapes rose following the landing of U.S. troops on Okinawa. The U.S. Pacific military newspaper *The Pacific Stars and Stripes* also reports frequently on alleged assaults by base personnel. See also George Feifer, *Tennozan: The Battle of Okinawa* (Boston: Houghton Mifflin, 1992); Miyashita Harumi, "Beigun ni yoru sengo Okinawa no josei hanzai" (Crimes against Okinawan women by American soldiers since World War II), in *Josei no jinken sonchou e no torikumi wo motomeru apiiru* (Appeal to undertake respect for women's human rights), ed. Takazato Suzuyo and Itokazu Keiko (Okinawa: Women's Group to Act for the Removal of Bases and the Military, 1996), n.p.

37. Takazato Suzuyo, "Beigun kichi—josei e no bouryoku" (American bases—violence toward women), in *Josei, bouryoku, jinken* (Women, violence, and human rights), ed. Watanabe Kazuko (Tokyo: Gakuyo Shobo, 1994), 178–92 (esp. 181). See also Saundra Pollock Sturdevant and Brenda Stoltzfus, "Olangapo: The Bar System," in Sturdevant and Stoltzfus, *Let the Good Times Roll*, 45–47 (esp. 45).

38. Nicholas Kristof, "Fearing GI Occupiers, Japan Urged Women into Brothels," *New York Times*, 27 October 1995, A1+.

39. E-mail correspondence with Bernie Provido, Department of Public Health Services, Guam, 24 April 1996.

40. Chow, *Writing Diaspora*, 7.

41. Interview with Dr. Gorvind Kelkar, director of the Gender and Development Center of the Asian Institute of Technology, 11 March 1996.

42. The figure of up to 300,000 child prostitutes is given in the Web site link of the 1996 World Congress Against Commercial Sexual Exploitation of Children (http:// www.childhub.ch/webpub/csechome/226e.html); the figure of 20,000 child prostitutes comes from Gitta Sereny, *The Invisible Children: Child Prostitution in America, West Germany, and Great Britain* (New York: Random House, 1985).

43. Union of International Associations (UIA) Web site, "Trafficking in Children for Adoption," (http://www.uia.org/uiademo/pro/f3302.html).

44. U.S. military Vietnam War testimony is quoted in Susan Brownmiller, *Against Our Wills: Men, Women, and Rape* (New York: Penguin, 1975), 110.

45. Wendy Chapkis, *Beauty Secrets: Women and the Politics of Appearance* (Boston: South End Press, 1986), 53–54.

46. Andrew Sachs, "Child Prostitution: The Last Commodity," *World Watch* 7 (July– Aug. 1994), 26, 29.

47. Personal communication with Yoshioka Shiro, international section head, Campaign to Stop the Prostitution of Children and Protect Their Rights (CASPAR), Japan, 13 July 1996.

48. Personal communication with Ellis Shenk, former director of ECPAT-USA, 3 June 1996.

49. Rey Ventura, *Underground in Japan* (London: Jonathan Cape, 1992), 164.

50. Egan, "Mail-Order Marriage."

51. Tsurutani Hisashi, *The Japanese and the Opening of the American West*, trans. Betsey Scheiner and Yamamura Mariko (Tokyo: Nippon Housou Shuppan Kai, 1977), 167–68.

52. Gayatri Chakravorty Spivak, "Can the Subaltern Speak?" in *Marxism and the Interpretation of Culture*, ed. Cary Nelson and Lawrence Grossberg (Urbana: University of Illinois Press, 1988), 271–313 (quote on 296–97).

53. Cha, *Dictée*, 81.

54. Chapkis, *Beauty Secrets,* 57–58.

55. Homi Bhabha, "DissemiNation: Time, Narrative, and the Margins of the Modern Nation," in *Nation and Narration,* ed. Homi Bhabha (London: Routledge, 1990), 291–322 (quote on 316).

56. See Linda Martín Alcoff, "The Problem of Speaking for Others," in Judith Roof and Robyn Wiegman, eds., *Who Can Speak? Authority and Critical Identity,* ed. Judith Roof and Robyn Wiegman (Urbana: University of Illinois Press, 1995), 97–119 (esp. 113).

57. Chow, "Violence," 93.

58. Sturdevant and Stoltzfus quote the Filipina women's leader Adul de Leon on the subject: "When you return to the States, you will have a hard time with the women's movement there. They spend all their time arguing about whether prostitution can be a free choice" ("Disparate Threads of the Whole," 300).

59. Amy Ling, "Discrimination against Asian Americans," in *Kyogi to Chinmoku: Nichibei to Nikkei Gensetsu o megutte* (Misrepresentation and silence: U.S.-Japan and Nikkei discourses), ed. Lynn Thiesmeyer and Yuji Suzuki (Tokyo: Eichosha, forthcoming).

60. Ann Laura Stoler, *Race and the Education of Desire: Foucault's History of Sexuality and the Colonial Order of Things* (Durham, N.C.: Duke University Press, 1995), 32.

61. It can also be assumed that the children fathered by American purchases of teenage or adult women's sexual services may in turn serve American purchasers of child sex. See Enloe, *Bananas, Beaches, and Bases:* "Of the approximately 30,000 children born each year of Filipino mothers and American fathers, some 10,000 are thought to become street children, many of them working as prostitutes for American pedophiles" (87).

62. Chow, *Writing Diaspora;* Shi-xu, "Ideology: Strategies of Reason and Functions of Control in Accounts of the Non-Western Other," *Journal of Pragmatics* 21:6 (June 1994): 645–69.

63. Mohanty, "Under Western Eyes," 52.

64. U.S. Congress, "Human Rights Abuses of Burmese Girls and Women," Senate Concurrent Resolution 12, House Concurrent Resolution 21, *Congressional Record,* 104th Cong., 1st Sess. (4 May 1995), S6182.

65. Chow, *Writing Diaspora,* 167.

66. Ibid., 30, 34.

4. Bloody Mary Meets Lois-Ann Yamanaka: Imagining Asia/Pacific—from *South Pacific* to Bamboo Ridge

Rob Wilson

and if especially
those insistent mushrooming discourses
on life for all Pacific
spell genokamikaze through and through—
then I'll gather up this debris; up, once
all over again: for you, Island.
—Russell Soaba, "Island: Ways of Immortal Folk"

"*South Pacific* will run forever!" Walter Winchell once remarked of the Rodgers and Hammerstein musical. But from Suva to Papua New Guinea to the local site of Bamboo Ridge in Hawai'i, Pacific-based writers have challenged these James Michener–like national productions of Asian/Pacific and indigenous cultures with local constructions of place, sublanguages, and alternative grounds of identity. In this chapter I counter the global machinery of cultural texts like *South Pacific* and *Blue Hawaii* with interior constructions of transnational Asia Pacific as place and identity and posit the turn within local literary culture in Hawai'i toward expressing and coalescing into some kind of oppositional regionalism. This Pacific regionalism, at its most powerful reimagining of place, nation, and language in Maori novels such as Keri Hulme's *Bone People* (1983) and Patricia Grace's *Potiki* (1986), signal works of Hawai'i's "local literature" such as Milton Murayama's *All I Asking for Is My Body* (1975), John Dominis Holt's indigenous pastoral novel *Waimea Summer* (1976), and trenchant poetry collections such as Michael McPherson's *Singing with the Owls* (1982), Eric Chock's *Last Days Here* (1990), and Lois-Ann Yamanaka's *Saturday Night at the Pahala Theatre* (1993), would implicitly fracture the white nation-state imagination in its tropological sway over the Pacific.[1]

Running through my discussion of the "local" Pacific will be four strands of thinking surrounding related contemporary concerns of language, nation, and place: (1) the attempt to resist "symbolic domination"[2] by the norms, tropes, and genres of literary culture imported and imposed from the mainland or from Europe; (2) the poetic "recreolization"[3] of English as a connotative signifier of bonds to local culture and multiethnic community worth preserving for purposes of expression and sense of control (hence the building up of a polylingual literature of the local and minor); (3) the contradiction-ridden yet coalitional articulation of what Raymond Williams calls the "bond to place" within a globalizing economy of transnational circulation that would construct and produce the local/locality into a tourist icon and decenter formations of class-based resistance; and, given this globalizing transnational economy, (4) the need for cultivating "bonds to place" in order to build what I call "critical regionalism" within a postmodern culture of simulacra, image spectacle, and sign-flux.[4]

For an American audience newly conscious of a global destiny, *South Pacific* conjures Pacific space into a settler's paradise of primitive enchantment, racial harmony, and (to be sure) military necessity. This "musical play" opened in 1949 and ran for close to 2,000 performances, won the Pulitzer Prize for drama in 1949, and set box office records as it traveled across the United States. Based on two racially tormented love stories from James A. Michener's Pulitzer Prize–winning book *Tales of the South Pacific* (1946), the play's fable of primordial racial and cultural encounters reactivated by the Pacific war, as Patricia G. McGhee has observed, "was well known to audiences when it auditioned in Boston in 1946."[5]

Michener, a popular novelist who gave something like $13 million over twenty years to various institutions, including the University of Iowa (for its writing program), and wrote about seemingly every landscape under the sun, still receives ample royalties from *South Pacific*.[6] As late as March 1994 the musical was still being performed by the Army Community Theater at Fort Shafter in Honolulu: that the U.S. military needs to keep performing *South Pacific* as a fantasy of Pacific space imposed upon Hawai'i and its Asia/Pacific characters is the cold war master narrative I want to expose and contest.

South Pacific, as a fable of cold war necessity, absorbed the Pacific into its master narrative of militarization and technological development. This story may have ended in October 1990 when, among related events of postindustrial dismantlement and internal dissent, a presidential order ended the bombing of Kaho'olawe island in Hawai'i. This special locus of what Davianna McGregor calls "spiritual and cultural identification" for the Hawai'ian sovereignty struggle was demilitarized and reclaimed for indigenous usage after having been targeted since World War II as a bombing and gunnery range.[7] Why associate *South Pacific* with the struggle for indigenous sovereignty and place-bound identity that is occurring in contemporary Hawai'i?

Although situated in the northern Pacific and strategic to the expanding American commercial presence across the Pacific Ocean at least since the sandalwood, fur, and whaling trade of the 1820s and the imperial rivalries with France and Great Britain in the 1840s, Hawai'i has long played "South Pacific" to the cultures and power of Northern capital, whether sugar money from California, bibles and whaling ships from Boston, or the hotel resort interests from Indonesia and Japan. This is palpable in the sugar rhetoric of Mark Twain, who urged, as a journalist in 1866, that "if California can send capitalists down here in seven or eight days time and take them back in nine or ten [via commercial steamships], she can fill these islands full of Americans and regain her lost foothold" in the Pacific.[8] American sugar interests did so around the coaling station of Pearl Harbor, to be sure, importing Asian labor and, in time, displacing and diminishing native peoples and outlawing Hawai'ian as a language of public instruction en route to annexation under the imperial presidency of William McKinley.[9]

Set on some unspecified generic colonial French Pacific island in World War II, the 1958 movie version of *South Pacific* "was filmed on Kaua'i, with scenes at the Berkmyre estate overlooking Hanalei Bay, Lumaha'i Bay, Ha'ena, Kalapaki Beach, and Barking Sands, plus one brief scene on O'ahu" and, even more so than the play, helped to evoke a white mythological fantasy of "one enchanted evening" in paradise for an American mass tourist audience soon to disembark from their planes in the new state of Hawai'i.[10] Via the pidgin-speaking persona of Bloody Mary, as I will discuss, American innocents (like Nurse Nellie) were offered a disfigured embodiment of far-flung Asian/Pacific cultures willing to be absorbed, acculturated, and contained in their global economy of signs. Hollywood (what some people in Hawai'i like to call "Haolewood") cooperated with the Department of Defense to produce and install a "concrete fantasy" and images of the American Pacific as *South Pacific*.

By the "tropological sway" of *South Pacific* in the imagined nation-state community, I imply something like what Antonio Gramsci theorized as the workings of "concrete fantasy" within the "national-popular" imaginary: a collective interpretation of the national community that, in times of organic crisis and micropolitical struggle, can give way to alternative interpretations and, in our specific case, allow for changes in the dominant self-representation of U.S. culture and its role in the Pacific.

Postwar inscription of local places and peoples into some "concrete fantasy" of the American Pacific can still regenerate cultural capital for travel writers of the up-market "tourist gaze" from Simon Winchester to Paul Theroux: in *Pacific Rising* (1991), Winchester is delighted that one of the sacred sites for tour guides on Kaua'i is "where Mitzi Garner washed that man right out of her hair."[11] For a postmodern global audience, driven by pastiche and simulacra, such an allusion could almost count as a historical deep memory binding consciousness to place and self to history. But for the

Macintosh- and Toyota-driven vision of Winchester's transnational Asia Pacific, Hawai'i (like the entire Pacific Basin) figures in as "vanishing wilderness" and people-emptied landscapes of wilderness sublimity that once "had mystic associations with long-vanished Hawaiian cultures"—in short, as the charming flora and fauna of "the Old Pacific."[12] There are no primordial sentiments of Hawai'ian nationhood or first possession, no cultural nationalists like Haunani-Kay Trask to disturb Simon Winchester's "concrete fantasy" of Old Pacific paradise for the *Conde Nast Traveller*.[13] No complex micropolitical thematics of the Hawai'ian sovereignty struggle disturb tourist Rimspeak.[14]

In *Happy Isles of Oceania* (1992), an archive of latter-day mythology of white cultural (by no means *first*) possession, Theroux reveals a fundamental condescension toward the cultures of the Pacific, as in his comments on the novelist Somerset Maugham as his Euro-American precursor in Samoa: "Maugham was another writer who had sanctified a place by using it as a setting; he had done the islands a great favor—made them seem [*sic*] exotic and interesting."[15] Without "sanctification" by the cultural capital and mythology of Western writers, painters, anthropologists, travelers and moviemakers, these "places without history" in the Pacific do not exist. At best, the Pacific beckons these Western writers as a submissive earthy woman of color waiting to be inscribed/awakened into Edenic trope, engendered into tropical submission, and inculcated into higher English, as in the pedagogy of Paul Gauguin's French-Tahitian travelogue *Noa Noa*. While Vilsoni Hereniko and Teresia Teaiwa reveal the erotic-maniacal fantasies of Euro-Americans who still seek to find some pristine island/woman in the Pacific in their co-written play *The Last Virgin in Paradise,* other writers are still searching to find what Hereniko and Teaiwa debunk.[16] Theroux desires "the apotheosis of the South Seas: distant, secluded, empty, pristine—ravishing in fact"[17] at a time when ethnography as a social science grows increasingly skeptical of its own ability to objectify, trope, describe, and salvage non-Western cultures in any redemptive way. Similar attitudes link Louis Bougainville's Venus-struck *Voyage* to Theroux's pioneer-like kayak—with its dog-eared copy of Malinowski's *Sexual Life of Savages* and self-pitying male hunger for paradise-on-earth figured as some "happy island" (troped as a dark submissive woman) in the vast vacancies of Oceania.

Given this tropological lineage, it may not appear so strange that most American movies made in or about Hawai'i, from World War I's *Martin Eden* (1914) to the postwar *South Pacific*, "took place aboard aircraft, ships, boats, or submarines," as Robert Schmitt outlines in *Hawaii in the Movies, 1898–1959*.[18] This perspective from the ocean toward the native shore presupposes the ongoing militarization of local space from the cold war American gaze: an aesthetic-commercial "sanctification" of Pacific Ocean localities from within defensive optics and global codes of representation.

Blue Hawaii (1961), a widely circulated movie that popularized anew the "paradisal interpretation" of Hawai'i as a mass tourist garden of exotic/erotic delight in the "South Pacific," at least tried to turn Elvis Presley into a place-bound Pacific resident.[19] Elvis's detailed knowledge of local custom and idiom (expressed in a mildly southern pidgin accent) allows him to drop out of his wealthy family's "Great Hawaiian Fruit Company" and pineapple production into the key business of the fiftieth state's future, namely, mass tourism. Chad Gates gets a job as a guide for "Hawaiian Island Tours," escorts and croons five haole women around the islands, and finally marries his half-Hawaiian, half-French sweetheart, Maile, at a wedding on Kaua'i that is fit for a (rock) king. To the dismay of his southern racist mother (played by Angela Lansbury), Elvis hangs out with native beach boys, speaks scraps of pidgin, surfs, and longs to waste his fortune crooning *aloha* to Maile and his knee-slapping friends in a little grass shack at "Hanauma Bay." Elvis at least gets close to, if circling around, the local culture of Bamboo Ridge.

For the most part, the azure-deep photogenic landscape of Hawai'i—as in an array of postmodern television series starring Hawai'i-as-place, from "Hawaiian Eye" (1959–63), "Hawaii Five-O" (1968–80), "Big Hawaii" (1977), "Magnum PI" (1980–88), "Aloha Paradise" (1981), "Hawaiian Heat" (1984), "Jake and the Fatman" (1988–90), "Island Son" (1989), and "Raven" (1991) to "The Byrds of Paradise" (1995)—figures mostly as an Edenic backdrop to some imagined ethnoscape of racialized, exoticized, blatant Orientalizing-of-the-local plots (local Japanese usually play shifty-eyed Yakuza and Hawai'ians and Samoans play nightclub bouncers or gophers).[20]

This "tourist gaze" upon a Pacific locality as the exotic/erotic site of tourist fulfillment is palpable in the tackiest Elvis-croons-in-Hawai'i movie ever made, *Paradise, Hawaiian Style* (1964), which uses a soporific plot about Elvis and the plight of his tourist shuttle company. The movie offers banal calypso-like music but features primal Pacific events such as Samoans, Tongans, and Tahitians playing ever-smiling Hawai'ians dancing the hula. This performance takes place at the just-opened Polynesian Cultural Center, the real star of the show. Perspective upon place and culture is, from first to last, rendered through the gaze of United Airliners and tourist company helicopters (piloted by a singing Elvis) sweeping over vast native-emptied rain forests of Kaua'i and over the tourist-thick resort hotels and azure Pacific waters from the Royal Hawaiian to the Kahala Hilton: tourist heaven as "paradise, Hawaiian style."

Twentieth Century Fox's lavishly filmed *South Pacific*, directed with escapist exaggeration and occasionally ludicrous "ever-present [colorizing] filters" by Joshua Logan, which drench the yellow Pacific in red, white, and blue hazes, premiered at the height of the cold war, when U.S. military hegemony across the Pacific had solidified into nuclear normality and what Russell Soaba calls the "insistent mushrooming discourses"[21] were doing their anti-

Soviet work.[22] Circulation of *South Pacific* through the cultural arteries of the American imaginary was aggravated with the advent of another technology, the LP album of *South Pacific,* which proved to be a blockbuster as well. The VCR and Ted Turner's television network's penchant for singalong musicals in the American grain have prolonged *South Pacific*'s afterlife into the 1990s, even as the Johnston Atoll (Kalama Island) in the far-flung "South Pacific" is used to incinerate chemical weapons left over from North Atlantic struggles.[23] As cinemascope spectacle, cultures of the North Pacific and *South Pacific* fuse into a fantasy of Edenic enchantment, boundary blurring, and Asian/Pacific otherness here figured as that broker of local beauty and commercialization of native custom, namely, Bloody Mary. Mary's broken-English slogan for the emerging transnational Asia Pacific lifestyle is: "Native Skirts Fo' Dollah."

South Pacific is far more than a heterotopia of "escapism" and harmless space of cross-cultural otherness, as some critics have claimed of the movie genre.[24] Mythology of racial and cultural superiority was produced to ratify the American presence in this postwar musical appropriation of the South Pacific and to assuage the labor of Asian/Pacific boundary negotiation the operatic music mystifies. Cultural domination takes place in enchanted dreamscapes of blue and red suffused on so-called Bali Ha'i.

This labor of possession, which "takes place on two islands in the South Pacific during the recent war," seems harmless enough in its symbolic-fantasy fusions of transnational bodies across racial, class, and national divides.[25] While the pidgin-speaking, bootlegging, go-between character Bloody Mary negotiates over the marriage of local culture and the body of her Tonkinese/ Tonganese daughter to Joseph Cable, a swooning ex-racist Marine lieutenant from Princeton, Emile De Becque joins his French colonial presence as landed aristocrat ("Is all this yours?") and antifascist hero to the cockeyed smarmy new-world optimism of Nurse Nellie ("He's a cultured Frenchmen— / I'm a little hick").[26] Dominating the Japanese and subordinating Pacific peoples to commercial and military enterprise from Papua New Guinea to the Bikini Atoll, American and French administrators work together to represent, construct, and install *their* "South Pacific" into an enchanted "Bali Hai" playground fit for Euro-American romance, commodity worship (see Lamont Lindstrom on the Western fantasy of the cargo cult as a universalizing of the commodity fetish to Melanesian natives), sexual contamination, danger, passion, and, above all, hegemonic military might.[27]

American innocents "have to be taught" to savor Proust's novels of landed gentry and to sip cognac on "some enchanted evening" in a white settler's manor. But they also have to overcome a 300-year legacy of racial prejudice that Ensign Nellie Forbush brings with her from Little Rock, Arkansas, to categorize the peoples of Polynesia by racial color. In Michener's short story, American racism is overt, as Nellie (played with nervous charm by Mitzi Gaynor in the musical) muses on the sexual contamination of the French émigré. Like his colonial predecessors from the time of Bougainville, Emile De Becque had been enchanted by "the Venus of Tahiti": "Emile De Becque, not satisfied with Javanese and Tonkinese women, had also lived with a Polynesian. A nigger! To Nellie's tutored mind any person living or dead who was not white or yellow was a nigger. . . . Her entire Arkansas upbringing made it impossible for her to deny the teachings of her youth. Emile De Becque had lived with a nigger. He had nigger children."[28]

Nicholas Thomas argues that "local appropriation for local ends" in the Pacific "must all ultimately be seen in the global context of European dominance."[29] Thus, like many uneven global/local exchanges within colonial contexts of commercial dependency and metropolitan administration, a global/local bargain does get struck. Natives of the South/North Pacific from the Solomon Islands to Guam will have to be taught the market system, technological warfare, geopolitics, and, above all, the unchallengeable militarization of local space and identity by global powers from the far-flung polities of Europe, America, and Japan. Americans, for their part, will have to be taught to sing along with the U.S. Department of Defense and the Commander in Chief of the Pacific Command (CINCPAC) and to take up the burden of French plantation colonialism done over in Nellie's lesser key of *innocent disavowal.*[30]

Michener, a prolific mythographer of national settlement as democratization, has become a whipping boy for the "local literature" movement emerging in Hawai'i—not so much for *South Pacific* as for his novel *Hawaii,* which came out in 1959 and attempts to legitimate, in one panoramic gaze of triumph, Hawai'i's march from primordial emptiness through missionary culture to the imagined community of a liberal statehood. *Hawaii* proved relevant to mapping the "real nexus" of cultural labor and national imagining such popular literature is involved in. As the *New York Herald Tribune* blurb on *Hawaii* has it, "James A. Michener tells the whole story of the people, Polynesian, American, Portuguese, Chinese, Philippine, Japanese, who have mingled to make our fiftieth state."[31] Dedicated to "all the people who came to Hawaii," including indigenous ones in a grand telos of Hawai'ian modernity as prolonged Americanization, *Hawaii* narrates the movement of Asian/Pacific cultures into what I call the "melting pot sublime." According to Michener's commonsense liberal view, multicultures will mix and amalgamate races and customs into the transcendent fusion of the nation-state. As such, it proves inadequate to describe the Asian/Pacific dynamics of the local literature movement in Hawai'i.

"Local" culture critics have been less sanguine about *Hawaii* as a "masterpiece" of historical production and have worked to unsettle such fanta-

sies of place and offshore tactics of cultural representation. Michener's "con-
trived pidgin English" in *Hawaii*, as Stephen Sumida contends, has served
to mystify the dynamics of local culture and indigenous possession. It has
also served to denigrate local perspectives as substandard, minor, and in-
sufficient to grasp the dynamic of historical progress or articulate their own
values and place in the metropolitan system. "The inference is that Hawaii's
pidgin vernacular is the identifying mark of a savage, a fool, or a simpleton,"
Sumida cautions.[32]

Michener's Bloody Mary represents exactly such a transnational body
who merges Toganese superstition and Tonkanese-Chinese venality into a
toxic Asian/Pacific brew of bad English, stinking body, and clownish man-
ners. Given her crass, fawning pursuit of the "saxy Lootellan" from "Phil-
adelia" money and Princeton cultural capital for her younger-than-spring-
time daughter, Liat, Bloody Mary plays the disfigured Asian/Pacific body
of mangled English and opportunistic hybridity. She integrates native costumes and customs (a melange of hula skirts, betel nuts, shrunken heads,
and boar's teeth) to capitalist appropriation and absorption into the wartorn world system: "Look, Lootellan, I am rich. I save six hundred dolla'
before war. Since war I make two thousand dollah."[33] As a bluntly enchanted native eager to Westernize and commodify all social relations, including her own French-speaking Catholic daughter, Bloody Mary will have to
be taught to smooth and lighten "her skin as tender as Dimaggio's glove,"
but, above all for a residually Puritan white culture, to "use Pepsodent":

> Men [singing Seabees]:
> Bloody Mary's chewing betel nuts,
> She is always chewing betel nuts,
> Bloody Mary's chewing betel nuts—
> And she don't use Pepsodent.
> (She grins and shows her betel-stained teeth.)
> Now ain't that too damn bad.[34]

The American makings of this Pacific racial hierarchy and neocolonial
division of labor in *South Pacific* are articulated in Michener's short story "Fo'
Dolla," which provides the musical its political structure: "It was only proper that as a Tonkinese [from French Indochina] she [Bloody Mary] should
exercise her endowed rights over the inferior Melanesians. Like a true grand
dame, she cleared the way for the greater nobility, a white lieutenant, to step
ashore."[35] If a Melanesian "savage" in blood, Liat would be unacceptable; if
Chinese, then the cultural and racial border in the Pacific becomes negotia-
ble through sexual contact and marriage, the unimaginable extreme of Eurasian contract. "Were Bali-hai and all its people merely a part of the grim and
brooding old cannibal island? Were Liat and her unfathomable mother mere-

ly descendants from the elder savages? No! The idea was preposterous. Tonkinese were in reality Chinese, sort of the way Canadians were Americans, only a little different."[36] Cable, however, must die before such a Hollywood-taboo marriage can be consummated.[37]

The violence of international war by outsiders destroys and displaces Pacific space and uproots whole cultures in the name of military necessity, as later at the Bikini Atoll. But this history is not glimpsed in the scene where the Lono-like[38] Cable (in his first appearance to Bloody Mary, he descends from the clouds) still fears that Miss Liat is too close to *cannibal* blood, too ambiguously *Tonganese*, "too far away from [movie stars of] Philadelphia, PA" with their Ivory soap skin.

South Pacific, like Michener's later blockbuster epic of Hawai'ian locality, worked as spectacles in the American-pop tropological grain. The people of the Pacific are enlisted into Western mores and the contradictory history of Hawai'i is inscribed into Michener's myth of Hawai'i as multiracial heaven. By no means foundational as a discourse, *South Pacific* comprises part of a tropological intertext through which the local North/South Pacific, displaced and disfigured into subjugated local knowledges, circulates and tries to affirm counterclaims to identity, language, community, nation, and place. If the seamless makings of the *South Pacific* nation can be called into question as *cold-war cultural artifact*, then the transnational production of Hawai'i into ex-primitive icon, from Hollywood to Asia-Pacific Economic Co-operation (APEC), can be challenged and undone.[39]

As Gramsci has demonstrated, to grasp the function and circulation of "culture" in any formation of "national-popular"[40] hegemony as well as the makings of subaltern resistance, we must look to "the real nexus," that is, to the specific contexts of a work's social creation and reception as well as to its absorption in particular cultures, spaces, and histories.[41] Such a *real nexus* between cultural representations and the apparatus of material power, soliciting national consent in contexts of monetary and military coercion, is suggested in the opening sequence of *South Pacific*. Superimposed over the swaying palms of a timelessly spectacular tropical sunset emptied of other narratives and prior peoples, the paragraph reads: "The Producers thank the Department of Defense, the Navy Department, the United States Pacific Fleet, and the Fleet Marine of the Pacific for their assistance in bringing this motion picture to the screen." Militarization of the Pacific Ocean puts huge infrastructural demands on the environment and disrupts local place and vision. U.S. geopolitical possession, at that time, remained intact, albeit expanding, some twelve years after the war as *South Pacific* moved from novel to play to movie and went global. Natives have to be taught to rethink their long-occupied Pacific spaces as "off limits" and "Navy property." Natives have to be taught to take part (even if they only play silent, goofy, or, at best, smiling backdrop to the psychological complications of Western romance) as warriors (and cargo carriers) in the global battle for "enemy-held islands." Opposing such representations, there are countermappings of the Pacific war in poems and songs by displaced island peoples.[42]

Racial prejudice toward Pacific peoples in Michener's Nurse Nellie is no cultural anomaly from the Eisenhower-era bigotry of Little Rock. Through his Peeping-Tom narrator Tommo in *Typee* (1843), Herman Melville as interpreter of the early American Pacific had associated the Polynesians of Hawai'i with "Negroid" blood and woolly headed Fijians. This romance turned Melville's fantasmatic Pacific native Fayaway into an olive-skinned, blue-eyed, smooth and lovely goddess who stepped out of the Greco-Roman mythologies of earthly paradise more than out of Marquesan culture.[43] As Paul Lyons has argued, a racial binary structured American fears of being tattooed and cannibalized by Pacific natives like the one-eyed chief Mow-Mow and thus reverting into black "savages."[44] Melville lamented the "fatal impact" of Western civilization on indigenous Pacific cultures and the arrogant violence of national agents like U.S. Navy Captain David Reynolds; nonetheless, he also described King Kamehameha III as "a fat, lazy, negro-looking blockhead, with as little character as power,"[45] and he separated the more "voluptuous Tahitians" and "European cast" Marquesans from "the dark-haired Hawaiians and the woolly-headed Feejees [who] are immeasurably inferior to them."[46] That is, the racial binary of American writers in the Pacific, for which the foundational text is Melville's fantasy-haunted *Typee* (based on experiences in Nukuheva and Hawai'i in 1842), involves the trauma of Pacific islanders reverting to cannibalism and, furthermore, longings and fears by whites of "becoming native" and expressing this degeneration via an embrace of tattooing as a way of writing the Pacific body.[47] By the turn of the nineteenth century, after the monarchy of Queen Liliuokalani was toppled, Jack London (with true Anglo-Saxon delight) still found "niggers" everywhere his white characters gazed across the colonies of Melanesia (see, for instance, "The Inevitable White Man").[48] "Melanesians. Polynesians. Tonks! They're all alike," says one of Michener's American sailors, dreaming of repossessing his white "hot number in cold Minneapolis," as he simplifies the complex cultures of the Pacific in "Fo'Dolla."[49]

Given the 400-year imperial outreach by Western powers to cross and claim the Pacific Ocean for metropolitan purposes, island geography is not a physical given but a cultural projection. From conquest to contest, the Pacific is a space inscribed with power, class struggle, and polity, overrepresented by outside powers, encoded with (white/native/multicultural) mythology, and circulated through the "mimetic technologies" of global capital as *South Pacific*—the movie, not the place.[50]

To invoke the cultural politics of Gramsci, for whom complications of place, location, and class alignment are always crucial to the formation of national popular identity, "East and West are arbitrary and conventional, that is historical constructions, since outside of history every point on the earth is East and West at the same time."[51] Pacific geography, and the taken-for-granted orientations of "East" and "West" as binary terms, are driven, in Gramsci's skeptical view, "from the point of view of the European cultured classes, who, as a result of their world-wide hegemony, have caused them to be accepted everywhere." The result has proved formative for peoples affected by this (Orientalizing) self-knowledge: "Japan is the Far East not only for Europe but also perhaps for the American from California and even for the Japanese himself, who, through English political culture, may then call Egypt the Near East."[52]

As geopolitical meaning gets sedimented into binary geographical terms like "East" meeting "West" or into that contemporary signifier of all-purpose indeterminacy, "Asia/Pacific," and the subordination of "Pacific Basin" to "Pacific Rim," these historically burdened signifiers come to occlude what Gramsci would track as "specific relations between different cultural complexes."[53] Given the "real nexus" of global power and struggle for international as well as internal hegemony over its own peoples, U.S. representations of the "South Pacific" as an enchanted yet inferior place would absorb Pacific space, both North and South, into the workings of America's own imaginary geography and geopolitics.

If only in the reimagined space and genres of culture as "minor literature," colonial binaries are breaking down, the global codes of capitalist space-time can get scrambled, and a third, or *in-between,* space can emerge. Gilles Deleuze imagines the nomadic movement across continent and ocean as a *deterritorialization:* "American literature operates according to geographical lines: the flight towards the West, the discovery that the true East is in the West, the sense of the frontiers as something to cross, to push back, to go beyond."[54] Deterritorializing geography back into mythology, Deleuze concludes that, in the watery reaches of Pacific space, "Captain Ahab has a whale-becoming." Similarly, the "fugitives" from European (De Becque) and American (Nellie) binaries of race and national fantasy may find new life in the Eurasian hybridity of the postwar Asian/Pacific.[55]

Seeking to undermine these unconsciously hegemonic constructions of local Asia/Pacific cultures by people of liberal will like Michener, Theroux, and Winchester—which I have troped into the genre of *South Pacific*—with more interior constructions of place and dynamics of multicultural identity, my aim has been to posit the makings of an oppositional regionalism in the Pacific. Such "minor literature" fractures the settler nation-state imagination and reclaims location as ground of place and vision. Enacting "critical regionalism" and minority languages that refuse to be assimilated into or explained by myths of multicultural "American" identity, the Pacific lo-

cal has emerged as a distinctive place, a ground of commitment and identi-
ty and language. Hawai'i, as I claim, stands for some "trojan horse" of Asian/
Pacific localism imploding within the national imagination of the United
States.

Bamboo Ridge, as place and cultural symbol, sits in the middle of one of
the most heated real estate markets in the world. Since the days of King Kamehameha (who, in the military wake of Cook and Vancouver, first unified
the islands into nation status), governing groups have drawn power, legiti-
macy, and structure from possessing (in contracts and symbols) the land in
Hawai'i, the 'aina. This ground is contested and claimed within various symbolic heritages and affiliations of power. Adhering to the real nexus of locality at Bamboo Ridge posits a way of *reimagining* relationships between region, nation, and globe in which difference is not negated or reified but
constructed, negotiated, and affirmed. The local has materialized into alternative narratives and counterclaims upon the "American Pacific."

At another extreme, native Hawai'ians seek to possess, bond to, and preserve the land as locus of cultural identity. These Hawai'ians' claims would
fracture the unifying myths and legal status of sovereign territory—the imagined unity—of the U.S. nation-state. For example, Dana Naone Hall's pro-
test poems of place are forceful in their evocation of Hawai'ian mythology
and Hawai'ian "signs" mobilized against transnational resorts and golf cours-
es bent on taking over the beachscapes of Mau'i.[56] Any stance of "critical
localism" has to struggle, not only globally but locally, with/against forces of
transnational simulation. Carolyn Lei-Lani Lau writes in a poem that fractures her Chinese-Hawai'ian American identity as a diasporic Chinese into
more Hawai'ian claims of counter-American allegiance:

> in spite of the plantations and pineapple fields,
> the tourists
> and military,
> Hawai'i never became the 49th state[57]

Caricatured representation of Pacific values, sense of place, and embodiment (as in the squatting body of Bloody Mary, named after an alcoholic
Western drink) is being replaced by the interiorized, grounded, and tension-
packed Hawai'i Creole English of Lois-Ann Yamanaka: that "transcendent
tita" whose Bamboo Ridge Press book *Saturday Night at the Pahala Theatre*
(1993) has caused a sensation in Hawai'i.[58] Her poetry has brought local poetics into sharper focus, especially in relation to Hawai'ian thematics and
Asian-American norms, and her work has been avidly anthologized on the
mainland.[59] As in some *Spoon River Anthology* of pidgin personae, in Yamanaka's reimagined world of Pahala, sister and sister clash for domination, males
intimidate and exploit and initiate women, Titas rule, mother abuses daugh-

ter, races clash and mix and fuse into the dynamic working-class community of a Big Island plantation. Pidgin expression is not the exception but the
rule, in love, in family, in ethnic interaction. The plantation world of Pahala
opens out to mountain ("Haupu Mountain") and ocean ("Glass").[60]

In desublimating personae of crazed Deleuzian pidgin English like "Tita:
Japs" and "Tita: The Bathroom," local Japanese identity is viewed as hardly
one of purity or ethnic wholeness but one of self-division, self-hatred even:
a longing to be othered into haole cultural styles (from Cher to Judy Gar-
land) ranging, at another extreme, into the deeper Hawai'ian place values and
resonances in poems such as "Pueo" and "Glass." In "Yarn Wig," the range
of voices is playful and acute, the humor devastating toward local style as a
mixture of aspiration and abuse, local custom and mass mediation. The title poem similarly details the disruptive if not abusive effect of mainland
pornography on gender relations in the plantation town of Pahala on the Big
Island.

In one of the quasi-Hawai'ian poems of place, "Glass," pidgin becomes a
symbolic vehicle for a deeper probing into place-as-history and into reaches of the numinous world of the sacred, incarnated by the "glass floater" given
up by the Pacific Ocean, "light blue and cool in the shade of the naupaka
bushes."[61] Bernie, the *kupuna*-like taxidermist, becomes an older initiator of
the main female character, Lucy. He initiates her not into sexual domination
but into the wild animal and spiritual energies of the place. It is a place that
he respects and knows intimately, as is demonstrated in the trip out of the
plantation smallness to the greater natural world of "Haupu Mountain." This
respect is also revealed in the trip to the ocean:

> Us get in the Jeep and pass the cow pasture
> by the just burn sugar cane field.
> Then us pass Punalu'u and Honoapu Mill.
> Bernie go slow through Naalehu
> then Waiohinu by the Mark Twain monkeypod tree.
> Bernie tell me stories about every stone wall,
> every old graveyard, every stream,
> and even the monkeypod tree.[62]

Tapping into deeper memories and ties to place as appropriated and enriched
by layers of indigenous and settler cultures, Yamanaka is no cultural *purist*
but rifely postmodern in her Asian/Pacific/American identity tactics—not
only in the full-out Deleuzian quality of crazed pidgin voice but in the full
range of lower culture: the "My Eyes Adore You" playing on the eight-track
in WillyJoe's yellow Datsun; corn beef patties with rice eaten in front of the
"Ed Sullivan Show"; vanilla Cokes and Sonny and Cher looks; or Donny
Osmond and Captain and Tenille tapes.[63] "Tita: User" offers a cornucopia of

local appropriations and circulations of American-pop culture in the Asian/
Pacific community of the Pahala Theatre. "I was encouraged [by Faye Kick-
nosway, Eric Chock et al.] to write in the voice of my place without shame
or fear," Yamanaka claims in her biographical statement for *Charlie Chan Is
Dead*.[64]

Lois-Ann Yamanaka vanquishes Michener's slobbering Bloody Mary with
a grounded vision of compassionate interiority. The voices of staunch singularity in her poems range from Tita and Kala to the pathos of the Willy-
Joe character, whose lack of Standard English does not disable him from
emotional depth, complexity of insight into place, family, and his loved one,
Lucy. Lucy gives him another language, finally, in the lyric memorialization
of her poem "Name Me Is," where both find voice and affirm it in its own
peculiar and distinctive Hawai'ian Creole English:

> I IS.
> Ain't *nobody*
> tell me
> otherwise.[65]

Like Milton Murayama, John Dominis Holt, Gary Pak, Zack Linmark, Michael McPherson, Juliet Kono Lee, Haunani-Kay Trask, and others, Lois-Ann
Yamanaka has learned "to write in the voice of [her] place without shame
or fear."

Notes

1. Works cited include Keri Hulme, *The Bone People* (New Zealand: Spiral/Hodder and
Stoughton, 1984); Patricia Grace, *Potiki* (Auckland: Penguin, 1986); Milton Murayama, *All
I Asking for Is My Body* (San Francisco: Supa Press, 1975); John Dominis Holt, *Waimea
Summer: A Novel* (Honolulu: Topgallant, 1976); Michael McPherson, *Singing with the Owls*
(Honolulu: Petronium Press, 1982); Eric Chock, *Last Days Here* (Honolulu: Bamboo Ridge
Press, 1990); and Lois-Ann Yamanaka, *Saturday Night at the Pahala Theatre* (Honolulu:
Bamboo Ridge Press, 1993).

2. On the "symbolic domination" achieved via distinctions of language, taste, and
"cultural capital," see John B. Thompson, *Studies in the Theory of Ideology* (Berkeley:
University of California Press, 1984), 48–61.

3. See Charlene J. Sato, "Linguistic Inequality in Hawaii: The Post-Creole Dilemma,"
in *Language of Inequality*, ed. N. Wolfson and J. Manes (Berlin: Mouton, 1985), 255–72.

4. On "bonds to place" as ground of transnational resistance, see Raymond Williams,
"Decentralism and the Politics of Place," *Resources of Hope: Culture, Democracy, Social-
ism*, ed. Robin Glade (London: Verso, 1989): "But *place* has been shown to be a crucial
element in the bonding process—more so perhaps for the working class than the capi-
tal-owning classes—by the explosion of the international economy and the destructive
effects of deindustrialization upon old communities. When capital has moved on, the
importance of place is more clearly revealed" (242). Katharyne Mitchell has made a su-
perb study of transnational disruptions of place-bound identity in Vancouver on the
northwest Pacific coast of Canada. See "Multiculturalism or the United Colors of Capitalism?" *Antipode* 23 (1993): 263–94. In a related global/local study, see David Harvey,

"From Space to Place and Back Again: Reflections on the Condition of Postmodernity," in *Mapping the Futures: Local Cultures, Global Change,* ed. Jon Bird, Barry Curtis, Tim Putnam, and George Robertson (London: Routledge, 1993), 3–28.

5. See Patricia O. McGhee, "*South Pacific* Revisited: Were We Carefully Taught or Reinforced?" *The Journal of Ethnic Studies* 15 (1988): 124.

6. On the philanthropic and American liberal writing habits of James Michener, who sold the film rights to his novel *Hawaii* "for $750,000, the highest price paid for a picture property up to that time," see A. Grove Day, *Mad about Islands: Novelists of a Vanished Pacific* (Honolulu: Mutual Publishing, 1987), 237–46.

7. See Jon Yoshishige, "U.S. Vote Brings Kahoolawe Home," *The Honolulu Advertiser,* 11 November 1993, A1. For related decolonizing struggles, see David Robie, *Blood on Their Banner: Nationalist Struggles in the South Pacific* (Leichhardt, NSW: Pluto Press Australia, 1989).

8. Mark Twain, *Letters from Hawaii,* ed. A. Grove Day (Honolulu: University of Hawaii Press, 1975), 12.

9. See Michael Dougherty, *To Steal a Kingdom: Probing Hawaiian History* (Waimanalo, Hawai'i: Island Style Press, 1992), 165–79.

10. Robert C. Schmitt, *Hawaii in the Movies, 1898–1959* (Honolulu: Hawaiian Historical Society, 1988), 73.

11. Simon Winchester, *Pacific Rising: The Emergence of a New World Culture* (New York: Prentice Hall, 1991), 368.

12. Ibid., 366–71.

13. On the native-centered nationalism of Haunani-Kay Trask, see the essays in her collection *From a Native Daughter: Colonialism and Sovereignty in Hawai'i* (Monroe, Maine: Common Courage Press, 1994). On her vision of literary decolonization in the Pacific indigenous region, see her two essays in *Inside Out: Literature, Cultural Politics, and Identity in the New Pacific,* ed. Vilsoni Hereniko and Rob Wilson (Boulder, Colo.: Rowman and Littlefield Press, 1999). A more flexible vision of Hawai'ian national identity is offered in hybrid terms in John Dominis Holt, *On Being Hawaiian* (Honolulu: Ku Pa'a Press, 1995), and in his novel *Waimea Summer.*

14. For a summary of recent configurations between state and nation, see Chieko Tachihata, "The Sovereignty Movement In Hawai'i," *The Contemporary Pacific* 6 (1994): 202–10; *Ka Leo O Ka Lahui Hawai'i: A Compilation of Materials for Educational Workshops* (Honolulu: Ka La Hui, Hawai'i, 1993); Hawaiian Sovereignty Advisory Commission, "Final Report," 18 February 1994, Honolulu.

15. Paul Theroux, *The Happy Isles of Oceania: Paddling the Pacific* (New York: G. Putnam's Sons, 1992), 350.

16. Vilsoni Hereniko and Teresia Teaiwa, *Last Virgin In Paradise* (Suva, Fiji: Mana Publications, 1993).

17. Theroux, *Happy Isles,* 398.

18. Schmitt, *Hawaii in the Movies,* 6.

19. "*Blue Hawaii,* a [1961] film that was never intended as serious commentary [on Hawai'i] but one that attracted huge audiences because of its star—Elvis Presley—and its evocative title, had a greater impact upon popular impressions of the island than any other film ever made. In a sense, this is regrettable, as its portrayal of Hawaiian society, while blandly complimentary, is a blurred amalgam of Hawaiian, Samoan, and Tahitian culture overlaid with borrowed Southern notions of hospitality, aristocracy, leisure, and race. Despite these shortcomings, however, it does project an essentially paradisal interpretation and stands, thus, as a major factor in the popularization of this view of the islands" (Paul F. Hooper, *Elusive Destiny: The Internationalist Movement in Modern Hawaii* [Honolulu: University of Hawaii Press, 1980], 22).

20. Hooper, *Elusive Destiny,* 22–28. See also Ed Bark, "Isle 'Byrds' Worth a Look,"

Honolulu Advertiser, 3 March 1994, B1 (includes catalog of television series set in Hawaiʻi); Ed Rampell, "The Tackiest Films Ever Made about Hawaii," *Honolulu Weekly* 2 (15 April 1992): 4–5.

21. Russell Soaba, cited in Gilian Gorle, "The Theme of Social Change in Papua New Guinea, 1969–1979," *Pacific Studies* 18 (1995): 95–96. Soaba's poem "Island" is forthcoming in the journal *Kava.* On the Euro-American nuclearization of the Pacific, specifically Hawaiʻi, see Rob Wilson, "Postmodern as Post-Nuclear: Landscape as Nuclear Grid," in *Ethics/Aesthetics: Post-Modern Positions,* ed. Robert Merrill (Washington, D.C.: Maisonneuve Press, 1988), 169–92.

22. Rick Altman, *The American Film Musical* (Bloomington: Indiana University Press, 1987), 197.

23. See William A. Callahan and Steve Olive, "Chemical Weapons Discourse in the 'South Pacific,'" in *Asia/Pacific as Space of Cultural Production,* ed. Rob Wilson and Arif Dirlik (Durham, N.C.: Duke University Press, 1996), 57–79.

24. Altman, *American Film Musical,* 62.

25. Oscar Hammerstein and Joshua Logan, *South Pacific: A Musical Play* (New York: Random House, 1949), 1.

26. Ibid., 10.

27. See Lamont Lindstrom, *Cargo Cult: Strange Stories of Desire from Melanesia and Beyond* (Honolulu: University of Hawaii Press, 1993).

28. James A. Michener, "Our Heroine," in *Tales of the South Pacific* (New York: Fawcett Crest, 1974), 138.

29. Nicholas Thomas, *Entangled Objects: Exchange, Material Culture, and Colonialism in the Pacific* (Cambridge, Mass.: Harvard University Press, 1991), 184.

30. On the critical desublimating of American imperial acts of possession, see Amy Kaplan and Donald Pease, eds., *The Cultures of United States Imperialism* (Durham, N.C.: Duke University Press, 1993).

31. James A. Michener, *Hawaii* (New York: Random House, 1959). For local idolatry of Michener as national hero, see Melissa Sones, "Portrait of an 'Average' Guy," *Honolulu Advertiser,* 27 January 1986, D1–2.

32. Stephen H. Sumida, *And the View from the Shore: Literary Traditions of Hawaiʻi* (Seattle: University of Washington Press, 1991), 81.

33. Hammerstein and Logan, *South Pacific,* 120.

34. Ibid., 18–20.

35. Michener, *Tales of the South Pacific,* 184.

36. Ibid., 191.

37. On the Hollywood narrative codes that forbid the full representation of miscegenation between white males and Pacific native women, as well as the semiotic dance around such erotic and political censorship of interracial unions, see Glenn Man, "Hollywood Images of the Pacific," *East-West Film Journal* 5 (1991): 1629; Luis I. Reyes, *Made in Paradise: Hollywood's Films of Hawaiʻi and the South Seas* (Honolulu: Mutual, 1995). The ill-fated lovers, Luana and Johnny, in *Birds of Paradise* (1932) are prototypes of this alluring but forbidden consummation; and the punishment is often death by volcano (the movie was based on a play from 1912 and was redone and set in Hawaiʻi in 1951; it also gave its name to a 1995 television show, "The Byrds of Paradise," which dealt with conflicts between visiting tourists and disgruntled islanders refusing the erotic gaze).

38. Lono was the Hawaiʻian god of harvest fertility whose myths and narratives were projected onto Captain James Cook: this is a complicated and contested issue of whites "becoming Lono" in their own fantasy if not in the pragmatic symbolism of the Hawaiʻians (see Gannath Obyeskere, *The Apotheosis of Captain Cook* [Princeton, N.J.: Princeton University Press, 1995]). For a novelistic treatment, see O. A. Bushnell, *The Return of Lono: A Novel of Captain Cook's Last Voyage* (Honolulu: University of Hawaii Press, 1971).

39. During the postwar era, when the Asia/Pacific region became CINCPAC's staging ground for phobias of communism in Russia, China, North Korea, and Vietnam, the American "territory" of Hawai'i had to be taught the dangers of international communism as threat to labor, trade, and freedom. In *Big Jim McLain* (1952), John Wayne played the un-American hunting agent sent out from Washington, D.C., to Honolulu for "Operation Pineapple" to ferret out communist labor organizers, secret agents, and fellow-traveling University of Hawaii professors: "An island espionage ring [international communist and seeking to block trade and communication to the 'Far East' via poisoned Pearl Harbor waters and labor blockages in Honolulu] has Duke seeing red!" reads the Warner Brothers blurb (see Schmitt, *Hawaii at the Movies*, 60; Rampell, "Tackiest Movies Ever Made about Hawaii," 5). *Big Jim McLain* was released just as the "Hawaii 7" labor leaders were going to trial for violations of the Smith Act as communist threats to the U.S. government, thus House Un-American Activities Committee agent Jim McLain flies to Hawai'i to uncover international machinations and expose communist takeovers of Hawai'ian labor, shipping, and trade: Wayne/McLain does so, but the worldwide network of left-wing terrorist criminals gets off via Fifth Amendment pleas to Senator Joseph McCarthy's panel. "Duke" does end up marrying a lovely haole divorcée (Nancy Olson) and bops around the ethnoscape with Korean War hero James Arness, from the Royal Hawaiian Hotel to the pre-memorial USS *Arizona* to the leper colony on Molokai to Hotel Street dives and a communist meeting place at what looks to be—what else—Hanauma Bay!

40. For an unpacking of this Gramscian concept, see David Forgacs, "National-Popular: Genealogy of a Concept," in *The Cultural Studies Reader*, ed. Simon During (London: Routledge, 1993), 177–90. As applied to specifically American national-popular contexts, see Donald Pease, "New Americanists: Revisionist Interventions into the Canon," *boundary 2* 17 (Spring 1990), 1–37.

41. Antonio Gramsci, *Selections from Cultural Writings*, ed. David Forgacs and Geoffrey Nowell-Smith, trans. William Boelhower (Cambridge, Mass.: Harvard University Press, 1985), 356.

42. For counterviews of the Pacific war in various genres of local oral circulation, see Lamont Lindstrom and Geoffrey White, "Singing History: Island Songs from the Pacific War," in *Artistic Heritage in a Changing Pacific*, ed. P. Dark and R. Rose (Honolulu: University of Hawaii Press, 1993), 185–96.

43. Herman Melville, *Typee* (New York: Penguin, 1972), 133–36.

44. See Paul Lyons, "Literary Tourism and the Discourse of Cannibalism from Herman Melville to Paul Theroux," *Arizona Quarterly* 51 (1995): 33–62.

45. Melville, *Typee*, 258. On imperialist dynamics of the U.S. presence in the Marquesas and commercial outreach into the Pacific as relating to racial injustices at the Jacksonian national core, see John Carlos Rowe, "Melville's *Typee:* U.S. Imperialism at Home and Abroad," in *National Identities and Post-Americanist Narratives*, ed. Donald E. Pease (Durham, N.C.: Duke University Press, 1994), 255–78.

46. Melville, *Typee*, 252.

47. See Paul Lyons, "Literary Tourism and the Discourse of Cannibalism," *Arizona Quarterly* 51 (1995): 33–62.

48. Reprinted in Jack London, *South Sea Tales*, ed. A. Grove Day (Honolulu: Mutual Publishing, 1985).

49. Michener, *Tales of the South Pacific*, 193–94.

50. Stephen Greenblatt argues in *Marvelous Possessions: The Wonder of the New World* (Chicago: University of Chicago Press, 1991) that "engaged representations . . . are relational, local, and historically contingent" (12) and that "in the modern world-order it is with capitalism that the proliferation and circulation of representations (and devices for the generation and transmission of representations) achieved a spectacular and virtually inescapable global magnitude" (6). In other words, the global systems of representation,

by this very magnitude and the far-reaching power of circulation, took dominion over more local systems of representation.

51. Antonio Gramsci, *Selections from the Prison Notebooks*, ed. and trans. Quintin Hoare and Geoffrey Nowell Smith (New York: International Publishers, 1971), 447.

52. Ibid.

53. Ibid.

54. Gilles Deleuze and Claire Parnet, "On the Superiority of Anglo-American Literature," *Dialogues*, trans. Hugh Tomlinson and Barbara Habberjam (New York: Columbia University Press, 1987), 37.

55. Ibid., 44.

56. See Dana Naone Hall, "Ka Moʻolelo o ke Alanui" (The story of the road), which recovers Hawaiʻian history of a Mauʻi road as a means to resist its closure for tourist resort usage, in *Hoʻomanoa: An Anthology of Contemporary Hawaiian Literature*, ed. Joseph P. Balaz (Honolulu: Ku Paʻa, 1989), 34–36. Haunani-Kay Trask, in "Coalitions between Natives and Non-Natives," *From a Native Daughter: Colonialism and Sovereignty in Hawaii* (Monroe, Maine: Common Courage Press, 1993), disqualifies all non-Hawaiʻians from claims to being "Hawaiian in spirit" or practicing and expressing an ethic of *malama aina:* "Immigrants to Hawaiʻi, including both *haole* (white) and Asians, cannot truly understand this cultural value of *malama aina* even when they feel some affection for Hawaiʻi. Two thousand years of practicing a careful husbandry of the land and regarding it as a mother can never be and should never be claimed by recent arrivals to any Native shores. Such a claim amounts to an arrogation of Native status" (248).

While I support the move toward self-determined Hawaiʻian sovereignty and respect Hawaiʻian cultural nationalism as political force, I contend that, given the cultural "hybridity" of postmodern identity formation, the virtually Hegelian *binary* oppositions that often drive Trask's political vision of Hawaiʻian sovereignty—throughout her political rhetoric, if not in her poetry, she opposes "Western" against "Native," "Local" against "Indigenous," "Precontact" against "Colonized"—cannot be that *purely* separated, by conscious choice, at the level of everyday culture and identity. Identity is not just a matter of blood but of mixture, invention, and political commitment.

57. See Carolyn Lau's poem "Haʻina ʻia mai ana ka puana" (Let the story be told), in "A North Pacific Rim Reader," *Chicago Review* 39 (1993): 168–74, as well as Haunani-Kay Trask's poem "Koʻolauloa," in *Light in the Crevice Never Seen* (Corvallis, Oreg.: Calyx Press, 1994), 80. On poems of recuperated Hawaiʻian identity, see the work of Joseph Puna Balaz, John Dominis Holt, and Puanani Burgess.

58. David K. Choo, "Fishing for a Local Voice: Bamboo Ridge and the Search for an Island Literary Identity," *Honolulu Weekly* 3 (20 October 1993): 7.

59. Yamanaka's work is anthologized in Jessica Hagedorn, ed., *Charlie Chan Is Dead: An Anthology of Asian American Fiction* (New York: Penguin, 1993). *Saturday Night at the Pahala Theatre* has already won literary awards on the mainland.

60. Yamanaka, *Saturday Night at the Pahala Theatre*, 94–96, 106–7.

61. Ibid., 107.

62. Ibid.

63. Ibid., 111–15.

64. In her biographical note in Hagedorn, *Charlie Chan Is Dead*, Yamanaka claims, "I write in the pidgin of the contract workers to the sugar plantations here in Hawaii, a voice of eighteenth century [*sic*] Hawaii passed down to now third- and fourth-generation descendants of various groups" (544). But Japanese contract laborers were not recruited and transported to Hawaiʻi until 1868. See also Ronald Takaki, *Strangers from a Different Shore: A History of Asian Americans* (New York: Penguin, 1989), 43.

65. Yamanaka, *Saturday Night at the Pahala Theatre*, 140.

5. Representing the "New" Asia: Dick Lee, Pop Music, and a Singapore Modern

C. J. W.-L. Wee

IN AN IMPLICIT CRITICISM of Francis Fukuyama, the political philosopher Chantal Mouffe says, "Not long ago we were being told . . . that liberal democracy had won and that history had ended." The event that matters is, of course, the collapse of communism. What caught some people off guard, however, was that "instead of the heralded 'New World Order,' the victory of universal values, and the generalization of 'post-conventional' identities, we were witnessing the explosion of particularisms and an increasing challenge to Western universalism," a universalism that is characterized as being "rationalist . . . individualist"[1]—the supposed culmination of the modern era ushered in by the Renaissance.

While Mouffe is referring to the burst of ethnic nationalisms—"the archaic"—that erupted in Eastern Europe, and to particularistic movements such as radical feminism, since the 1980s similar politico-cultural contestations or resistances against Western universalism have also occurred in the parts of East and Southeast Asia that experienced high rates of economic growth. Samuel Huntington, of Harvard's Olin Institute for Strategic Studies, has wrongly but influentially chosen to see this challenge as a "clash of civilizations" among Sinic (or Confucianist), Islamic, and Western civilizations.[2]

While the essentialist term "civilization" must be interrogated—as if the vastness of Asia could be a single, fixed cultural entity—a discourse on "East Asian modernity" emerged, claiming a status as a *counter-* or *alternative* model of modernity—a "regional" universalism—in which "traditional" Asian values of family-centeredness, self-control, frugality, and corporate identity were seen as the foundations for Asian success.[3] Within this discourse, some Asians argued that they had *indigenized* modernity and might escape the cultural deracination thought to be taking place in the West—perceived to be the consequence of its supposedly extreme, individualist modernity. The discourse thus espouses a *neotraditional modernity* that has a less-prominent role for individualist, bourgeois democracy. (The tensions indicated in that expression are intended.)

Despite Huntington's Orientalist approach to culture,[4] he rightly pronounced at the Pacific Rim Forum in Beijing in October 1994 that there is "an Asian 'Occidentalism' portraying the West in much the uniform and negative way which Western Orientalists allegedly once [but now no longer?] portrayed the East."[5] One of the focuses of transnational cultural theory[6] has been an examination of, among other things, the way in which non-European and non–North American groups or cultures use the local to resist Western hegemonic forces of modernity. The challenge for cultural analysis, as Anna Tsing says, "is to move from situated, that is 'local,' controversies to widely circulating or 'global' issues of power and knowledge and back."[7] Keeping in mind such a dynamic of resistance, in this essay I suggest that some postcolonial Asian states were playing a game of creating "frontier identities" in order to resist Western modernity through appropriating it. This occurs even while these states were engaged in the high-stakes, free-trade game that went on with the General Agreement on Tariffs and Trade (GATT)—now the World Trade Organization (WTO)—and the Asia-Pacific Economic Co-operation (APEC) forum. This context is important for understanding the regional success of a major Singapore musician, Dick Lee, who is well known in parts of Southeast and East Asia. I look at the way in which Lee's musical representation of a "new" Asia is oddly related to Singapore's ruling People's Action party (PAP) leadership's overall stand on Asian identity and, in particular, what might be called (pace Paul Rabinow) their version of a Singapore modern.[8] The PAP's position entailed culturally resisting even while being politically and economically involved with "globalization"[9]—the organization and exploitation of markets on a world scale[10]—through the reinvention of a local identity (or what British cultural critics might call a "heritage" culture) that seeks to preserve, not to eradicate, the tension between progress and restoration.

Dick Lee is relevant to these issues because he is the only Asian pop artist I know of who directly set out to depict—and, in some abstract sense, to territorialize—the vacant idea of Asia. He started off, in the late 1970s, writing and performing a combination of English-language pop and light jazz music. Beginning in the early 1980s, increasingly, he inserted significant local touches into his music. Lee's regional success really began with *The Mad Chinaman* (1989); in this release, he blended traditional Chinese and Southeast Asian music and older Chinese pop songs either to create his own compositions or to be played on top of more contemporary rhythms. The music thus makes gestures toward being world music—or at least toward being a quasi–world pop. What prevents

Lee from being labeled definitely as an Oriental world music artist is the too-knowing and sometimes (self-)parodic incorporation of the authentic into his music, an incorporation that simultaneously questions the status or need for the authentic while on another level proclaiming a true "Asianness."

In local markets, Lee sold fairly well with university and polytechnic students who appreciated the novelty of his hybrid pop-jazz music, despite the critics' scathing assessments. Japanese youth also liked the new sound of Lee's quasi–world pop. His own sophisticated, witty, and cosmopolitan personality—displayed, for example, in his chic Armani attire—gained in appeal as he began to foreground the Asian elements of his cultural makeup. Arguably, within Southeast Asia, only Singapore, with its specific Anglo-Asian cultural configuration, could have produced a star like Lee. Initially rejected by the usually humorless political establishment in Singapore for his populist send-up of local life, Lee has since become part of the state's approach to the national-popular. For instance, the Singapore Symphony Orchestra performed Lee's music in July 1995, in a program with the singers Sandy Lam of Hong Kong and Tracy Huang of Taiwan.

* * *

I move now to a discussion of the social and cultural context that framed Lee's music. It is important to note that while there existed a *generalized* discourse or rhetoric on Asian modernity and the East Asian economic "miracle" (as the World Bank calls it[11])—now problematized since the Asian financial crisis began in July 1998—not all the emerging East Asian nation-states use this discourse in the same way and with the same political purposes, despite the impression one received from the Western media.[12] Gerald Segal points out that at the 1993 United Nations conference on human rights in Vienna, Japan "distanced itself from fellow Asians' anti-democratic views,"[13] in which national development is prioritized over individual rights. Yet, some voices in Japan also expressed the idea that an emerging pan-Asia has its uses. Ogura Kazuo, Japan's former ambassador to Vietnam, writes that Western "universality is not something exclusively Western but rather something that arose out of the . . . West's collisions with other civilizations"; now that places like Taiwan and Hong Kong "are becoming models of economic development," "we in Asia must seriously search for values that we can present to the world as universal. In the process of this search, we must lend our ears not only to Okakura Kakuzo and Kitobe Inazo, author of *Bushido*, . . . but also to people like . . . Rabindranath Tagore and Sun Yat-sen."[14] This concept of an Asia Major propounds the plundering of Asia's cultural pasts for the treasures that could advance world civilization.

Singapore and Malaysia—the latter a largely Islamic country with a large Chinese minority that also (peculiarly) lays claim to what has been described as a neo-Confucian, or "Sinic," modernity[15]—despite (or perhaps because of) their relatively small sizes, have emerged as two of the most outspoken champions for the traditional-modern Asia. Singapore's former premier Lee Kuan Yew roamed the world spreading the good news of Asia's arrival. Singapore hosted the first WTO ministerial meeting in December 1996 because, as a journalist for Singapore's *Straits Times* puts it, "it would be 'symbolically appropriate' to host the first meeting in Asia as an acknowledgement of the region's growing importance in the world economy."[16]

What, then, did Asian pop music have to do with the new Asia's contestation over or demand for a space within the Western globalization project? In *Producing Pop*, Keith Negus argues that "informing the resistance to a global mass culture in various parts of the world has been the recognition that, over the last thirty years, much of this has been Anglo-American in origin and content."[17] Dick Lee recognizes in his, and in Singapore's, complex, postcolonial, Anglo-Asian identity the heritage (or baggage) of Anglo-American culture. The transnational West is part of Singapore's national culture, but it is also something Lee is contending with. He struggles with what the exact link between "transnation" and "nation" ought to be. Lee writes of his approach to pop in the liner notes to *Asiamajor* (1990): "I've always felt this need to find a musical answer to my identity problem. You see, coming from Singapore, where east truly meets west on an island largely of immigrants, there's always this thing about how we should dress, speak and sound. . . . Most Asian pop is written in the Western genre, but sung in the various Asian languages. Why not throw the traditional aspects in with the contemporary, add a few of my own touches, and mix them . . . to create a new kind of Asian pop."

Whether Lee manages a truly syncretic music or stays at the level of an unabashedly commercial and gimmicky pastiche—supported by outrageous costumes[18]—as some of his detractors charge, is a real issue. Yet, although Lee's picture of culture might look decentered, his creatively assembled version of Asia Major never lacks a grand combative narrative of progress in the face of anticipated Western skepticism. To him, Asia is not stuck in the past. We should not see Lee as simply a product of a global process called "post-modernity."[19] He sings, in the suitably electro-pop title track of *Orientalism* (1991):

> I think that it's time to show
> That all of us are no
> Caricatures or stereotypes,
> No token yellows!
> We simply have to be
> Assertive, make them see
> This is the new Asian
> Ready for the twenty-first century!

The new Asian is centered, dynamic, and progressive: he can be as modern as any westerner.

The song continues—in a domesticated rap style befitting Lee's pro-West resistance to the West—that we were once in "some kind of limbo"; now, however, the new Asian is both "east and west / forget the rest." There is no need anymore to choose between the two, the either/or of the culture of late colonialism that hid the desire for the Other.[20] The new hybrid is potentially everywhere: "Oriental—New York City / Oriental—Quezon City." Lee has found some freedom from an earlier postcolonial subjectivity that enforced a pretend whiteness and a sense of shame at a hidden but apparently ineradicable, backward Asianness; but now, "It's quite alright: / Be white inside," as long as you are also "turning on to Orientalism." I doubt that Lee is aware of how Edward Said uses the term "Orientalism"; the singer obviously gives it a positive meaning here.

The question of identity thus forms the core of Lee's music. The title track of *The Mad Chinaman* portrays an Ancient Mariner–type persona who stops all and sundry to listen to how the Mad Chinaman struggles with his "Traditional, / International" halves: the mariner asks himself, "how should I react? defend with Asian pride? Or attack!"

Lee's attempts to transcend his colonial origins mark him as "postcolonial." As Kwame Anthony Appiah has argued, "Postcoloniality is the condition . . . of a relatively small, Western-style, Western-trained, group . . . who mediate the trade in cultural commodities of world capitalism. . . . The *post* in postcolonial . . . is the *post* of . . . [a] space-clearing gesture."[21] Other Asian pop

CD cover for *Orientalism.* Note that the "t" is part of the Chinese characters for "China," meaning "Middle Kingdom." Lee's surname in Chinese is also shown. Courtesy of Music and Movement Private Ltd. (Singapore).

artists without Lee's agenda, such as the immensely popular Hong Kong stars
Aaron Kwok, Andy Lau, Jacky Cheung, and Leon Lai—the so-called Heavenly
Kings—borrow internationalized Western forms of music and choreography
without feeling the need to be "original"; Lee is dismissive of their form of
Canto-pop[22] precisely because of this indifference to cultural neocolonialism.
The Hong Kongers then were still colonial subjects, but they are clearly not
interested in transcending coloniality. (Lee's own work co-opts many types of
musical genres—but he takes it to be a contestatory co-optation.)

My use of the term "postcolonial" is different from the way it has been used
by some cultural critics, which has to do with the fact that the Singapore musician's anti- yet pro-West discourse does not emanate from an underdeveloped society struggling under the weight of a more-or-less direct neocolonialism, as has been the case for many African peoples in the aftermath of the
dismantling of colonialism proper. Gayatri Chakravorty Spivak has rightly
argued that "in the high-growth capitalist parts of Asia the cultural sector
[when compared to postindependence Algeria or India] is not that strategic
because within [contemporary economic rather than territorial] neocolonialism they are run much more by ministries of finance."[23] But what she over-
looks is how successfully Asian governments, such the one run by Singapore's
PAP government, generate a media-based knowledge both of the West and of
its own locally formulated national and regional cultural identities. Since 1960,
PAP leaders have taken the stance that culture need not be organic; and this
stance has been asserted in an aggressive, masculinist form that is a reworking
of the colonial masculinity that dominated much late-imperial British life.[24]
S. Rajaratnam, the first minister of culture and later deputy prime minister,
announced that year that "we do not regard culture as the opium of the intellectuals or as something to tickle the fancies of gentlemen or gentlewomen. For
us the creation of a Malayan culture is a matter of practical politics . . . [and]
nation-building."[25] Dick Lee's pop music functions within this state-generat-
ed, instrumentalist framework of cultural knowledge production in which
Western high and pop culture have been allowed to permeate Singapore on the
basis that the state could always manage culture if it became troublesome.

Lee himself belongs to the colonial-created, English-speaking Chinese minority that dominates the PAP government. Of financially comfortable background, he grew up in upper-middle-class Singapore. His early exposure to jazz,
contemporary pop, and Stephen Sondheimesque Broadway music—a privilege for those growing up in the late 1960s and 1970s—contributed to his Asian
pop style. Lee's background is also *peranakan*—that is, Malayan-born Chinese
who have imbibed of Malay culture—and he uses this Malayan background
to effect, quite apart from the folk and pop Chinese music he incorporates into
his work. His music contains a strong element of nostalgia for a Singapore of
the 1950s and 1960s. In addition, as occasion demands, Lee also pirates popu-

lar or folk Thai, Filipino, and Japanese tunes, sometimes arranged for contrast with a scat or bebop background. When he performs, rather than using Standard English, he deliberately uses colloquial Singapore English ("Singlish"), which is riddled with non-English expressions as another marker of the local.

Like other pop musicians, Lee uses videos to cultivate his public persona. His parodic, campy style contributes to a persona that consumes and contests the West.[26] On the cover of *The Mad Chinaman,* he appears in full Chinese opera regalia but with the army-style boots that were part of a trendy "street-wear" or "work-wear" look. Lee's knowing, and on occasion parodic, incorporation of different elements of Asian cultures has meant that he has avoided a claustrophobic and binding notion of Asian identity in his music; but sometimes this has led to frivolity. Lee's detractors regard him as a mere entertainer.

The (self-)parodic nature of Lee's public persona and his campy costumes form a sharp contrast with the masculinist, pure, and puritan white shirt and trousers of the 1960s and 1970s PAP cadre. Lee might contest the West, but his body is gendered along different lines from the dominant PAP masculinity. As I argue, while Lee may have been co-opted by the PAP government, it cannot be assumed that he is in easy collaboration with the state, any more than one should assume Singapore "simply" supports late capitalism as a Western client-state. These relationships are all, in different but interrelated ways, fraught with simultaneous collusion and resistance.

Popularly known simply as "Dick," Lee has written and performed in musicals, plays, and comic revues of varying quality in Singapore, Japan, and Hong Kong. He was one of the country's best-known personalities in the late 1980s and 1990s and hosted a television talk show in 1995. Lee's albums sold well locally, averaging perhaps 15,000 per release, which is considered high for a homegrown musician. Despite Lee's obvious success, public opinion about him is ambivalent: the English-speaking middle class often finds him not serious enough, while the Chinese-speaking population sometimes feels he is using their culture inauthentically. Representations of Asia by either the PAP government or by figures like Lee obviously are not always commensurate with actual popular sentiment.

The height of Lee's career so far has been the 1992 staging of *Nagraland,* termed, perhaps grandiosely, an "Oriental pop operetta." Mitsubishi Corporation spent six million Singapore dollars (just under four million U.S. dollars) on the operetta, which was staged in Japan, Singapore, and Hong Kong. The key members of the performing and production team, in keeping with the new Asia ideology, were all Asian: the choreographer was Malaysian; the director, Indonesian; and the production manager, Japanese. I return later to a fuller discussion of *Nagraland.*

The production of albums and CDs has been the mainstay of Lee's career.

Among his best-known albums are *Life in the Lion City* (1984); *Suriram* (a twelve-inch single, 1984); *Fried Rice Paradise* (1986); *The Mad Chinaman* (1989), arguably the most popular and creative work so far;[27] *Asiamajor* (1990); *Orientalism* (1991); and *The Year of the Monkey* (1992). The very titles are indicative of the pan-Asian and Singapore-Asian ideologies that he has chosen to valorize and stage.

As early as 1986, when Lee was twenty-nine, he stated that he wanted "to see if we can forge some kind of [more organic] Singaporean identity [as] . . . the Singapore government is . . . trying to *force* culture upon the people. . . . It must be spontaneous."[28] Presumably, Lee's work attempts such an empowering "spontaneity" in reforming Asian identity. In "The Windchime Song," from *Mad Chinaman,* Lee tells the listener to pay attention to the wind chimes common in many Chinese homes, as he or she will discover that "Somewhere deep inside our [racial?] memories / Lie the cultures . . . Our father's father's fathers / Handed down with hopes they'd *grow*" (emphasis mine). Lee is not advocating an attitude toward progress that eradicates the nonrational—for this attitude is part of the negative baggage left from colonial insecurity. Nonetheless, Lee feels that Asians must be as progressive as Westerners are, if Asians are to be able counterplayers. Presumably, he would not agree with Kant that humans must emerge from their "*self-incurred immaturity.*"[29] Asian mankind's *Bildung* must be a more inclusive one.

In "A Human Touch," from *Orientalism,* Lee poses a question for unspecified Asian leaders: "So, you think you know the score . . . With your new highways, and the foreign praise?" There is no need anymore for self-deprecation and reliance on foreign validation, as "the old colonial ways are gone"; now, "the future identity" will arise only from a simultaneous looking backward and forward—an action that will add the "human touch" to a mechanistic Asianized rather than Asian modernity.[30]

Lee's lyrics have at times been considered offensive: the song "Fried Rice Paradise," for example, was once taken off the airwaves "for being too specific in its sending-up of [Singaporean] things and places."[31] But despite his criticism of the coldness and high-handedness of the PAP government, Lee has been celebrated by the state. His musical *Kampong Amber* (in Malay, "Amber village") was a centerpiece in the 1994 Arts Festival, and he performed the penultimate number (ironically, the once-banned "Fried Rice Paradise") in the 1994 National Day variety show "Rhythm of the Nation."

Lee's regional (and especially Japanese) success has been noted not only by critics in Singapore but also abroad.[32] The *Los Angeles Times,* in a 1992 special feature on the "New Asian Order," said of Lee: "In appealing for Pan-Asian pop culture unity, Lee stands as the clearest symbol yet of an intriguing shift afoot in . . . the Pacific Rim: Popular culture in Asia, so long dominated by the West, is looking back East [even though the 'West may not know Lee yet'].["33] *Vogue Paris*, pretty much taking Lee at his own word, effusively (and uncritically) said of him: "The singer and actor has become a celebrity in Japan because he sings about the new Asian identity in English. He represents the upcoming generation which learned little or no Mandarin in school and assertively strives for an international Asian culture where dances from Bali and Taiwan meet the chants of Mongolia and the pop music of Malaysia."[34] The *Vogue* writer reduces the discourse on the new Asia into a simple description of "identity crisis" and the unproblematic cultural reality that is purportedly developing out of this crisis. Both quotations reveal how Lee was treated as representative of the new, more self-confident Asian who challenges Western cultural hegemony; this treatment suggests Lee's place within pan-Asian discourse in Singapore.

Plans were discussed for an assault by Lee on Broadway itself, possibly in conjunction with the Cameron Mackintosh group (which produced *Les Misérables*), a venture broadly supported by Singapore's National Arts Council.[35] Hard as it might be to achieve, the ultimate pop-cultural success would be to penetrate the metropole, repudiating Orientalist depictions of the East as an effeminate or feminized object.

* * *

Lee's music espouses what might be called a "neotraditional modernity" that, in Singapore, challenges Western progressivism of the sort that is often associated with modernization theory. He hopes for a modernity in which the tension between ethnocultural restoration and economic progress is *not* eradicated. Despite Lee's intentions, progress, as it were, remains in control of tradition rather than being in partnership with it, and this has implications when read against the PAP's program in the 1980s and early 1990s to discipline the national economic body via the discourse on Asian (previously "shared") values.

In its own odd way, Lee's music attempts to be "traditional" because it seeks to capture the past—the habits, customs, and attitudes that form the sources of Asia's "self." The music is *neo*traditional, as is the ideology that informs it, because Lee also believes that the past must be recovered selectively, excising its more "atavistic" urges. The new musical forms must include the progressive—the Western—and this needs to be mixed with Asian genres. Only thus can the past be modernized to fit into the booming cities of Southeast and East Asia, where new, modernist skyscrapers reach up, a sign of Asian virility. Singapore, not surprisingly, becomes the standard-bearer of such an indigenized modernity.

The clearly nostalgic element in the music partly results from the economic remaking of postwar Asia. At the same time, there is a note of pride in being as modern as the Western person. In a light, jazz-fusion piece entitled "ModernAsia" (on *Year of the Monkey*), Lee sings,

> You're going to enjoy the ride
> Through Wonderland. . . .
> ModernAsia
> Isn't what it used to be.

Modernity's homogenizing forces have worked: "In this new world, we're all the same." Or are we? Lee adds, "A spirit deep inside me remains." We still need the empowering recovery of our father's culture, as this ancestral spirit can help fuel the creation of Asian commonalties: "Now the journey has begun / Into a land that once was one / But is uniting once again." For Lee, there was once a unified, prelapsarian Asia. Conscious of the historical divisions within emerging Asia, he makes an appeal to his audience in a note in the album: "Let us take the pain of war and strife our parents faced, accept what we did to each other in a new way."

Lee refers not only to the Second World War but also to current Asian divisions. Even in "The Windchime Song," with its optimism that deep culture can be spontaneously recovered, he sounds a warning note: "Do you feel the stirrings deep inside / When you watch your neighbours as they war? / Do you lose your roots as they guard theirs?" The memories of various Asian pasts need to be reconstructed in light of the needs of a reconciliatory as well as progressive pan-Asian identity, which means that parts of the past must also be jettisoned. Asia has its distinct realities that need to be connected if a unified and powerful Asia equal to the West can be formed.

Lee's strategy in attempting to represent an emerging pan-Asia is to run a number of Asian languages and musical forms together and, if context permits, to use Singlish in place of Standard English. A simple example is "One Song" from *Asiamajor*. The tune ("Yin Dee") is something he picked up in Bangkok, and Lee's version, with his own lyrics, starts with the words for "welcome" in four different languages (Thai, Malay, Chinese, and English): "*Kap sawasdee kap, selamat datang, huan ying*, welcome." After this, Lee's heroic status as the herald of a new Asian order is revealed:

> I am an ambassador who brings . . .
> A song about freedom and about peace. . . .
> Our separate lands
> Are one from now on . . .
> And we'll sing one song.

The backup vocals are assembled from a variety of Asian ethnic or national groups, as might be expected; included are Thailand's Ekachai Uekrongtham, Japan's Tomoko Yamaguchi, and Singapore's Kay Hamid.

While it would be easy to dismiss as fantasy Lee's idea of a pan-Asia, I argue that it is the exigencies of cultural identity formation in Singapore that feed into his discourse. From the 1960s until the early 1980s, Lee Kuan Yew and his coleaders in the PAP tried to make industrial modernity (rather than high culture) the metanarrative that might frame what they perceived to be an empty "Singapore" identity. They hoped that in this way the country's extremely diverse population—the majority, but not cohesive English- and Chinese-speaking Chinese, Malays, Indians (largely Tamil), and "Eurasians"—to some extent could be homogenized and contained.[36] The inflammatory and—from the government's point of view—"primordial" issues of race and cultural difference were to be discouraged at all cost. In 1961, Lee announced that a nonorganic consumer culture, as Rajaratnam had already suggested, would be Singapore's national culture: "We are hoping to build a modern society in which . . . we will have the factories to make more . . . of the things which make life better. . . . Recitation of poetry and writing of essays are important things in a civilized society. But important also is the turning of screws and lathes. They make our modern world hum."[37]

By the early 1980s, however, this metanarrative and its related institutions—which were thought capable of containing "primordial" racial identities—were surrendered, and in their place an idea of *Confucian modernity* was erected that ran the risk of alienating the minority groups. This idea was then modified in the early 1990s and became more generic in its propagation of Asian values and modernity.[38] Thus, there came about an appeal to and a legitimization of the primordial—or the "traditional"—that had been vilified by the same government in the 1960s and 1970s but apparently without the elevation of the (supposed) values of a specific group: the Chinese. There was opposition. Some asked what had happened to the earlier idea of a society in which, as schoolchildren recited during school assembly every morning, "We, the citizens of Singapore, pledge ourselves as one united people, regardless of race, language or religion . . ." Was the ideal of a universal progress unencumbered by the baggage of different racial pasts to be forsaken?[39]

While bilingualism as an educational goal continued in the 1980s, the logic that motivated it changed. In the 1960s and the 1970s, English was considered the rational language of science and administration; the so-called mother tongues were confined to the private sphere of ethnic culture. From the 1980s on, the use of Mandarin (which is not the native language of most Singapore Chinese) was promoted increasingly as a public and rational language by the English-speaking, Chinese PAP leadership. The opening up of economic opportunities in China was one major reason for Mandarin's elevation. While this does not in itself account for the local rise of a pan–East Asianist discourse, it does indicate the historical vicissitudes of Chinese iden-

tity formation in Singapore. Modernity in this way was joined to the primordial; as the sociologist Kwok Kian Woon argues, "The instrumental learning
of the Chinese language and the promotion of a rationalized and mandarinized Chinese culture now become part of a cosmopolitan identity which can
claim to be both traditionally rooted and economically useful."[40]

Lee's music is symptomatic but not directly reflective of the ongoing ref-
ormations of politico-cultural issues in Singapore. He manages to resist as
well as to be complicit with the state's position on multiracialism. Lee's suitably popularized Singlish rap version of "Rasa Sayang" (in Malay, "to feel
love"), a popular folk song that appears on *Mad Chinaman*, seems comfortable with the older metanarrative of progressive national identity. The song
is a small-scale version of the triumphant British Whig's "Our Island Story," with its celebration of commerce and the triumph of universal history.
The multiracial rap team singing in "Rasa Sayang" unfolds a story where a
once jungle-covered island, with "only trees / And a lion or two enjoying the
breeze" has developed into an international country. The song continues,
"Everything we have has to be the best / Of the fabulous East and the Won-
derful West"; and "We can eat, eat, eat till we nearly drop / Then we all get
up and we shop, shop, shop." All are at peace with each other, and consumption binds all the races.

The yoking of progress and the past in the story of Singapore manifests
itself not only in the juxtaposition created by singing a traditional folk song
in the rap genre but also in the fact that the song cites as joint founders of
the nation both the legendary Sang Nila Utama ("The island has come very
far / All thanks to man named Utama") and the factual Sir Stamford Raffles
("We love that guy!"), who historically opposed the East India Company's
anti–free trade policies. In this song, race simply doesn't matter, as long as
we move on. But the coherence of commercial modernity falls away (or perhaps the inherent contradictions surface) when Lee considers his Sinic—that
is, racial read as cultural—heritage, the heritage that scholars like Harvard's
neo-Confucian champion Tu Wei-ming contend have fueled the new Asian
modernity.[41]

How is one to regard Chinese culture now that postcolonial and largely Islamic Southeast Asia has had to come to terms with China's reemerging power? Until, say, the 1970s, to the English-educated Chinese who rejected communism's modernity, China itself seemed a retrograde country, one that was
perceived to be far removed from Straits-born families like Lee's, imbued as
they were with the goals of imperial British reformism, which strived not to
be backward-looking. But the fact remains that Singapore is largely a Chinese
country, and this seems to demand new efforts at interpretation. Even in a
comfortably hybrid song like "Rasa Sayang," a Southeast Asian Chinese-ness
is potentially a problem: the ending of the video of "Rasa Sayang" has Lee in

CD cover for *Mad China-man*. The English-speaking Singaporean in "authentic" Chinese drag? Courtesy of Music and Movement Private Ltd. (Singapore).

Chinese opera attire standing in the center of a circle of people, including the non-Chinese rap team, who are dressed in similar outfits. The framing of the music seems to shift from the metanarrative of industrial modernity to one of Mandarinized Chinese-ness. In his album *Orientalism,* Lee explores these questions of Chinese-ness and comes up with diametrically opposite answers.

The first "answer" in *Orientalism* to the question of local identity comes up in an arrangement of a song by He Luding and Guan Lu that is often played during the Chinese New Year and now has the virtual status of a folksong. Lee titles his version of the song "Springtime" (first line: *Chun-tian li-lai fai-hua xiang*), and the first section is sung in Mandarin by Lee's mother, Elizabeth. A translation of the song is given; part of the first stanza goes: "In spring all the flowers are fragrant, / The warm sun shines in the sky, / Shining on my tattered clothes."

After Elizabeth Lee sings, her son offers a jazzy response in English, accompanied by a solo trombone. The idea of springtime is peculiar in always humid equatorial Singapore, where only the early morning sun is tolerable. Lee is ambivalent about the relevance of the image of Chinese life that is being touted: "Will I ever see a season change in front of me? Never ever!" The Singapore experience? "Weather hot and wet outside / That's reality!" And yet, the imagined landscape is attractive:

> Cherry blossom in my mind
> Blooming in suspended time
> Countryside of my design
> Etched in memory.

It is a China of no specific place or history, "etched in memory"; but where does this memory come from? Is it a "blood" affair, the "really you" of "The Windchime Song"? Is this recovery of Chinese "roots" a threatening one? The call of an essentialized identity, which coincides with the acknowledgment that culture is not nature, nor is it ahistorical, remains difficult to deal with.

The song that immediately follows picks up on the question of an originary Chinese identity. First, Lee sings, in Mandarin, a famous folksong, "Alishan" (*A-li shan*), that virtually every Chinese Singaporean Lee's age would know. Then, as in "Springtime," an English response follows. Alishan is a famous mountain in Taiwan, and the home of Taiwanese aboriginals rather than of the revered, truly Han Chinese. In his response, Lee completely identifies with this landscape of the mind that is not even, purely speaking, Chinese:

> Mountain is calling to me. . . .
> Alishan is my own
> I'll never leave home
> Alishan is where my spirit will be free.

Lee's conception here of what it means for him as an English-educated, Southeast Asian–born Chinese-Singaporean to identify with (a misread version of) China becomes incoherent.

There is a stark contrast in Lee's depiction of Singapore between, on the one hand, his conceptualization of it as a cultural entity that is part of a progressive, transnationally dynamic core and, on the other hand, his perception of its connection to a bound, static periphery—the latter "a site of [an] autochthonous cultural formation,"[42] as Anna Tsing would put it. One might also say that the aesthetic configurations of realism and myth clash in Lee's oeuvre. Perhaps restoration and progress cannot be as easily reconciled as Lee would like.

The contrast between realism and myth standing in for true identity is more apparent (and most unresolved) in Lee's *Nagraland*, first staged at the Tokyo Nakano Sun Plaza. Lee played Chris, a confused, Westernized Asian journalist who dreams of Nagraland and visits it with his girlfriend and a friend. They are from a contemporary Asian city, obviously Singapore, and the second scene of the musical depicts the charms of metropolitan life: singers in suits and hard hats cavort in front of skyscrapers and a flashing digital clock. Here is the world of the present. Nagraland turns out to be a version of Bali (though the island is at the same time, somewhat obscurely, also meant to be pan-Asian), with the natives going about in lavish costumes that resembled those of a production like *The King and I* and were designed by the Paris-based Singapore designer Yang Derong. With the gamelan in the background, the music is vaguely Indonesian and at times possibly Japanese.[43]

When Chris and his friends arrive on the island, they find themselves in the midst of a crisis. The minister of the interior is upset at the opening up of Nagraland by the government to Western-style development. The minister's wife appeals to Chris to publicize the danger posed by Western influence, reminding him that he hails from a formerly traditional culture: "Trust your heart," she says.

At a folk performance, Chris learns of the legend of Nagraland. The Dragon King Nagarabashti had become infuriated with his daughter, Princess Naira, because she had left her heavenly home and fallen in love with a mortal outsider, Prince Nursalam. In anger, Nagarabashti killed the prince and banished Naira to Nagraland. The legend indicates the violence that lies at the heart of the island. A beautiful young woman named Lia plays Naira. Predictably, our hero falls for Lia, the adopted daughter of the interior minister. The parallels between the real and the mythical start to unfold.

After Chris meets and falls in love with Lia, a rebellion breaks out. The minister flees into the mysterious jungle, taking Lia with him. At this point, the realistic narrative begins to break apart. A woman seer ties a sash around Chris, marking his renativization. Chris then sets off in search of Lia.

After Lia's rescue, Chris and Lia are transformed into Nursalam and Naira, who are confronted by the Dragon King Nagarabashti (a transfigured interior minister). The king/interior minister's wife and a rebellious son appear,

Scene from *Nagraland*. A Bali-oriented representation of pan-Asia. Courtesy of Music and Movement Private Ltd. (Singapore).

appealing to him to forsake the cycle of violence that, because of the legend, has always plagued the islands. The son throws himself on Nagarabashti's sword, bringing his father to his senses. The cycle of violence has finally come to an end. What one would perhaps expect, then, is for Chris as the reincarnated Nursalam to remain in Nagraland, possibly as the beneficent traditional-modern head of government.

Unexpectedly, this is not what happens. The operetta begins and ends with Chris awakened from sleep by his dream: "I need to go . . . / Back to my dream, to Nagraland"—to the origins of the "really you." At the end we learn that the woman in bed with him is Lia. Thus, the entire stage action is a recapitulation of events. Despite his longings for origin, Chris has returned to the jaded, deracinated metropolis; having reclaimed a now othered Southeast Asian identity from the frontier, he abandons it for the charms of the modern. In the dreamlike Conradian darkness of the Nagraland jungle, Chris discovered that tradition can harbor pointless, even savage, violence that results in a disorganized society.

The operetta oddly restages the mid- to late nineteenth-century British quest for colonial kingship, rather like Kipling's "Man Who Would be King" but without the warning signs of the dangers of such a kingship.[44] The rational, civilized man would be king over natives who recognize his stature because he is able to comprehend who they are and be a part of their world. What is further peculiar—discounting the Orientalist replay of the ahistorical, exotic East—is that an Anglo-Asian Singaporean occupies the white man's civilizing role. While the people in the city that Chris hails from stand in danger of deracination, they nevertheless must be careful of the source of rejuvenation from which they drink, as the work of civilization must be continued.

In looking at *Nagraland* and songs like "Alishan" and "Springtime," it becomes clear how difficult the task is of territorializing Asia as a single cultural entity. In the case of *Nagraland,* Asia is a primitive and possibly uncontrollable territory; in the case of the Chinese songs, Asia might be a static entity, but one that is restrained and possesses a high civilization. To be static is also to be long-lasting. Lee appears to prefer the nowhere and the misread aboriginal-seen-as-Sinic landscape of Alishan to the savage dynamism of Southeast Asia. As the song "Alishan" relates, "The high mountains will forever be green / The valley's water will forever be blue" (*Gao-shan chang-qing, jian-shui chang-lan*). The binarism of self/other is not simply to be taken as West/Asia but as a choice of either West/savage Asia *or* West/static Asia—and it is easier to assimilate static Asia into a workable politico-cultural model of neotraditional modernity. Perhaps this is why, until the Asian currency crisis broke in July 1998, Southeast Asia is invariably referred to as being part of the "East Asian success story"—more "successful" since China has joined the capitalist fray—rather than as part of "southern Asia." It makes transparent the Singapore success story (and presumably Malaysia's and Thailand's as well) by lumping it with the other mini-Dragons of Taiwan, South Korea, and Hong Kong. Ezra Vogel, for instance, thinks that while there are specific "situational factors" that account for East Asian industrialization, we must still "consider tradition [as] . . . this achievement cannot be separated from the institutional practices and underlying attitude . . . absorbed in growing up in their culture."[45] Static East Asia requires reassessment, as it is no longer as static as it used to be.

An illuminating song to look at alongside *Nagraland* is "North and South," from *Orientalism.* Strikingly, "North" and "South" are not used to refer to "developed" and "underdeveloped" regions but rather to southern or Southeast and East or Northeast Asia, entities perceived to be too long separated: "If North and South were to be reunited once again, / We'd be the people we should be." Lee thus sings about pan-Asian unity. But the pan-Asian future he envisions is curiously *East* Asian in its makeup: "Change your ways, alter everything / Yellow people of tomorrow!"; "North and South, out of the dragon's mouth / Spreading from the rising sun."

Embedded within "North and South" is a second song in either Indonesian or Malay (they are similar languages) that broadens the idea of who is to be conjoined in the new Asia:

> Ku ingin bersamamu
> Kesuatu tempat
> Dimana Utara dan Selatan bertemu
> Maukah engkau menikah denganku
> Disuatu tempat
> Dimana seluruh Umat Campur
> menjadi satu . . .

> (I desire to be together with you at a place where the north and south meet. Would you like to be married to me at a place where the mixed people [or "people of mixed marriages"] become one?)[46]

Unfortunately, the translation in the liner notes is inadequate—"*Umat Campur*" is more literally given as "Kingdom of Campur" rather than with the implied sense of "people of mixed marriages." Nevertheless, the fact remains that the "Yellow people" are the primary Asians the song refers to as making up the new Asia.

The complexities in Lee's work are in accord, as earlier argued, with the tangled history of Chinese-ness in Singapore and with the PAP government's deployment of the discourse on Confucian—later Asian—modernity, consensus, and communitarianism in national life: these were argued to be the grounding values of all the ethnic groups. Of course, "Asian" values may indeed *be* Asian—that is not the concern here; but, in this case, the government was specifically trying to achieve two purposes by using a discourse on

Asian values. The first was to maintain discipline and efficiency in the area of economic production; the second was constantly to keep Singapore in place in the larger Asian setting—tiny Singapore needs Asia, if not vice versa.[47] Being a part of Asia Major gives the Singaporean nation-state the ballast it needs to maintain pressure on the West to keep markets open to its exports. Furthermore, incorporating Chinese-ness into its new conceptualization of Asian values also meant that a reimagined regional community with China—one in which trade and investment are important—can be encouraged, even if it is fraught with political difficulties.

The fact that Singapore is such a small country means that its population finds it hard to escape the combined pressures of the (re)invented Asian past and the demands of development that the PAP government brings to bear. There is literally very little space to move around in. Lee is not free from these pressures, and his resistance to Western universalism, his neotraditional modernity, and his espousal of a positive Anglo-Asian hybridity all seem to be brought under the spell of government-sponsored "Asian values." Even in "Let's All Speak Mandarin," from *Mad Chinaman*, a send-up of the PAP's "Speak Mandarin" campaign of the 1980s, Lee falls into the trap of the deployed blood-call of essential identity; the background refrain runs: "Mandarin—let's all speak Mandarin. The sound that's happening inside my heart!"

* * *

During an earlier period of cultural history, the English, like many continental Europeans, found China, especially the person of Confucius, very attractive: "Confucius was the supreme apostle of the orderly status quo. It was the temper of the Augustans to find their Elysium not, as their descendants did, in the primitive innocence of the South Seas, but in the glories of a civilized past."[48] It is ironic, to say the least, that various figures in postcolonial Singapore and in the West returned to *chinoiserie* as a way of reenvisioning a national and, more ambitiously, regional selfhood that is rational but with historical continuity. Given this restaging of *chinoiserie,* I do not think that we can say the modernist impulse of the Enlightenment has given way unproblematically to postmodernity: history and historical memory are issues, but so is the commitment to a progressive narrative. The concerns in Southeast Asia, on both the Malay Archipelago and the mainland, are "modern"—having to do with national development in relation to foreign direct investment, international capital flows and free trade, and some (admittedly circumscribed) notions of progress—though these concerns are definitely complicated in a world where national barriers are harder to control. The new "East Asia"—or, alternatively, the United States's preferred term, "Asia-Pacific"—is unlikely to be a clear-cut "hegemonic Euro-American production"[49] but, at the least, more of a joint production.

What, then, can be said in conclusion about Dick Lee and the new Asian order to which those such as the PAP government seem committed? Does it transcend the level of pastiche and become a significant site of cultural practice and transformation? How much does the Asian financial crisis, inaugurated by the crash of the Thai baht in July 1998, change the direction of cultural production Lee's work gestures toward? Certainly, both Lee's work and Singapore itself cannot be seen merely as pastiche, even given the (sometimes not unreasonable) comments made that "the city resembles a clean and efficient theme park,"[50] the result of a deliberate, nonorganic process of nation building. Still, at many levels the nation coheres as a society, despite the still-existent multiracial tensions inherited from the colonial period.

Lee's music and the larger East Asian discourse on modernity used by the PAP government do represent a significant site of cultural practice, though Lee's music is itself harder to evaluate: the ideological element is a strong component in his work, but, given its witty, performative nature, his music does not always manage to be "serious" enough to uphold the pan-Asian ideology. The discourse proper was used to justify the idea of a nonindividualistic democracy,[51] and within the region it sought to offer potential models for a modernity that Vietnam, Cambodia, and Burma might aspire to.

The financial crisis, and the cries of "collusion, corruption, and nepotism" that followed, indicate that the actual transformative power of the East Asian discourse is uncertain in the long run. At the same time, it is important to recognize that Singapore—the least-affected country in Southeast Asia— having drunk of the wells of economic success, and artists like Lee who have benefited from this success, are unlikely ever to go back to any cultural expressions of third-worldism. However, the linking of the ethnic to economic survival in Singapore is tricky: it poses a constant problem, as it is never clear when the "irrational" card of a ethnicized identity might be overplayed in a multiracial society. A sign of this can be seen in one of Lee's latest Canto-pop albums, *Compass* (1995). The Chinese markets beckon, and it is not incidental that Lee's latest work is in a Chinese language in which the singer himself is not fluent. This suggests how strong the lure of emerging markets can be. Ethnic movements are perhaps always ambivalent; and in Singapore, even while a countermodernity was and still is being advocated, such movements do not forego all the ideals of progress of the Enlightenment.

Notes

Thanks to the participants of the "Symposium on Problematising Culture: Media, Identity, and the State in Southeast Asia" at the Institute of Southeast Asian Studies, Singapore, 28–29 November 1994, and especially to Ray Langenbach, Yao Souchou, and Lee Weng Choy. Thanks also to Kwok Kian Woon, Lauren Berlant, Bruce Robbins, Chua Beng Huat, Ronald Inden, Rani Moorthy, Kelvin Tan, Victor P. H. Li, and Gregory B. Lee. Glen B. Y.

Goei suggested the topic. Music and Movement Pte. Ltd. kindly gave me access to their Dick Lee materials. An earlier version of this essay appeared as "Staging the New Asia: Singapore's Dick Lee, Pop Music, and a Counter-Modernity" in *Public Culture* 8:3 (Spring 1996): 489–510.

1. Chantal Mouffe, *The Return of the Political* (London: Verso, 1993), 1, 2.

2. Samuel Huntington, "Now Watch the Faultlines between Civilizations," *International Herald Tribune*, 8 June 1993. Huntington's essay "The Clash of Civilizations?" (*Foreign Affairs* 72:3 [Summer 1993]: 22–49) has been well received in Southeast Asia. It was part of an Olin Institute project on "The Changing Security Environment and American National Interests."

3. During a 1994 visit to France, Prime Minister Goh Chok Tong told a journalist that the "Confucian values"—"such as promoting the family, motivating education, developing a liking for hard work and a sense of thrift"—that some people such as Singapore's Lee Kuan Yew and Harvard's Tu Wei-ming have argued underpin Singapore's success are universal rather than narrowly Asian, though these values seem to survive better in Asia (Jean-Pierre Clerc, "Eastern Approach," *Le Monde* section of *The Guardian Weekly*, 30 October 1994, 21).

4. See Huntington, "Clash of Civilizations?": "Differences among civilizations are . . . basic. Civilizations are differentiated from each other by history, language, culture, tradition and, most importantly, religion. . . . These differences . . . are far more fundamental than differences among political ideologies and political regimes" (25). Despite Huntington's gestures in the essay toward development in Asia, what Edward Said argues of (especially) French Orientalism applies here: "The Oriental is given as fixed. . . . No dialectic [between East and West] is either desired or allowed" (*Orientalism* [New York: Vintage, 1979], 308).

5. Samuel Huntington, "Emergence of East Asia Intensifies Conflicts with the West," *The Straits Times*, 4 November 1994, 34. See also Xiaomei Chen, "Occidentalism as Counterdiscourse: 'He Shang' in Post-Mao China," *Critical Inquiry* 18:4 (1992): 686–712.

6. See especially *Anthropology and the Analysis of Modernity*, ed. Paul Rabinow, special issue of *Cultural Anthropology* 3:4 (1988). Arjun Appadurai's essay "Disjuncture and Difference in the Global Cultural Economy" (*Public Culture* 2:2 [Spring 1990]: 1–24) is also very suggestive, but it places greater emphasis on the difficulties entailed in thinking through what the globalization of the imagination means.

7. Anna Lowenhaupt Tsing, "From the Margins," *Cultural Anthropology* 9:3 (Aug. 1994): 279.

8. Paul Rabinow, *French Modern: Norms and Forms of the Social Environment* (Cambridge: MIT Press, 1989).

9. "Globalization" is a buzzword in the business world. See *Business Week*'s special bonus issue on "21st Century Capitalism: How Nations and Industries will Compete in the Emerging Global Economy," 18 November 1994.

10. In 1988, Singapore expelled an American diplomat for allegedly meeting with antigovernment lawyers. The backdrop of this event was the detention by the government of twenty-two activists. The lawyers whom the diplomats met were representing the activists. The *Financial Times* opined: "The fracas between tiny Singapore and the mighty U.S. looks set to go down as one of the more improbable . . . diplomatic clashes. . . . All this is directed against a country which absorbs a quarter of Singapore's total exports, [and] provides about a third of its foreign investments" (quoted in Stan Sesser, *The Lands of Charm and Cruelty* [London: Picador, 1994], 46).

11. The World Bank, *The East Asian Miracle: Economic Growth and Public Policy* (New York: Oxford University Press, 1993).

12. See, for example, "Asian Values: The Scourge of the West," *The Economist*, 22 April 1995, 24–25.

13. Gerald Segal, "This Rhetoric about Clashing Civilizations Can Only Hurt Asia," *International Herald Tribune,* 6 October 1993, reprinted in *Asian Bulletin* 18:12 (December 1993).

14. Ogura Kazuo, "A Call for a New Concept of Asia," *Japan Echo* 20:3 (Autumn 1993): 39, 38, 40.

15. The Malaysian prime minister Dr. Mahathir Mohamad deployed a generalized idea of Asian values in his public discourse on modernity and human rights (e.g., "Mahathir Blasts Western Nations' Liberal Values on Human Rights," *The Straits Times,* 7 December 1994, 19) but will also speak on "Islamic" modernization.

16. Irene Ngoo, "S'pore Less Interested in Hosting 2nd WTO Meet," *The Straits Times,* 17 December 1994, 1.

17. Keith Negus, *Producing Pop: Culture and Conflict in the Popular Music Industry* (London: Edward Arnold, 1992), 7.

18. A Singapore magazine cited these two criticisms: "'This guy's not for real. He's got no talent. All he's got is money,' says a 30-year-old accountant. . . . 'He's for show only. He's part of that crowd of beautiful people all so covered with gloss. If that's who he is, it's still a bit too much. That super-duper [usage of] Singlish [i.e., colloquial Singapore English],' says a 28-year-old secretary" (*Go Magazine,* September 1989, 79).

19. For a critique of global arguments of the postmodern, see Yoshimoto Mitsuhiro, "The Postmodern and Mass Images in Japan," *Public Culture* 1:2 (1989): 8–25.

20. For work that deals with the "consumption" of the primitive Other within the imperial homeland, see Robert Young, *Colonial Desire: Hybridity in Theory, Culture, and Race* (London: Routledge, 1994); C. J. W.-L. Wee, "Kipling, a 'Primitive' National Identity and the 'Colonial' Condition at Home," *New Formations* 24 (Winter 1994): 51–65.

21. Kwame Anthony Appiah, *In My Father's House: Africa in the Philosophy of History* (New York: Oxford University Press, 1992), 149.

22. That is, Cantonese-Chinese pop music.

23. Gayatri Chakravorty Spivak, interviewed by Robert Young in "Neocolonialism and the Secret Agent of Knowledge," *Oxford Literary Review* 13:1–2 (1991): 221.

24. See Mrinalini Sinha, *Colonial Masculinity: The "Manly Englishman" and the "Effeminate Bengali" in the Late Nineteenth Century* (Manchester: Manchester University Press, 1995).

25. S. Rajaratnam, "Malayan Culture in the Making," in *The Prophetic and the Political: Selected Speeches of S. Rajaratnam,* ed. Chan Heng Chee and Obaid ul Haq (Singapore: Graham Brash, 1987), 119. The term "Malayan" is used rather than "Singaporean" because in the 1960s the PAP was working toward merger with Malaya (now West Malaysia).

26. Negus quotes David Howells, managing director of Peter Waterman Ltd.: "99 percent of people give answers that relate [music] to the visual. The extraordinary thing is that you see what you hear" (*Producing Pop,* 66). This statement holds true for Lee. During the launch of *Orientalism* in 1991, he appeared at a popular dance club, Zouk, dressed in trousers with feathers at the hem, Elvis Presley–style sideburns, and striped, Gary Glitter–type platform shoes (see Grace Fernando, "Birthday Boy Dick Lee Launches New Album," *The Straits Times,* 24 August 1991, 29).

27. Of this release, James Hale says: "Blending elements of Indonesian, Chinese, Indian and Malay pop and folk songs, plus adding rap and singing in English has made 'The Mad Chinaman' one of the most adventuresome and satisfying albums in years" ("Singapore Singer Now Rocks Abroad," *The Japan Times,* 3 August 1990). *Mad Chinaman* marks the moment Lee broke into the difficult Japanese market: "Dick Lee . . . has been given as much space in music magazines in Japan during the past six months as The Rolling Stones. Lee, 33, has won so much attention solely on the basis of his album 'The Mad Chinaman'" (Shig, "Lee Leads World Music Boom in Asia," *Asahi Evening News,* 30 June 1990).

28. Lee, quoted in "A Day in the Life of Dick Lee," *Asia Magazine,* 29 June 1986, 54.

29. Immanuel Kant, *Political Writings,* ed. H. Reiss, trans. H. B. Nisbet (Cambridge: Cambridge University Press, 1970), 54.

30. Lee's lyrics here can be read as a response to the PAP government's policy, until the 1980s, of consistently tearing down much of old Singapore to create more commercially viable buildings; current "restoration" activities have been criticized as giving buildings a theme-park appearance.

31. *Go Magazine,* September 1989, 79.

32. Lee's photo appeared on the cover of *Billboard* (18 February 1992), and he was cited in the caption as one of "the artists . . . who helped the Japanese music industry achieve its fastest growth in two decades." Lee also did well in 1991 as he won Best Newcomer Award in the International Music Toll organized by Radio Television Hong Kong.

33. Teresa Watanabe, "In the East, Pop Audience Gets Icons of Its Own," *Los Angeles Times,* 19 May 1992.

34. Laure de Gramont, "In Search of an Identity," *Vogue Paris* (suppl.) 741 (November 1993): 26–27. It must be noted that, with the exception of a minority who attended the more elite mission schools, most people of Lee's age who gained even a lower-secondary-school education muster passable Mandarin.

35. Tommy Koh, a former ambassador to the United States and then-chairman of the council, said, "I told Dick that anything I can do to help him fulfill this [Broadway or West End] ambition, I'll do it." The *Asiaweek* writer added, "[Koh] is trying to get Lee and Mackintosh together" ("It's Glamor Time!: From Rock to Musical, Top Acts Light Up the Asian Stage," *Asiaweek,* 3 November 1993, 41).

36. C. J. W.-L. Wee, "Contending with Primordialism: The 'Modern' Construction of Postcolonial Singapore," *positions: east asia cultures critique* 1:3 (Winter 1993): 715–44.

37. Cited by Alex Josey, *Lee Kuan Yew* (Singapore: Donald Moore Press, 1968), 172, 173.

38. On Confucian modernity, see Robert Elegant, "The Singapore of Mr. Lee: 'Confucian' Ethics, Asian Values," *Encounter,* June 1990, 22–29.

39. Regarding opposition to the state's endorsement of the primordial or the traditional, S. Rajaratnam, then in retirement, protested in a letter to the press: "At this rate, there will be a long queue of Singaporean citizens proclaiming Sikh identity, Jewish identity, . . . Cantonese identity, Hokkien [Fujian] identity—and goodbye Singapore identity" ("Raja Wants Revival of a 'Singaporean Singapore,'" *The Straits Times Weekly* [overseas edition], 17 March 1990, 3). The fear was that "communalism," as the British called it, might again rear its ugly head.

40. Kwok Kian Woon, *Social Transformation and the Problem of Social Coherence: Chinese Singaporeans at Century's End,* Department of Sociology Working Paper No. 124 (Singapore: National University of Singapore, 1994), 32.

41. See, e.g., Tu Wei-ming, *Confucian Ethics Today: The Singapore Challenge* (Singapore: Federal Publications, 1984); idem, ed., *The Triadic Chord: Confucian Ethics, Industrial East Asia, and Max Weber* (Singapore: Institute of East Asian Philosophies, 1991).

42. Tsing, "From the Margins," 282.

43. In the liner notes to *Year of the Monkey,* Lee says that he used "(in part) the *gamelan* scale of Indonesia, which coincidentally is similar to the Japanese Koto Scale." This mix-and-match is consonant with Lee's pan-Asian theme.

44. See Wee, "Kipling."

45. Ezra F. Vogel, *The Four Little Dragons: The Spread of Industrialization in East Asia* (Cambridge, Mass.: Harvard University Press, 1991), 92.

46. Thanks to Wong Seng Tong for help with the translation.

47. Chua Beng Huat, *Culture, Multiracialism, and National Identity in Singapore,* Department of Sociology Working Paper No. 125 (Singapore: National University of Singapore, 1995), 14–21.

48. William W. Appleton, *A Cycle of Cathay: The Chinese Vogue in England during the Seventeenth and Eighteenth Centuries* (New York: Columbia University Press, 1951), 41.

49. Rob Wilson and Arif Dirlik, "Introduction: Asia/Pacific as Space of Cultural Production," *boundary 2* 21:1 (Spring 1994): 7.

50. Jay Branegan, "Is Singapore a Model for the West?" *Time*, 18 January 1993, 36. See also Sesser's chapter "Singapore: The Prisoner in the Theme Park," in *The Lands of Charm and Cruelty.*

51. Beng-Huat Chua, *Communitarian Ideology and Democracy in Singapore* (London: Routledge, 1995).

6. Killing Motherhood as Institution and Reclaiming Motherhood as Experience: Japanese Women Writers, 1970s–90s

Fukuko Kobayashi

IN A COMIC STRIP that appeared in the March 8, 1994, issue of the *Daily Yomiuri*, an old man asks a newlywed couple when they plan to have a baby. The husband of the couple answers: "Don't be so medieval. We aren't going to have children! They have no place in a solid economic arrangement like marriage!" The inspiration for this comic strip is obviously the statistics showing a marked decline in the childbirth rate in Japanese families. Throughout the 1970s, the average number of children per family stayed around 2, but in 1989 it dropped to 1.57, reflecting various new phenomena in Japanese society: namely, the higher cost of living, the more pleasure-oriented lifestyle of Japanese families, the damaged natural environment, and, above all, the changing attitudes of Japanese women seeking more activity outside home. The media reaction to the statistical output was somewhat comical, resulting in the so-called 1.57 shock all over the country. There is no alleviating this trend, however, for in 1993 the figure dropped further to 1.46.

In explaining why the statistical figure was so shocking to the general Japanese public, the media emphasized the prospect of a shortage among the younger Japanese labor force in contrast to a growing population of the aged. But the other and perhaps more pressing concern, particularly to the male members of society, stems from their recognition that the foundation of the long-standing patriarchal order of Japanese society—namely, the cherished ideal of Japanese women as loving mothers and motherly wives—is finally eroding due to Japanese women's collective gesture of refusal to conform to this ideal.

With this situation in mind, it is interesting to note that during the 1970s and early 1980s, when the imperative that Japanese women be "good wives and wise mothers" was still quite strong, many of the serious women writers of the time—Ôba Minako, Takahashi Takako, and Tomioka Taeko—were prophesying in their works the advent of the changes we are seeing now. Their works are filled with female characters who counter and oppose the conventional motherly types popular in earlier fiction. Vicious, selfish, and often with a tendency for aggression verging on murderous impulses against any small infants or children near them, these characters reflect the authors' deep-seated antipathy toward anything to do with the prevailing assumption of motherhood as women's natural calling.

First, I will focus my attention on the authors just mentioned, whose work I interpret as an attack on motherhood as an institution, to use Adrienne Rich's well-known phrase. Then, I will examine works by a younger generation of women writers, such as Hikari Agata, Yoshimoto Banana, Yamada Eimi, and Tsushima Yûko. These writers show a common concern with the more or less positive side of motherhood and child rearing, and I interpret their work as an effort to reclaim motherhood as experience, to use another of Rich's phrases.

* * *

Before turning to the individual works, let me sum up the specific conditions of motherhood in Japan prevalent around the 1970s and early 1980s. Historically, women in Japan have always been valued more as mothers than as wives. As noted by the anthropologist Nakane Chie, due to the long Confucian tradition the Japanese family has always had as its foundation the "vertical relationship" of parent and child rather than the "horizontal relationship" of husband and wife. Furthermore, during the period of the 1970s and early 1980s, and coinciding with the nation's unparalleled high economic growth, most Japanese men worked extremely long hours, so that their wives tended to rely solely on their children for emotional fulfillment. Another factor that emphasized the importance of the maternal role is the "examination hell" that produced a host of "education mamas" who prized their children's academic standing above anything else. All these factors added up to create uniquely close ties between mother and child, often resulting in stifling relationships between the two. Besides, due to the cherished memory of the elaborate care shown by their own mothers, Japanese men tended to demand that their wives be a sort of mother surrogate to them, and they would continue to act irresponsibly and childishly in their wives' presence. Hence, the often talked-about image of the quietly enduring motherly Japanese wives prevailed.

Luckily, Ôba Minako (1930–   ), the first woman writer I will discuss, seems to have had little to do with the aforementioned requirements as Japanese wife and mother. Soon after her marriage, Ôba went to Alaska with her businessman husband, and they lived there with their daughter for ten years. It was during this period that Ôba produced her award-winning first work, "Sanbiki no Kani" (Three crabs),[1] which played a significant role in setting the tone for much of the serious Japanese women's fiction in the ensuing decade or so.

The protagonist of the novella is Yuri, a middle-class housewife and mother, who lives with her husband and daughter in a U.S. town. One evening, out of sheer boredom, Yuri sneaks away from a party she is giving for her husband's pseudointellectual friends. She wanders into a deserted amusement park where she meets a strange man who is identified throughout the story as a "pink shirt." She ends up sleeping with him for no special reason and, the narrative suggests, without any guilt or sense of consummation; afterward, Yuri simply goes back to her former life, baking cakes, playing bridge, and so on. Like most of Ôba's works, "Sanbiki no Kani" has as its central theme the essential purposelessness and solitariness of modern people's lives; hence, Yuri is by no means drawn as a happy person. But, overall, her character and lifestyle must have possessed a fresh appeal to Ôba's female Japanese readers, for Yuri is allowed a degree of freedom and selfishness little known to the average Japanese woman of her time. She is permitted an occasional affair or two without much worry about losing her status as wife and mother. Yuri's story is plausible chiefly because it takes place in the exotic location of a faraway U.S. town.

Soon after her return to Japan, Ôba wrote *Tsuga no Yume* (Dream of hemlock),[2] a novel more in the realism genre, that deals with two female characters, both living in Japan as wives and mothers. Although seemingly opposite in type, both female characters are portrayed as selfish. Nobue, who spends much of her time on her family's affairs, such as her children's academic achievement and her husband's promotion in his company, is rightly condemned by her daughter for "using" her family "for her own ego-fulfillment."[3] Okon is the more erratic character, playing mah-jong every night and using sleeping pills to put her children to sleep. Unlike Yuri, both women are ultimately punished for their selfish behavior: Nobue goes insane when she learns her businessman husband has refused to take a more lucrative position, while Okon sees her children permanently handicapped as a result of neurological damage from the sleeping pills.

In both stories, Ôba clearly shows that the popularly held concept that women's happiness lies in satisfying their maternal "instinct" is a myth: women as mothers can be as self-centered as men or as troubled by life's meaninglessness as men. Ôba's women, basically confined to the conventional role of wife and mother, show little power in resisting such myths: their attempts to act on their own initiative end either as a mere temporary act of transgression, in Yuri's case, or in an unexpected catastrophe, as for Nobue or Okon.

Compared with Ôba's women, Takahashi Takako's (1932–   ) heroines display more control over themselves and their immediate environment. Often single or divorced women, they deliberately choose to live independent, solitary lives, and if they happen to solicit any outside ties, they do so with the intent of doing some malice to those they approach.

Sakiko, the heroine of "Ronri ûman" (The lonely woman),[4] who lives alone in a shabby rented apartment, is thrilled by the recent fire at a nearby elementary school playground. Imagining the "fresh young bodies" of the schoolchildren burning in the fire gives her abundant pleasure, for children to Sakiko are nothing but "useless creatures who have no other ability than to raise noisy screams."[5] More and more involving herself in the police investigation into the cause of the fire, Sakiko finally comes to fantasize that she herself is the very criminal that caused the fire.

Another secretive and even more malicious heroine of Takahashi's is Hisao in *Sora no Hate made* (Toward the end of the sky).[6] She finds sadistic pleasure in tormenting the girl Tamako, whom she raises as her own daughter. Tamako's real mother is Yukie, who used to be Hisao's close friend in high school. Hisao has kidnapped Tamako for the sole purpose of tormenting mother and daughter, both of whom represent what Hisao heartily detests: the world of conventionality and "healthy-mindedness."

In one of her essays commenting on the male convention of categorizing women as "witch-types" and "mother-types," Takahashi expresses her view that there are only two kinds of women—those who are awakened to their selves and those who are not. In Takahashi's argument, the women who are content in the prescribed role of wife and mother are obviously the ones yet to be awakened to their true selves. The disturbingly destructive women in Takahashi's works, then, can be regarded as the author's attempts to shock the majority of Japanese women out of their collective sleep.

The heroines of Tomioka Taeko (1935–   ), the last of the three authors I discuss in this section, are similar to Takahashi's in preferring independent, individualistic lives. Kyôko in *Nami utsu tochi* (Heaving land)[7] well exemplifies such a character. Although married to a man who somehow shows up only once in the novel (in the last scene, where the two are playing tennis together), as a professional poet she seems to be able to live on her own and as she pleases. Like the majority of Tomioka's heroines, Kyôko is childless by choice, expressing her wish outright that her mother had not given birth to her. Kyôko is having an affair with a married man who typically has no capacity for uttering any meaningful words to her and therefore is treated by her as a mere sex partner. In fact, many of the male-female relationships Tomioka depicts exhibit a similar pattern, demonstrating the author's profound disillusionment about any satisfactory male-female relationships in Japan.

Tsushima-san, the unmarried heroine in another of Tomioka's novels, *Shokubutsu-sai* (Plants fair),[8] is a bit different. She and her young lover, Natsuki, are bound not only by sexual appetite but by their common motive to get rid of the overwhelming presence of the memory of their own mothers. While the mature Tsushima-san is successful in her attempt, the childish Natsuki is not. Natsuki's mother, Misako, is married to a prosperous businessman and has long been believed by Natsuki to be his aunt. It turns out that Natsuki is actually Misako's illegitimate son, raised as a son of his grandmother. When Natsuki learns this, he attempts to rape Misako to show that he refuses to accept her as his mother. But Misako pursues a relationship with him, as if to compensate for all the lost years they should have been together. She even gets a divorce to be near Natsuki, as his mother and his lover, causing Natsuki to complain to Tsushima-san that the only way to get rid of his mother is probably to kill her. Since the story is narrated by Tomioka with wry humor, it is not as sensationally melodramatic as it may sound, but it is evident that in Misako's crazy infatuation with Natsuki, Tomioka caricatures those Japanese mothers who stifle their children with their overpossessiveness and overconcern.

Each of these writers shows that Japanese women are at odds with their traditionally assigned role and that Japanese families, as the bedrock of the country's patriarchal order, are in the process of disintegration. In this sense these works can be regarded as emergent feminist texts. But what is troubling about them is that in their severe attack against motherhood as institution they seem to negate not only the myth of Japanese women as perfect mothers and motherly wives but also everything connected with women's maternal capacity. Indeed, one senses in these works that the mere idea of women's procreative function is perceived as repulsive to them. In this respect, these authors share what Marianne Hirsch points out in *Mother/Daughter Plot* is the common tendency in early feminist discourse—"the fear of and discomfort with the body," particularly the maternal body, "as a pervasive discomfort among women and within feminism," due to their shared feeling that "nothing entangles women more firmly as pregnancy, birth, lactation, miscarriage, or the inability to conceive."[9] Furthermore, the totally negative ways in which all mothers are portrayed in their works suggest that these writers might be subject to what Rich calls "matrophobia," or "a woman's splitting of herself" in her "desire to become purged once and for all of [her mother's] bondage to be individuated and free."[10]

As Hirsch argues, the mere one-dimensional negation of everything connected with maternity in order to achieve thorough demystification of the prevailing ideology concerning motherhood is inappropriate and can only lead to a different type of objectification of mothers. Hence, what is urgently needed is to explore "mother's double or multiple consciousness"[11] in its fuller complexity.

Four of the younger generation of Japanese women writers seem to approach the theme of motherhood from another perspective. Tsushima Yûko, Hikari Agata, Yamada Eimi, and Yoshimoto Banana started their writing careers in the 1980s. Of the four, Tsushima deserves special attention.

* * *

Although Hikari, Yamada, and Yoshimoto seem to be a disparate group of writers, they share a common interest in exploring new forms of familial ties, namely, mother-child relationships. In two of Hikari Agata's (1943–92) best-known works, *Uhohho Tankentai* (The ahem! expedition party) and *Yukkuri Tokyo Joshi Marason* (Slow-paced Tokyo women's marathon),[12] groups of divorced mothers and their children bond together to overcome various difficulties that confront them. In her preoccupation with broken families, Hikari reminds us of the so-called minimalist writers of the United States during the 1980s, such as Ann Beattie and Bobby Ann Mason, some of whose works Hikari herself translated into Japanese and published in an anthology. However, the characters in Hikari's works seem far more hopeful than those depicted by U.S. minimalist writers. As one of the children in *Uhohho Tankentai* says, the mothers and children in Hikari's fiction are "the explorers of a new territory,"[13] where both can be individualistic and yet tied with mutual understanding.

A similarly pioneering air pervades the relationships depicted in works by Yamada Eimi (1959–   ) and Yoshimoto Banana (1964–   ). In *Jeshî no Sebone* (Jessie's backbone), a sequel to her best-selling first work *Bedtaim Aiz* (Bedtime eyes),[14] Yamada weaves motherhood and child rearing into her favorite theme of interracial romance. As in Yamada's earlier work, the young heroine Koko is extremely candid in expressing her sexual desire toward her African-American lover, Rick. However, she cannot monopolize Rick, for he brings into their life a boy named Jessie, whom Koko discovers is Rick's son. Obliged to take care of Jessie while Rick is away, Koko is at first annoyed with the boy, who remains quite antagonistic toward her. However, by the end of the story they are bound together by something akin to love, which is achieved only when both regard each other as individuals. Koko is here experiencing surrogate motherhood—an experience through which she herself can grow.

In the case of Yoshimoto's sensationally popular work *Kitchin* (Kitchen),[15] it is the heroine, Mikage, who is taken care of by her surrogate mother. Mikage, left alone after her grandmother's death, receives love and care from the "mother" of Yûichi, a young male friend of her dead grandmother. It turns out that Yûichi's "mother," Eriko-san, is actually his father who has surgically become a woman. Later, when this lovingly caring Eriko-san is suddenly murdered in a bloody fight at a bar where he works, Mikage gives love and care to the bereaved Yûichi. By turning a male into the central figure in the kitchen, a symbol of care and a nurturing spirit traditionally associated with maternal love, Yoshimoto suggests that not only women but also men can acquire maternal virtues.

These three writers appear so different from those discussed in the preceding section that one wonders what could have happened to cause such a marked change. One may recall here what Kurt Vonnegut once called the "canary-bird-in-the-coal-mine theory of arts": just like the canaries that chirp when they smell gas in coal mines and sound their notes of alarm to the people around them, the earlier writers may have been sounding their alarm against the one-sided celebration of motherhood during the 1970s and early 1980s, whereas the latter may be sounding their alarm against the mere one-sided rejection of motherhood that has become more noticeable of late.

What should be borne in mind, however, is that any attempt to place high value on maternal virtues can easily turn into the elevation of the old form of motherhood as an institution. Such fear is particularly valid in Japanese society, where the institution of motherhood has been so powerful and persistent that it will not disappear easily in the foreseeable future. Especially in the cases of young writers such as Yamada and Yoshimoto, whose fictional worlds seem somewhat out of touch with the mundane reality of everyday life, one wonders to what extent they are critically aware of the harsh reality that generations of Japanese women have had to confront as mothers in a patriarchal society. Even those brave new heroines created by Yamada and Yoshimoto may enact the old roles of "good wives and wise mothers" in this new discourse of social ability.

* * *

Tsushima Yûko (1947–   ), the last writer to be taken up in this essay, is uniquely valuable as a writer concerned with the representation of motherhood and child rearing. Belonging to the generation that falls between the oldest and the youngest writers discussed above, she is situated in the best position to explore the positive sides of motherhood without losing sight of the inherent dangers of its overvalorization. Among Tsushima's numerous works dealing with motherhood, *Chôji* (Child of fortune)[16] is the most useful text for our purpose as it shows her double perspective on motherhood better than any of her other works.

Published in the late 1970s, *Chôji* presents two female characters who represent the opposing types of Japanese women of the period. One is Shôko, wife of a well-established lawyer and a devoted mother of two children, a model "good wife and wise mother" of her time. The other is her younger sister, Kôko, who is in fact the central character of the novel. A resolute non-conformist, she is divorced from her selfish, irresponsible husband, Hatanaka, and on her own continues to raise her daughter, Kayako, in a shabby apartment.

Kôko is not particularly unhappy with her situation, for she can earn money, teaching piano to children in a private music school, and occasionally meets different men, even though she has no intention of establishing permanent ties with any one man. Her main cause of trouble is her sister, Shôko, who meddles in her affairs. Covertly labeling Kôko a bad mother, Shôko persuades Kôko's daughter to move away from Kôko and into her home in order to prepare for the entrance examination to the prestigious private junior high school Shôko's daughter attends. Kôko, aware that her somewhat erratic and unconventional lifestyle has been creating a gap between her and her daughter, cannot stop Kayako from moving away. She now sees Kayako only on weekends, when the girl returns to visit with her.

Kôko's life changes drastically when she discovers that she is pregnant as a result of a casual affair with Osada, a friend of her ex-husband. Without much hesitation, Kôko decides to keep the baby. From then on, Kôko lives in two distinct worlds: the everyday reality of piano teaching, Shôko's persistent demand that she have an abortion, and Kayako's failure in her entrance examination; and an imaginative world in which she dreams of taking care of her new baby with the help of Kayako, a time she imagines will be free and innocent, just like the old days when she played with her elder brother who was mentally retarded but kindhearted.

The final twist comes when Kôko finds out from her doctor that her pregnancy was merely a product of her own imagination, that those undergoing severe stresses of various kinds can develop this kind of pathological condition. However, Kôko knows, and the reader does too, that she was actually transformed during that period. Imagined or not, she was bodily and mentally changed, feeling a fetus inside her, "her celestial bodies" stirring "inside her womb."[17] Hence, even after the surprising revelation, we see Kôko somewhat differently: a woman stronger and firmer in facing the reality around her. This is never more evident than at the time when Kôko flatly refuses a marriage proposal from Osada, who obligingly comes to see Kôko with Hatanaka. Condescendingly, both men try to display themselves as generous saviors of the poor woman so desperately in need of someone to depend on as to falsely imagine being pregnant.

As Rebecca Copeland observes, Kôko's intention to keep her illegitimate child can be interpreted as her act of revenge on her meddling sister as well as on the society Shôko represents.[18] I would argue that Kôko's decision to keep her baby also signifies her effort to maintain her own autonomous universe away from the dominant value system of the larger outside world—

the world preoccupied with continous upward mobility and materialistic achievement. Shôko's "peaceful well-ordered" world is repugnant to Kôko precisely because it is a microcosm of the outside world in which Kôko has no wish to participate. Wholly geared toward securing a perfect environment for her children's successful academic performance, Shôko has no room in her life for anything Kôko would deem important and valuable. Thus, while Shôko pities Kayako when she finds out that the young girl has to do her share of domestic chores at home, it is Kôko's belief that a child can grow into maturity by sharing many things that his or her mother goes through in everyday life. This line of thinking may also lie behind Kôko's reasons for allowing her daughter to come into contact with the men she sleeps with by bringing them home with her. In the one-dimensional life pattern of some-one like Shôko, an irreproachable "wise mother" and "education mama," such an act is an outrage. In fact, Shôko's house seems to have little trace of any man's existence—even her husband seems absent from it most of the time since he never appears in the story.

The narrative suggests that the root of Kôko's worldview can be found in her childhood experience with her disabled brother, who died at the age of fifteen. In fact, of all her family her brother was the only one with whom she could feel genuine warmth and security. Though he was unable to partici-pate in any "meaningful" conversation, Kôko could feel his love and his ready instinct to protect her from harm. The story implies that Kôko felt so strongly about her brother partly because she was too young to understand the full implications of his mental condition but also because she herself tended to feel alienated from their family, given that her mother was always holding her sister, Shôko, in higher esteem for her conventionality.

It may safely be assumed that Kôko's imaginary pregnancy, occurring right after Kayoko leaves home to live with Shôko, resulted from her unconscious urge to regain a version of the lost world of innocence she had with her broth-er. With her "pregnancy" Kôko could feel close to another being; she could feel a nonverbal bonding in a kind of pre-Oedipal space. That it turns out to be a fantasy of her own creation clearly signifies the impossibility of escap-ing from the world of language once it has been entered.

It should be noted that Kôko does not lose the memory of this pre-Oedi-pal world. Rather, it remains, as it should, an important part of her from which she can recover a sense of wholeness necessary to oppose the ever-increasing societal pressures that fragment her. In revealing to Kayako the painful fact of her own imaginary pregnancy, Kôko also talks about her dead brother and the nature of their relationship, and she asks Kayako to remem-ber that there was such a person once in her mother's life, a person who happened to be Kayako's uncle. In this way, Kôko passes on to her daughter a spiritual legacy, potentially paving the way for their damaged relationship to recover.

Indeed, it is Kôko, not Shôko, who retains the more vivid memory of their dead mother. Kôko's lonely state during and after her supposed pregnancy brings her into the hitherto unexplored world of the inner consciousness of her mother, who had to endure the loneliness of bringing up three children after her husband died of a heart attack while with a lover on the beach.

By exploring Kôko's rare experience of imaginary pregnancy side by side with the conventional motherhood represented by the figure of Shôko, Tsushima extends in *Chôji* a radical critique of the existing institution of motherhood, while simultaneously reclaiming the experience of motherhood with its emphasis on the mother-daughter bond.

Julia Kristeva, in her illuminating essay "A New Type of Intellectual: The Dissent," expresses her belief that while pregnancy can be considered a "threshold between nature and culture," maternity can be considered a "bridge between singularity and ethics." Kristeva further argues that a woman can "find herself at the pivot of sociality—at once as a guarantee and a threat to its stability."[19] At a glance, the staunchly nonconformist, unconventional Kôko may appear to signify a small threat to Japanese patriarchal society, but it is evident that she is also envisioned by Tsushima as a guarantee of a particular kind of society—a society where the dichotomies of "nature and culture," or "singularity and ethic," are not in such extreme opposition as they seem to us now. Thus, with *Chôji*, as with many of her other texts that deal with motherhood, Tsushima shows us that the maternal body can be a fertile ground for feminist discourse that is at once subversive and creative.

Notes

1. Ôba Minako, "Sanbiki no Kani" (Three crabs), 1968, in *This Kind of Woman: Stories by Contemporary Japanese Women Writers*, trans. and ed. Tanaka Yukiko and Elizabeth Hanson (New York: Perigee Books, 1984), 89–113.

2. Ôba Minako, *Tsuga no Yume* (Dream of hemlock) (Tokyo: Bungeishunjûsha, 1971).

3. Ibid., 174.

4. Takahashi Takako, "Ronrî Ûman" (The lonely woman), in *Ronrî Ûman* (Tokyo: Shûeisha, 1977), 5–48.

5. Ibid., 39.

6. Takahashi Takako, *Sora no Hate made* (Toward the end of the sky) (Tokyo: Shinchôsha, 1973).

7. Tomioka Taeko, *Nami Utsu Tochi* (Heaving land) (Tokyo: Kôdansha, 1983).

8. Tomioka Taeko, *Shokubutsu Sai* (Plants fair) (Tokyo: Chûokoronsha, 1973).

9. Marianne Hirsch, *The Mother/Daughter Plot: Narrative, Psychoanalysis, Feminism* (Bloomington: Indiana University Press, 1988), 166.

10. Adrienne Rich, *Of Woman Born: Motherhood as Experience and Institution* (New York: W. W. Norton, 1986), 236.

11. Hirsch, *Mother/Daughter Plot*, 166.

12. Hikari Agata, *Uhohho Tankentai* (The "ahem!" expedition party) (Tokyo: Kawade Shobô Shinsha, 1998); idem, *Yukkuri Tôkyô Joshi Marason* (Slow-paced Tokyo women's marathon) (Tokyo: Fukutake Shoten, 1984).

13. Hikari, *Uhohho Tankentai,* 42.

14. Yamada Eimi, *Jeshî no Sebone* (Jessie's backbone) (Tokyo: Kawade Shobô, 1987); idem, *Bedtaim Aiz* (Bedtime eyes) (Tokyo: Kawade Shobô, 1986).

15. Yoshimoto Banana, *Kitchin* (Kitchen) (Tokyo: Fukutake Shoten, 1988).

16. Tsushima Yûko, *Chôji* (Tokyo: Kawade Shobô Shinsha, 1978); idem, *Child of Fortune,* trans. Geraldine Harcourt (Tokyo: Kôdansha International, 1983).

17. Tsushima, *Child of Fortune,* 43.

18. Rebecca Copeland, "Motherhood as Institution," *Japan Quarterly* 156:39 (January–March 1992): 108.

19. Julia Kristeva, "A New Type of Intellectual: Dissent," trans. Sean Hand, in *The Kristeva Reader,* ed. Toril Moi (New York: Columbia University Press, 1986): 292–300.

7. The Melting Pot of Assimilation: Cannibalizing the Multicultural Body

Sneja Gunew

Cannibalism is never just about eating but is primarily a medium for nongustatory messages.
—Peggy Reeve Sanday, *Divine Hunger,* 3

Through oral dietary satisfaction, there emerges, beyond it, a lust for swallowing up the other, while the fear of impure nourishment is revealed as the deathly drive to devour the other.
—Julia Kristeva, *Powers of Horror,* 118

DURING MY EIGHTEEN YEARS of researching ethnic minority writings in the Australian context, I discovered a film produced by the Department of Immigration in the 1950s called *No Strangers Here.* It formed part of a campaign to educate the general public into a greater tolerance toward the large numbers of immigrants who were rather precipitously thrust into Australia during and after World War II. The film is set in "Littletown," a small Australian rural town, in the immediate postwar period. Narrative point of view is provided by the editor of the town's newspaper, a genial and overweight liberal. The story begins when he receives several anonymous letters, signed "a true Australian," contending that foreigners are not wanted in Littletown. As the editor perambulates through the town kissing babies and talking to women working in their gardens, he notices what is evidently a group of strangers walking the streets. The groups consists of two parents, a son, and a daughter, all good-looking but conspicuously foreign. A voice-over traces their backgrounds briefly as refugees from totalitarian, wartorn Europe. Their exact provenance is carefully not specified. Suffice it to say that they clearly gesture their astonishment at the abundance of material objects around them: food and particularly a bicycle, which the father obviously craves.

Remarkably quickly they find their niches. The father works in the local brickworks, the son goes to school, and the fetching daughter ends up as an aide in the local hospital, where she sets aflutter the hearts of the male patients and doctors. The mother remains in the home, where the editor decides to pay her a visit. He enters her home with the immortal words, "Please tell me the story of your life!" On the brink of answering, or performing a kind of reponse, the mother rushes to the oven, where something urgent is evidently calling for attention. She offers the editor a slice of homemade cake, and he in turn requests the recipe and laboriously copies it down, translating her gestures and broken language into phrases like "enough to cover sixpence."[1] This transaction proves to be the answer to his question. The recipe is published under the heading "Easy to Mix" and the townswomen respond appropriately. The film ends with a multicultural food festival where the running joke is that, due to the editor's labors, the local women offer the immigrant woman her own cake as a special treat to make her feel welcome.

This somewhat risible example is an accurate metaphoric and metonymic delineation of the ideology at the heart of postwar migration in Australia and the various attempts to manage it. The film signals assimilation in certain ways, notably linking it to the digestive model from which the term derives. Crucially, the mother offers food instead of words. Food, as we know, has long been the acceptable face of multiculturalism; indeed, there is a long tradition of food as a signifier for cultural difference—and not only in Australia. The very term "melting pot" employed in the United States is another echo of this link. To put it more forcefully, no matter how one labors to lift the rhetoric, the apparently positive connotations of multiculturalism are invariably limited to food. Cultural diversity translates into the enrichment of national cuisines as a balance to the rhetoric of "immigrants taking away jobs." Rather than seeing this nexus in terms of loss and negativity or simply as an expression of the subjugated status of ethnic minority groups, in this essay I analyze some of the implications of the conjunction of food and cultural difference. Since a number of texts will be drawn from Australian minority writers, a prefatory explanation is required that in Australia the term "multiculturalism" has a particular configuration and resonates in specific ways. Briefly, whereas in Australia the primary difference indicated by the term "multiculturalism" refers to Australians who are not of Anglo-Celtic (English and Irish) or Aboriginal backgrounds, in other parts of the world, such as Canada, the United States, and the United Kingdom, "multiculturalism" is more clearly a code word for racialized differences.[2] More precisely, "multiculturalism" is usually reserved for what are known as "visible minorities," or, alternatively and broadly speaking, non-Europeans. There is nothing fixed, natural, or self-evident about any of these terms and the differences they supposedly name.[3] These taxonomies and terms are brought into play through sociopolitical and discursive practices. They are highly relative and historically and culturally very specific.

In a world where racialized differences and their bloody entourage of oppression have given way to the equally obscene battles around "ethnic cleansing," one of the few seemingly benign representational systems of these "multicultural" differences has been food. The local multicultural food festival has become a standard safe (and even safety) device for acknowledging the different histories and traditions that comprise the demographic diversity of most nations. This celebration of gustatory diversity is a common spectacle across those nations that acknowledge their multiculturalism, albeit in the most conservative ways. In Homi Bhabha's phrase, the "people as one" are momentarily staged in the mutual assimilation of each other's food.[4] One might also observe that there is an excessive energy employed to convert those cultural differences into gastronomic ones. I argue here that we don't simply become *like* each other by eating each other's food (akin to donning each other's clothing) but that eating each other's food is often a barely sublimated way of simply eating each other. The significance of this process varies and is by no means always a mark of dominance or disrespect, a matter of dehumanizing or commodifying the other. Cannibalism, as analyzed by anthropologists such as Peggy Reeves Sanday,[5] has many meanings, including those associated with sacred awe and respect. Using psychoanalytic concepts as well, particularly the work of Julia Kristeva, I suggest further that while food signifies actual bodies, it also stands in for—indeed, contends with—language itself. Thus, the dominant culture engages with multicultural cuisine as a way of not acknowledging multicultural words. In this essay I focus on the permutations of the feast in relation to strangers and hosts and on the overdetermined field of mother-daughter relations where mother tongues and mother's cooking are conspicuously in conflict with the formation of separate subjectivities.

The notion of the feast or banquet as a locus for suspending the tensions between "us" and "them" is a much-explored territory in anthropology.[6] The feast is where guests (no matter that outside this process they are the greatest of enemies) are welcomed and hostilities are suspended. Bizarre instances of this come to mind, such as stories about World War I in which the opposing sides came together for Christmas celebrations. Such ancient laws of hospitality are, one imagines, less easily invoked now. One thinks as well of the instances (apocryphal or not) in which these laws of the banquet are violated, as in the terrible story that is the prelude to the *Oresteia,* in which a father is unwittingly served his own children and the great cycle of intrafamilial revenge begins. These transgressions indicate the shadowy side of the paradigm of the feast as the sanctuary or locus of arrested conflict, one that has often been acknowledged but perhaps not traced in the multicultural formation. It has also been noted that just who is the host and who is the guest becomes to some degree interchangeable. As Julian Pitt-Rivers points out in a seminal essay:

[The inversion involves] a transformation from hostile stranger, *hostis,* into guest, *hospes* (or *hostis*) . . . from one whose hostile actions are assumed to one whose hostility is laid in abeyance. The word *hostis* claims therefore as its radical sense, not the obligation to reciprocal violence, but the notion of "strangeness" which underlies this transition. The further extension to *host* is perfectly congruent, since strangeness is logically reciprocal, whether it enjoins distrust or hospitality. Both senses of the word, *l'hôte,* are conserved in French which must find other ways to distinguish between host and guest.[7]

Using the word "host" in a Judeo-Christian framework already reveals the next stage in the signifying chain, namely, the hidden cannibalism that lurks below the feast, particularly a sacramental one, in which the host or guest may as easily *be* the feast as partake of it. It is this series of displacements and the symbolic logic entailed therein that is explored here by tracing the stages of the multicultural stranger at the feast of the host country.

As Mary Douglas's work illustrates, the shared meal is one trope for sorting out who belongs and who doesn't.[8] In the first stages of the scenario of immigration and diaspora, these worlds of food coexisted in mutual intolerance and undisguised disgust. Food was used to assert impenetrable boundaries—the other could literally not be stomached. Foreigners were associated with taboo foods: they ate dogs, cats, offal, or other dishes outside the arbitrary rules imposed by the host culture.[9] Although I cite Australian examples for the most part, I begin by referring briefly to a text with which many North Americans are familiar, Maxine Hong Kingston's *Woman Warrior.* As with many multicultural texts that strive to find both common ground and grounds of difference, *The Woman Warrior* offers numerous references to food. While everyone eats, the way one eats or what one eats can signify an absolute parting of ways. In Kingston's text, for example, as a way of registering her own cultural split (growing up Chinese in America), the narrator describes being nauseated by and unable to stomach her family's food. She finds it so revolting that she almost gives up eating:

We'd have to face four- and five-day-old leftovers until we ate it all. The squid eye would keep appearing at breakfast and dinner until eaten. Sometimes brown masses sat on every dish. I have seen revulsion on the faces of visitors who've caught us at meals.

"Have you eaten yet?" the Chinese greet one another.

"Yes, I have," they answer whether they have or not.

"And you?"

I would live on plastic.[10]

The mother is characterized as being a great—indeed, epic—eater: "My mother could contend against the hairy beasts whether flesh or ghost because she could eat them." This prowess forms part of the mother's resilience to any trials she encounters and is particularly prominent in her narrative of herself as a "ghost-buster," not only of the ghosts or baleful ectoplasms encountered within the mother country, China, but also of the ghosts or foreigners in the new world. The mother securely retains the boundaries of her subjectivity even in America, the place of dislocation. She maintains China and the subjectivity forged in that language, that symbolic in the Lacanian or Kristevan sense, in the new terrain. And she eats anything and everything, including, metaphorically, her daughter, who after all is part "ghost" and who struggles for most of the book to detach herself from her mother's powerful and controlling presence. The denouement for this release of her own subjectivity comes in one of the most disturbing scenes in *The Woman Warrior* when the narrator encounters her hated alter ego (I'll return to this later). What we note now is the lurking shadow of cannibalism, particularly as refracted through Kristeva's analysis of the processes of abjection where the subject, unable to separate from the maternal, is unable to maintain the boundaries necessary for subject formation.

Australia's immigrant history dates most significantly from the postwar period in which dislocated "reffos" (short for refugees) and DPs (displaced persons) registered their alienation from the dominant culture by foraging pathetically for "real" bread, which wasn't white or spongy. Lily Brett's collection of linked stories, *Things Could Be Worse*, is structured around a group of Holocaust survivors of the Lodz ghetto. Now upwardly mobile with all the trappings of material success, they survive in Melbourne and are observed through the eyes of one of the daughters, Lola, who has inherited her own set of problems. The following is a classic mother-daughter exchange:

> Renia [the mother] bought four loaves of bread a day for the birds in her garden. She bought rye, white sliced, wholemeal and vienna. She walked to Acland Street to get the best bread.
>
> She always had plenty of bread in the house. The few stories about Renia's past that she shared with Lola were about bread. She used to say, "Lola darling, you don't know what it is to be without bread. . . . You know, Lola, there were some people in the ghetto who killed people so that they could have their bread. Mrs. Berg, my high-school teacher, didn't report the death of her daughter. She kept the body with her for two weeks so she could claim her daughter's rations. Finally, the neighbours couldn't bear the smell and told the authorities."[11]

In the terms of the classic aphorism "We are what we eat," food and bodies function as each other's doubles, mirrored in turn by the symbiotic relations between mothers and daughters where, in a grotesque inversion, the dead daughter serves to keep her mother alive. In a later story in the same collection we encounter the following significant performance: "Lola often bent over the rubbish bin. She tore clumps of bread from a loaf. One piece of bread in her mouth, one piece into the bin, some more for her, and a few crusty pieces for the rubbish bin. Lola had to finish the loaf. It would have been damaging evidence. Another couple of bites, and the last piece could go into the bin."[12] Like the birds her mother feeds with the best bread, Lola too craves this maternal nurturing but in ambivalent ways. Clearly, as in the case of Kingston's narrator, the children of immigrants, those who have tried to adjust to the new world, to some extent demonstrate their different positionality through an overdetermined consumption and rejection of the food of both the motherland and the mother.[13] While on the one hand the "real" bread (endorsed by the mother's culture) is required by the daughter, on the other hand it is also necessary to "waste" it, to stage its superfluity.

Another example comes from a story by the Hungarian-Australian writer Inez Baranay:

> We've all got a black-bread-and-salami story. Our smelly stinky reffowog lunches. All the other children have their white soft sandwiches filled with stuff we have to find out about, vegemite—peanut butter—devon, and they swap half of this for half of that. But we have coarse thick black bread with spicy garlicky sausage and we throw it away or hide it or we eat it with shame defiance resignation we flavour it with revenge secrecy pride . . . we can't swap with them all we can do is share latvian bread polish sausage serbian pickle hungarian salami italian ham greek cheese . . .
>
> *They* are soft white bland even children and *we* are black lumpy spicy prickly children we cause strange smells in your nose strange sounds in your ears and in your belly indigestion discomfort embarrassment. They are real-australians. We are new-australians, would-be australians, non-australians.[14]

In what we will come to recognize as a repetitive process of figurative convergence, the children *are* the food, a food whose difference offends the nostrils of the host culture.

Just as this story involves a mechanism of exchange, so too is the next step of the immigrant as food on the road to assimilation by the dominant culture compactly staged. We have embarked on the process that transforms the nauseous taboo food into ethnic cuisine, a desirable marker of gastronomic richness and diversity that also acts as proof that the nation is an open and tolerant one, a guarantee of its cosmopolitanism. As Baranay states later in the same story: "Wog food becomes exclusive food becomes trendy food becomes city food becomes food.'"[15] How can there be racism or intolerance of any kind when we are all prepared to troop down to the local Vietnamese or Sri Lankan restaurant? Assimilation is figured in its most literal form. We have all learned to digest each other, and we are well on the way to having multiculturalism represented in popular culture as primarily the food festival, where difference is domesticated and arrayed for appropriation as smorgasbord. In another, more random example from popular culture, testifying to the unself-consciously invoked ubiquity of this conjunction, the Canadian national *Globe and Mail* newspaper ran an "ethnic success-story" in which a child of Ukrainian-Canadians buys a failed McDonald's site and sets up the first of a chain of successful urban Toronto bakeries. As the reporter put it: "That's the classic recipe for success. You start with immigrants, add hard work and the yeast of Old World culture, throw them in the urban oven and bake for one generation. The result is rich in every way, just like the sourdough rye at Future Bakery."[16] Once again, the multicultural body becomes figured as food, indicating simultaneously that the insistence on invoking food whenever multiculturalism is represented in a positive way is not quite so benign as it may at first appear. The negative interpretations of multiculturalism are legion and usually take the form of representing it as the "balkanizing" and divisive virus that infects the social or political body. That's another story entirely, one of contamination and pathology. We are left here with an interesting chain of displacement and condensation in terms of food, subjectivity, and sacrifice.

Why sacrifice? In her brilliant study on starvation, Maud Ellmann traces the metaphors of self-willed starvation and illustrates the ways in which they reveal the displacement of food by speech and writing via the mediating spectacle of the disappearing body: the fleshly body is transmuted into text. Among the many provocative ideas she puts forward, Ellmann suggests that oral processes function as a mechanism for knowledge acquisition, as in the example of the infant who puts everything into its mouth as a means of getting to know it. Oral processes thus constitute a primary mapping between self and other. Here, eating both marks and is perceived as the first violation of the boundaries of the ego: "Our first experience of eating is force-feeding: as infants we were fed by others." Ellman goes on to say: "*All eating is force-feeding:* and it is through the wound of feeding that the other is instated at the very center of the self."[17]

From Kristeva's work on abjection we are familiar with the link between the formations of subjectivity and oral processes. The abject comes into play when boundaries cannot be maintained, when the separation from the maternal cannot take place and meaning collapses.[18] Often this is figured in not being able to ingest food, tantamount to a refusal to be born or to acknowledge oneself as a separate being. As a (belated) rebellion against being ejected from the maternal, the subject refuses to take in anything, including food, that threatens the sovereignty of its bodily limits. Indeed, the process of birth may be perceived as one of the most archaic and threatening reminders of cannibalism. In other words, that the mother could as easily devour the offspring, assimilate it, as she could give birth to it; and, from the other perspective, the child is the archetypal parasite that devours the mother from within, threatens *her* boundaries. The subsequent "proof" of this desire is that in their first months or years of breastfeeding, infants "eat" their mothers.[19] Thus, when we "admit" food, who are we eating and, simultaneously, to what are we giving birth? Recall the mother-daughter exchanges in *The Woman Warrior* and Brett's stories. The mothers symbolically eat their daughters, refuse to give them a separate existence. The daughters vomit up themselves (give birth to themselves in this fashion) or, alternatively, expel the maternal body. In these inverted, demonic birth scenes, what emerges? Among other things, language—in the form of speech and writing.

Let us return to the encounter between the narrator in *The Woman Warrior* and her alter ego, the unnaturally good Chinese girl who never speaks and whom the narrator therefore torments in the school washroom in order to force her to speak: "She was baby soft. I thought I could put my thumb on her nose and push it bonelessly in, indent her face. . . . I could work her face around like dough. . . . I reached up and took the fatty part of her cheek, not dough, but meat, between my thumb and finger. . . . Her skin was fleshy, like squid out of which the glassy blades of bones had been pulled. . . . Her skin seemed to stretch. I let go in horror. What if it came away in my hand? . . . I hated her fingers. I could snap them like breadsticks."[20] Here is a scenario of abjection in which boundaries between self and other collapse and in which the self translates the other into food in order to be able to consume her, by now a familiar process. Thereafter, the narrator is paralyzed and bedridden for a year; she is rendered speechless, subsequently emerging from this ordeal as a writer. The mark of sanity and cultural assimilation is that the body of the undesirable alter ego is consumed and transmuted into speech. As part of the process, the foreign and visibly different aspects of the body of the narrator are screened or camouflaged through her ability, finally, to project the familiar language of the dominant culture.[21] As Ellmann puts it: "Speech is a form of fasting, and writing represents an even fiercer abstinence than speech."[22] From desiring to fast by rejecting the maternal food, the narrator fasts in a different mode by writing in the ghostly language, and in the process she finally succeeds in separating from the mother tongue and the mother.

Further pursuing the links between food and language, in Kristeva's *Powers of Horror* we have the following passage: "Through the mouth that I fill with words instead of my mother whom I miss from now on more than ever, I elaborate that want, and the aggressivity that accompanies it, by *saying*. . . . There is language instead of the good breast."[23] The mother is figured as food, a substance seemingly at odds with language/speech. In her study of abjection, Kristeva traces the subject's separation from the maternal and semiotic into the symbolic dimension and the acquisition of language. The degree to which the body becomes a clean and proper one signifies its entry into the fully symbolic, the law and language. As part of this process, Kristeva and others have traced a type of rivalry between food and language.[24] The disruption of the symbiosis between self and other is signaled by language, the mark of absence and difference.[25] The process tracked by Kristeva and other psychoanalytic critics entails one journey, but what happens to the mother tongue when one is involved in the diasporic scenario? What happens to the first language, which must be buried and suppressed to function in the new world? One possible answer is that it is turned back into food, or, perhaps, that it comes to signify waste and is excreted in the stages of abjection. Food and language are to some extent each other's doubles, and both function as the bedrock of subject formations.

The Polish-Australian poet Ania Walwicz's simulation of automatic writing techniques functions to signify some of those semiotic repressed elements that lend themselves very well to psychoanalytic readings. The following extract is from Walwicz's first novel, *red roses,* a meditation on the mother-daughter relationship, among other things.

> *she is cooking my text* in here it's all about her and not about her it's about this and this this cooking the baking all chopping i like to prepare for people i like to watch them eat *i eat them too their words* i am eating o worlds i eat eater her sin eater off my chest melted butter she is beating a child it just comes over me heavy frying grated sliced and sliced finely sliced chopping text and chopping slice into thin strips *to be eater and eating* to be cooking she's always in her place in frying a mix through a whisk to be doing i am doing short cuts and fine cuts in a slice and toss tossing in a stir and fry i am doing in oiling oily in a steamer and simmer pressure cooker for minutes in hot water in a drain and slice making mushroom love in a toss but not too much over not overdoing or saying just a mix in diagonal in raw prawns in a shaking take care roughly chop a chop in a dice and scatter cooked crab lemon wedge flip over griddle done and lightly film until risen and rise in may baking powder chowder wire rack she is strangling tomatoes and beating vienna schnitzels she is frying away beating an egg my egg in egg nog flips in pepper toast and cakes she is making a torte and a king *i am eating my mother she always wanted to cook and feedie getting into my gullets entering going though* going there wasn't ever enough separateness there was mesh in a mesh to eat hot cakes on a fat thursdays in with filled with jam there's only one mix in text there's no going away *she is holding me tight in my enter mouth directing my tongue* feeder plates in drop batter in little water in a steamer in a heater her dinners got less and less until there wasn't any at all none and nothing.[26]

Many images converge and collapse here: the child is being beaten, as are the ingredients for the meal. The meal itself is either the child or her text or, in a classic dream reversal, the child eats the mother or ingests the mother in order to separate from her and create her own text. Figured graphically in this text is Ellmann's notion, referred to above, of all feeding as constituting in some respects force-feeding.

In "translate," another piece by Walwicz, the narrator searches for her lost mother tongue, Polish, using images from a lost (possibly orphaned) childhood in which old toys/lost words also acquire the demonic features of nightmares, the return of the repressed: "loss lost language lost tongue pickled don't you lose this keeping . . . foreigner has some extra at back of head is another country my old words sleep wait."[27] The indigestible Polish words— "lost language lost tongue pickled"—are transformed into a foreign dish that could perhaps not enter the ear but could be assimilated via more traditional ways. Anglophone readers may not be able to absorb the Polish words the narrator spews, but we can contemplate eating her pickled tongue.[28] Another prose poem, "europe," begins, "I am europe deluxe nougat bar i'm better than most i'm really special rich and tasty black forest cake . . . in me is europe i keep it i got it i get it in me inside me . . . you can go to europe but you can't be europe like i am i suck my finger and i taste europe i touch europe."[29]

Here we return to the signifying chain with which we began, the notion that in symbolic exchange or substitution food is offered not in place of language but in place of the body. In theory this could happen as well to the foreign language, but it happens instead to the foreign tongue (as we know the language of dreams can sometimes be quite literal). The desire appears to be that the multicultural body should be assimilated in the sense of being eaten. And so it is, symbolically; and once again the paradigm of the Christian communion comes to mind. By offering their symbolic bodies, the multicultural other can be accepted as a legitimate part of the society. In an enigmatic interview titled "Eating Well," Jacques Derrida speaks about the "sacrificial structure" in relation to structures of authority and legitimation pertaining to the passage from animal to human. The "Chief of State," as he puts it, must be an eater of meat who must be prepared to be consumed himself; and this process of "carno-phallogocentrism" involves the "interiorization of the phallus and the necessity of its passage through the mouth, whether it is a matter of words or things, of sentences, of daily bread or wine, of the tongue, the lips, or the breast of the other."[30]

Kristeva speaks of the process of sacrifice in relation to circumcision as a ritual symbolizing disconnection from the maternal and a reconnection to God. She links it with the dietary prohibitions in Leviticus and their reference to the sacred word. Food is implicated here in the setting up of sexual difference as the basis or precondition for speech, and readers are referred to the example given at the beginning of this essay. I have also looked at this mechanism from the reverse direction, namely, that the multicultural body inside the host body acts as a kind of parasite, using the analysis traced by Michel Serres where the parasite also impinges on sound and hearing.[31] The parasite functions as the "noise" that disrupts language as meaningful communication.[32] Hearing the incomprehensible foreign tongue is mediated and transformed by sight into the acceptably exotic foreign dish. There is a continuum here with the familiar performance of ethnic dancing, where the body becomes a spectacle that can be devoured by the eyes of spectators at the multicultural food festival.[33]

What are we left with? The multicultural body in the exchange of communion threatens to disrupt the clean and proper boundaries of subjectivity—its own and those of the host nation. It retreats into the role of Kristeva's deject, who obsessively and repetitively erects boundaries to shore up the slipping self that refuses to stay in place.[34] The deject is often described as obsessed with language. In the move from food to language, the multicultural body deterritorializes the language from within, as Deleuze and Felix Guattari have shown in their classic study of Kafka.[35] The German employed by the Prague Jews disrupts the German master language from within. In a comparable move, we contemplate the disruption of postcolonial English by the former Empire and in settler colonies by ethnic minority groups. Thus, we have Creole, "dialects" (as they are disparagingly called) and the panoply of "new literatures in English" displacing both "clean and proper English," as well as the representations created by canonical English writers who were invoked to map the imaginary dimensions of the imperial world.

We might also encounter the secret feast as distinct from the food festival and with it return to the displaced mother tongue and sublimated multicultural body. Ellmann again: "In writing, language is emancipated from the mouth and ultimately from the body as a whole."[36] In a host country where multicultural food and multicultural bodies are consumed in inverse proportion to multicultural words, it may be that the sense of community is maintained by the secret feast held not for outsiders but to weld insiders.[37] Here we have the migrant or multicultural text written for the community itself, not in the host language, such as English, but in the mother tongue.[38] Even when written in English, these "parasites" serve to corrupt the language from within—and so we have terms such as "literatures in the new Englishes" and "urban dialects," acknowledging a new hybridity. In this new mechanism the multicultural body urges its nonassimilation, its indigestibility, its incommensurability, to the extent that we may notice what we are eating, seeing, and hearing and what this may in turn signify in relation to legitimate and illegitimate writing.

Notes

This essay forms a first attempt at exploring what clearly must be a much longer work in which I am far more alert than I have been to cultural differences within the symbolic constellation I trace here. At the moment there appears to be a remarkable similarity in the way this mechanism or process plays itself out across very disparate cultures. But then I am only looking at texts in English.

1. A sixpence in the old British imperial system would be equivalent to a U.S. dime.

2. Sneja Gunew, "Multicultural Multiplicities: U.S., Canada, Australia," in *Cultural Studies: Pluralism and Theory,* ed. David Bennett (Melbourne: Melbourne University Press, 1993), 51–65.

3. Sneja Gunew, "Postcolonialism and Multiculturalism: Between Race and Ethnicity," in *The Yearbook in English Studies,* vol. 27, ed. Andrew Gurr (Reading, U.K.: Modern Humanities Research Association, University of Reading, 1996), 22–39.

4. Homi Bhabha, "DissemiNation: Time, Narrative, and the Margins of the Modern Nation," in *Nation and Narration,* ed. Homi Bhabha (London: Routledge, 1990), 291–322.

5. Peggy Reeve Sanday, *Divine Hunger* (London: Cambridge University Press, 1987).

6. See Arjun Appadurai, "Gastro-politics in Hindu South Asia," *American Ethnologist* 8:3 (August 1990): 494–511; Mary Douglas, *Implicit Meanings* (London Routledge and Kegan Paul, 1975), 249–75; William Boelhower, *Through a Glass Darkly: Ethnic Semiosis in American Literature* (New York: Oxford University Press, 1984); Julian Pitt-Rivers, "The Stranger, the Guest, and the Hostile Host: Introduction to the Study of the Laws of Hospitality," in *Contributions to Mediterranean Sociology: Mediterranean Rural Communities and Social Change,* ed. J.-G. Peristiany (The Hague: Mouton, 1968), 13–30.

7. Pitt-Rivers, "Stranger, Guest, and Hostile Host," 20–21.

8. Douglas, *Implicit Meanings,* 249–75.

9. L. K. Brown and K. Mussell, eds., *Ethnic and Regional Foodways in the United States* (Knoxville: University of Tennessee Press, 1984).

10. Maxine Hong Kingston, *The Woman Warrior* (New York: Vintage, 1989), 92.

11. Lily Brett, *Things Could Be Worse* (Melbourne: Meanjin/Melbourne University Press, 1990), 73–74. Brett is an Australian Jewish writer now living and writing in New York City. Her latest novel, *Just Like That* (Sydney: Picador/Pan Macmillan Australia, 1996), deals with the tug between New York and Australia, among other themes.

12. Brett, *Things Could Be Worse,* 146.

13. This has clinical support as well. See Léon Grinberg and Rebecca Grinberg, *Psychoanalytic Perspectives on Migration and Exile* (New Haven, Conn.: Yale University Press, 1989), esp. chap. 17.

14. Inez Baranay, "You Don't Whinge," in *Beyond the Echo: Multicultural Women's Writing,* ed. Sneja Gunew and Jan Mahyuddin (Brisbane: University of Queensland Press, 1988), 26–27.

15. Ibid., 28.

16. J. Barber, "Local Boy Provides a Glimpse of the Future," *Globe and Mail,* 22 April 1994, A5.

17. Maud Ellmann, *The Hunger Artists: Starving, Writing, and Imprisonment* (Cambridge, Mass.: Harvard University Press, 1993), 35–36.

18. Julia Kristeva, *Powers of Horror: An Essay On Abjection* (New York: Columbia University Press), 2.

19. A number of essays in the collection *Disorderly Eaters* invoke the Hansel and Gretel story as a particularly telling example of the uneasy boundary between mothers eating, rather than nurturing, their children, as well as the reverse movement of children annihilating, in this instance, the "bad" mother or witch. The fact that they throw the witch into her own oven suggests multiple symbolic possibilities. See Lidia Corti, "*Medea* and *Beloved:* Self-Definition and Abortive Nurturing in Literary Treatments of the Infanticidal Mother," in *Disorderly Eaters: Texts in Self-Empowerment,* ed. Lillian Furst and P. W. Graham (State Park: Pennsylvania State University Press, 1992), 61–78; P. Medeiros, "Cannibalism and Starvation: The Parameters of Eating Disorders in Literature," in ibid., 11–27. One recalls as well Erich Neumann's Jungian analysis of the maternal in which he quotes an old Roman proverb, "The oven is the mother" (*The Great Mother: An Analysis of the Archetype* [1963; Princeton, N.J.: Princeton University Press, 1972], 286). For a quite

different, though related, analysis of food linked to child-sacrifice as a symptom of a coercive public sphere, see Rey Chow, "We Endure, Therefore We Are: Survival, Governance, and Zhang Yimou's *To Live*," *South Atlantic Quarterly* 95:4 (Fall 1996): 1040–64.

20. Kingston, *Woman Warrior*, 176–77.

21. For an enlightening and comprehensive thematic survey of food in Asian-American writing, see Sau-ling Wong, *Reading Asian American Literature: From Necessity to Extravagance* (Princeton, N.J.: Princeton University Press, 1993).

22. Ellmann, *Hunger Artists*, 47. One recalls here the familiar parental injunction, "Don't speak with your mouth full."

23. Kristeva, *Powers of Horror*, 41–45.

24. Ellmann, *Hunger Artists*, 46. Gilles Deleuze and Félix Guattari, in *Kafka: Toward a Minor Literature* (Minneapolis: University of Minnesota Press, 1986), 19–20, also note the link between food and speech. Once again the clinical evidence is also there in Grinberg and Grinberg, *Psychoanalytic Perspectives*, chap. 11.

25. Some of these questions were sparked by a question that continues to haunt my work on the semiotics of minority representation, namely, what happens to the mother tongue in relation to second-language acquisition from psychoanalytic theoretical standpoints. See Sneja Gunew, *Framing Marginality: Multicultural Literary Studies* (Melbourne: Melbourne University Press, 1994).

26. Ania Walwicz, *red roses* (Brisbane: University of Queensland Press, 1992), 30–31 (emphasis added).

27. Ania Walwicz, "translate," in *boat* (Sydney: Angus and Robertson, 1989), 83–84.

28. This is even more the case in the video *Europa* (1987, Media Productions, Deakin University, Geelong, Australia, dir. Peter Lane, 24 min.) in which the prose poem "europe" forms one of a tryptych of pieces performed by Walwicz. The visual material incorporates a very pickled ox tongue on a plate.

29. Ania Walwicz, "europe," in *boat*, 71–72.

30. Jacques Derrida, "'Eating Well'; or, The Calculation of the Subject: An Interview with Jacques Derrida," in *Who Comes After the Subject?* ed. E. Cadava, P. Connor, and J.-L. Nancy (New York: Routledge, 1991), 113.

31. Michel Serres, *The Parasite* (Baltimore: Johns Hopkins University Press, 1982).

32. Sneja Gunew, "Against Multiculturalism: Rhetorical Images," in *Multiculturalism, Difference, and Postmodernism*, ed. G. L. Clark, D. Forbes, and R. Francis (Melbourne: Longman Cheshire, 1993), 38–53. This connection of the foreign as noise rather than meaningful communication or music is depicted in complex ways in Annie Proulx's novel tracing ethnic histories in the United States, *Accordion Crimes* (New York: Scribner, 1996). See also Jacques Attali, *Noise: The Political Economy of Music* (Minneapolis: University of Minnesota Press, 1985).

33. There is a particularly complex treatment of this in Trinh T. Minh-ha's film *Surname Viet Given Name Nam* (see Trinh T. Minh-ha, *Framer Framed* [New York: Routledge, 1992]). There is also the illuminating study by Deborah Root of the West's aestheticization, commodification, and consumption of cultural difference, *Cannibal Culture: Art, Appropriation, and the Commodification of Difference* (Boulder, Colo.: Westview Press, 1996).

34. Kristeva, *Powers of Horror*, 8.

35. Deleuze and Guattari, *Kafka*, 16–27.

36. Ellmann, *Hunger Artists*, 47.

37. Gunew, *Framing Marginality*. My thanks to Mayfair Mei-Hui Yang for sending me her article "Gift Economy and State Power in China" (*Comparative Studies in Society and History* 31:1 [January 1989]: 25–54), which charts some of the same mechanisms I have traced here. Those with whom one can do business (insiders) are described as being "cooked," while outsiders are described as "raw."

38. A conspicuous example of this within recent Australian cultural history is the publication by the Greek Australian poet Π. O. (Pi. O.) of his epic poem *24 Hours*, a text of some 740 pages in which he evokes the history of Fitzroy, an inner-city suburb of Melbourne that is characterized by its ethnic mix. The language of *24 hours* comprises a unique tour de force in that it manages to capture with unerring accuracy a phonetic transcription of the many "dialects" the area has produced, thus deterritorializing the language from within. See Π. O. (Pi. O.), *24 Hours* (Melbourne: Collective Effort Press, 1996).

8. Dropping the Towel: Images of the Body in Contemporary Thai Women's Writing

Susan Fulop Kepner

IMAGES OF THE BODY in twentieth-century Thai women's writing are particularly striking in the work of five authors: Boonlua, Suwanee Sukhontha, Botan, Sri Dao Ruang, and Anchan.[1] In this essay I demonstrate the ways in which these women, the last three of whom are alive and still writing, not only paved the way from the "ladies' novels" of the early twentieth century to the realistic novels and short stories of the past thirty years but initiated the "re-embodiment" of women in Thai fiction.

An Agreeable Mirror

From the 1880s to the 1930s, Thai novels strongly reflected the characterizations and conventions of English and French nineteenth-century fiction. Thai men who studied in England during the reign of King Chulalongkorn (1868–1910), greatly impressed by writers from Dickens and Trollope to producers of penny dreadfuls, first translated their favorite works, then adapted them, and finally wrote original Thai novels using the techniques and patterns they had practiced.[2] Thai women did not go abroad to be educated until the 1920s, at the earliest, but they too read Western fiction, studying at home with governesses or in convent schools, where their favorite authors included Jane Austen, the Brontës, and Sir Walter Scott. One of the authors whose work is examined here, Boonlua, realized in midlife the adolescent ambition to translate her beloved *Ivanhoe* into Thai.

For decades, modern Thai fiction was almost entirely an upper-class avocation. It was easy to transplant the themes, characterizations, and social values displayed in the English novel to the world of the late nineteenth-century Siamese aristocracy. Dozens of early Thai novels written by women (and men) could well have begun with the first line of Jane Austen's *Pride and Prejudice:* "It is a truth universally acknowledged, that a single man in possession of a good fortune must be in want of a wife." Indeed, had that novel been translated into Thai (which to my knowledge it has not been), its characters and their vocations, avocations, and obsessions would have been thoroughly enjoyed and approved by Thai readers.

In general, Thai women writers in the modern era (1880 to the present) have been expected to write wholesome stories that are not only entertaining but uplifting and instructive to young females. Male writers have been given somewhat more latitude with respect to the depiction of realistic human beings, their emotions, and activities; but they, too, operate within the confines of a relatively "decent" literary ethic. Until very recently, explicit descriptions of sexual activity have been entirely confined to pornography, which has been differentiated from "literature."

The Body and Its Pleasures in Classical Literature

Women's bodies, as presented in dance-dramas and poetry written from the thirteenth through the eighteenth centuries, are celebrated in terms of ideal features: blackest, most lustrous hair, palest complexion, darkest eyes, with "[skin] beautiful as burnished gold . . . the pupils in their eyes . . . as black as those of a three-day old fawn."[3] Indeed, the image of a "young doe" is still used to describe a beautiful young woman.

Negative descriptions of women's bodies were more imaginative, as in this description of evil female spirits, from the same work: "[They are] always naked and their bodies smell from every pore. Flies alight on their bodies and burrow into their flesh. . . . Only sinews and skin barely cover their bones. They are famished. They cannot find anything to eat. When they [give birth] . . . they eat their babies' flesh. And still, they do not feel full."[4]

Plain but worthy women have their place in Thai writing. For example, a female character in *Phra Aphai Mani,* a tale composed by the eighteenth-century poet Sunthorn Phu, is highly intelligent, proud, steadfastly loyal to her sovereign Phra Aphaimani—and famously ill favored: "There was a thirty-four-year-old spinster named Wali who had a swarthy complexion. She was so ugly that not a man bothered to look at her. Her face was pock-marked and not a shade of beauty could be found on her. . . . [She] inherited the lore of the ancient folk which she thoroughly studied with diligence. . . . Having committed everything to memory, she burned all the texts. . . . people regarded Wali as a prophetess."[5]

An important component of Wali's unattractiveness is her dark, pock-marked complexion. If smallpox would one day be defeated, the unfortunate condition of "swarthiness" would always stand in the way of a Thai woman in literature (or in life) being considered an outstanding beauty. Although the emphasis on pale skin as the chief arbiter of beauty did not originate with the interference of Europeans, two centuries of exposure to European and American economic and (to a lesser extent) cultural hegemony—enhanced during the latter half of the twentieth century by omnipresent images on television and in the movies of white people having fun and getting rich and powerful—has done nothing to reduce the prestige attached to pale skin. Oil and watercolor images of nineteenth-century Thai women with very fair and distinctly Eurasian (or frankly Caucasian) looks have graced the covers of books about women for the past two decades. This trend was propelled by the work of two artists, both male: Chakrabhand Posayakrit and Arunothai Somsakul, whose delicate, exquisite miniatures have been described by Herbert P. Phillips as "[removing] people from the here and now . . . placing them into fantasies of life during the reign of King Chulalongkorn (1868–1910), a period perceived as [modern] Thailand's golden age, toward which there is a profound sense of nostalgia."[6]

Western influences aside, in Thailand, as everywhere else in Asia, relative "whiteness" has long been an identifying characteristic of the woman who does not have to toil in the fields, suffering the darkening and coarsening effects of sun, wind, and rain. Moreover, since Thai Buddhism teaches that everyone is born into the place he or she has earned through the deeds of previous lives, the fact of having been born into a life of privilege—with the soft, pale skin that is emblematic of such a life—enhances the significance of, and the preference for, light skin.

For centuries, classical dancers at court exaggerated their whiteness with heavy, chalk-white makeup. Other women attempted to live up to another favored image, the "burnished gold" referred to in the poem above, through the cosmetic use of turmeric (the ingredient most responsible for the color of commercial curry powder), which was sometimes applied over the entire body. Teeth already darkened by betel chewing were rubbed with a black paste that made them sparkle darkly and contrast nicely with the gold color of the turmeric.

Until the end of the nineteenth century, after the topknot had been cut at puberty the majority of adult Thai women wore their hair very short, in a kind of crew (or brush) cut. Very old women wearing this hairstyle may still be seen in Thailand.[7] In a nice example of the cyclical nature of fashion, at the close of the twentieth century some Thai women's great-granddaughters sport nineteenth-century hairstyles. Traditional dress consisted of a calf- or ankle-length lower garment and at least one upper garment. When women went bare-breasted, they did so in deference to hot weather and the demands of infants, not the dictates of fashion.

There is an interesting linguistic dimension to the breast, in that the Thai word for it is *nom,* meaning "milk." (The same word is used for "breast" and "milk" in most Southeast Asian languages.) It is thus impossible to divorce function from form, much less from language. There are no equivalents to the many English words designating and denigrating breasts. Many years ago, on holiday at the seashore, my young sons were taught by a mischievous Thai male friend to mutter *"nom yaay"* ("big breasts," but literally "big milks") under their breath whenever a woman with large breasts walked by on the beach. This seemed to them both daring and hilarious. Yet, the expression *nom yaay* was always very different in quality from, say, "big tits," because of two paramount, underlying, indivisible concepts: *milk* and *mother.*

In *A Child of the Northeast,* Kampoon Boontawee's novel of village life in the 1930s, a young boy named Jundi remarks about some young women he has observed in the village his family is visiting.

> "That [headman's] daughter is all right . . . but they have plenty of ugly girls here, too. A couple of them had real sour faces, and when they bent over to give us the rice, they had big floppy breasts."
> "You fool," [his uncle] said. "Those weren't girls. They were young women with babies."[8]

Jundi, the village scamp, has a frankly and frequently expressed interest in breasts; indeed, he is known to scrutinize the houses of young women for wide cracks between wallboards through which he can spy on them as they undress. But as he grows, he learns from men as well as from women the "context of the breast"—a naked breast is not necessarily a sexual signal.

In classical Thai dance-drama, the female body is covered but stories are rich in erotic allusions and permeated with a reverence for the delights of the senses. R. J. Owens recalled a conversation about Thai literature with the author Boonlua, who was also a literature professor and critic: "She told me that she had been lecturing to a group of students on classical Thai Literature. 'I don't know what to do with them[,]' she said sadly[.] 'They are so innocent and inexperienced and unimaginative. Thai literature is sophisticated, ironic, earthy and courtly, like Chaucer's. Imagine,' she said, beginning to heave with laughter, 'an old woman like me having to explain indirectly to all these youngsters what the stories are all about! What's wrong with the youth of today that they are so ignorant!'"[9]

Ignorance of the young aside, pride in the classical literary tradition has never faltered. However, when Thais began to write Western-style fiction in the late nineteenth century, because these were new genres and imitation was at first a necessity, they emulated not only the literary style but the conventions of Victorian writing in their own first efforts at short stories and novels. Additionally, the cautious depiction of bodies and sexuality in early modern Thai literature reflect a real fear of revealing any aspect of Thai culture that might seem "uncivilized" to Western colonial powers.

The Body Politic

From at least the mid-eighteenth century on, there was a good deal of justifiable anxiety about the possibility that England or France would invade and colonize Siam, claiming that the Siamese (like the Malays, Burmese, Lao, Cambodian, and Vietnamese peoples before them) would be better off under the "civilizing" influence of a European power. Scot Barmé has written: "[King] Mongkut [1851–68] told his officials of the need for the Thais to become more 'civilized' (*siwilai/rung ru'ang*). . . . *People who wear no upper garments seem naked;* the upper torso looks unclean, especially if the person . . . is sweating. . . . Since Siam is a civilized country and understands civilized ways, we should not cling to the ancient ways of our forefathers who were forest people. Let everyone, therefore, wear upper garments when coming to royal audience."[10]

With this dictum in mind, it is easier to understand the bitter reactions of Thais to the musical stage play and film *The King and I* and particularly to Yul Brynner's portrayal of their beloved king. Brynner's character sings and dances—unimaginably undignified behavior for a king—and, even worse, he is *naked from the waist up.*

Not only was there a "body politic" but, according to ideas developed by the Thai historian Thongchai Winitchakul, the Thai citizenry (at least the ethnic Siamese) experienced the nation as a (geo)body:

> A passage in *Ramakian*, the Thai version of the *Ramayana* . . . says: *All the cities are the body / the king is the mind / Which is the lord of the body.* The country, the kingdom, or the realm is always expressed as the royal property. . . . This means that territory . . . was a component of the royal body.
>
> When the geo-body displaced the premodern nonbounded, hierarchical realm, the manifestation of the royal body emerged in a new form. But it was still the royal body. . . . the king's extended body was now a little patchwork on a blue planet, no more the center of the universe or the southern continent of the Hindu-Buddhist cosmology. But in that semiological shift, the sanctity of royalness was transferred and transposed to the geo-body as well.[11]

Thongchai's ideas would have seemed quite reasonable to Boonlua, the first Thai woman writer whose work I examine. A "royal modernist," she was a descendant of the second king of the present Chakri Dynasty, now known generally as Rama II (1809–24); she received a Western education and began her career as an educator, author, and civil servant in 1932, the same year the absolute monarchy was overthrown. Quite consciously, she lived her life between two literary worlds, the classical and the modern.

Boonlua: Beautiful Heroines with Plain, Smart Friends

Boonlua's novels and short stories, most of which were written between 1960 and 1980, reflect several major influences: the Victorian novels she loved; her experiences working as an educator and writer through the difficult, interesting years following the overthrow of the absolute monarchy in 1932; and the profound, lifelong influence of her early exposure to classical Thai literature and Buddhism. The main characters in her work, particularly the early novels, represent the "ideal" of womanhood: gentle, yet strong; beautiful according to traditional standards, yet ever humble; biddable, yet possessing and displaying good character. The females in supporting roles are more interesting.

The best friend of the heroine in Boonlua's work is what I call the "authentic/nonideal" woman: a "real Thai" woman, by virtue of her virtues, but lacking the romantic attributes of a heroine. Always well bred, intelligent, and better educated than most of the women she knows, the heroine's best friend is outspoken and a bit sharp-tongued—but soft-hearted, despite her outward behavior. She is also plain and considered unikely to marry, both because of her plainness and her unfeminine tendency to speak her mind. In short, she is a woman much like Boonlua herself.

The novel *Thutiya Wiset* (the title is the name of a decoration the heroine is awarded for outstanding service to the nation) is loosely based on the life of Tanpuying La-iad Phibunsonggram, the wife of Field Marshal Plaek Phibunsonggram (usually referred to as "Field Marshal Phibun"), Thailand's prime minister during most of the years between 1938 and 1957. In this novel, Boonlua employs subtle, metaphorical descriptions of the body to advance some of her themes, including the powerful effects of physical attractiveness upon people's lives—both the attractive and the attracted—the importance of purity of motive; and the lonely realities of life that may underlie the appearance of beauty, power, and security.

As the story opens, Cha-awn is dressing for a grand party to honor herself and her husband, a rapidly rising star in Thailand's post-1932 military firmament. Descriptions of jewelry and clothing dominate the first two pages, a fact that unfortunately prevented my getting into this book for some years. I failed to get the point. Traditionally, the richness and colors of the fabrics in which a Thai woman is able to dress her body and the quality of her jewelry have been considered integral components *of* her beauty rather than additions to it. The body upon which necklaces, bracelets, earrings, and various other baubles are draped, clasped, wrapped, and pinned in the first pages of *Thutiya Wiset* seems, at first, to have no more importance, or more life, than a mannequin. At first reading, I found particularly irksome the constant murmurs of fawning female relatives: "How lovely! Oh, look, how lovely Cha-awn is tonight!"[12]

Several years after I first began this novel, I came to realize that this astute author knew exactly what she was about. The jewels signified everything that the world may know of a woman whose husband's career has carried her to the pinnacle of social prominence in society, while the tiny woman beneath the jewels (we are told that she is tiny) remains known only to herself and a small number of friends from childhood.[13]

At last sufficiently bedecked and bejeweled to go to the ball, Cha-awn sits beside her husband in the back of the limousine, musing on his fine looks. As she watches the dark streets of Bangkok rush past, she reminisces about their first meeting, when she was a girl living in her father's home.

Witun, a young army officer, had come to visit her father and accidentally saw Cha-awn frolicking in the pond beside the house. She was decently clad, of course—naked bathing would have been unthinkable—in a length of cotton (a *pasin*), wet and clinging, knotted over the gleaming wet skin of her young bosom. Witun was smitten at once with the charming child-woman paddling thoughtlessly about the pond, unaware that she was being watched.

Remembering that fateful day, Cha-awn feels her face grow hot with the memory of the shame she felt upon discovering that she was being watched: Would the young man think that she was "*klaa*"? "*Klaa*" is a word with several shades of meaning, among them "brave" or "bold" or "forward"; and since "forward" behavior could damage a young woman's reputation, as well as her perceived value in the eyes of potential suitors and their families, mothers continually reproved their daughters for behavior that could possibly be perceived as *klaa*.

General Witun's male body, in *Thutiya Wiset,* frankly demonstrates the beautiful and magnetic qualities of power and of the self-confidence and arrogance that are required to achieve it. In her youth, Cha-awn is self-conscious about her body and fearful of the appearance of sensuality; in middle age, her only consciousness of her body, besides dismay at the signs of aging (especially by comparison with her still-attractive husband), is to recognize it as the bearer of jewels and of the silk clothing onto which the decorations she has earned as her husband's wife will be pinned, for all the world to see.

In the same year *Thutiya Wiset* was published, an artist named Suwanee Sukhontha decided to turn to writing full-time and soon began making literary waves. In one of her short stories, a woman paddles about in the waters of a *klong* (canal) while a young man sitting on the bank observes her. Any similarity to Boonlua's gentle heroine emphatically ends here, however, for Suwanee's swimmer, like most of the (anti)heroines in her groundbreaking work, can only be described as unapologetically, unabashedly, enthusiastically . . . *klaa*.

Suwanee Sukhontha: The Towel Is Dropped

Turning from the writing of Boonlua, or of any Thai female writer before Suwanee, we are immediately aware of a great revision, or more accurately an extension, of the role of the authentic/nonideal Thai woman in fiction. Suwanee's own troubled, exciting, sometimes hilarious, and ultimately tragic life rolled onto the page, and the influence of her unself-conscious, radically new style was profound. In the late 1960s and 1970s, while busy publishing *Lalana*, the popular women's magazine she founded (in part to promote new women writers), Suwanee continued to write innovative, often uproarious short stories and novels that concentrated on the honest feelings of believable people.

"Snakes Weep, Flowers Smile"[14] is typical of Suwanee's "love-gone-wrong" stories. It includes lush nature imagery with plainly erotic over- or undertones; a faithless lover sullenly smoking cigarettes in the darkness; and a woman who suffers, thoroughly enjoying the titillating drama she has once again created. She knows that her distracted lover has a new, younger woman, one whose body she compares with her own, representing both as palm fronds, at opposite ends of their lives:

> [The night was] hot, stifling . . . but a breeze was beginning to blow in earnest, helping the old palm fronds to lower themselves into the dark pond.
>
> The young fronds rose up with dignity, gracefully flaunting their bright colors, their freshness, and their lovely shapes while the old ones withered, grieved, and sank.[15]

Here, Suwanee is clearly influenced not by the "license" of modern fiction but by the erotic nature imagery of her own literary tradition.

Later, the woman decides to seize her lover's attention with a dramatic gesture, and the towel is literally dropped.

> I took off everything but my thin underwear, tossing the other things in a heap and wrapping myself in a large, thick towel that belonged to him. He sipped his drink. A towel that other women had wrapped around their bodies, a towel that had fallen from their bodies. In a few moments I dropped it and jumped into the water. With a shock of revulsion, I felt the bottom mud seize my feet like the coils of a huge, cold snake. I quickly lifted myself to the surface and floated on my back among the roiling weeds. He sat and smoked, perhaps watching me.[16]

Another love affair has sunk to the bottom mud of the *klong;* in Suwanee's case, it is less a matter of art imitating life than of art keeping track of life. Despite the often controversial nature of her characters, plots, themes, and style, Suwanee received many literary awards, including a "best novel of the year" award for *His Name Is Kan,* the story of a self-sacrificing rural doctor and the spoiled city wife who ruins his life.

Suwanee's writing is often described as "male" in nature, which is to say that her style is earthy, frank, and rowdy, qualities women writers before her had avoided. In the story "On a Sunny Morning," the narrator briefly interrupts a serious tale of urban violence to offer some remarks on barbecued chicken: "Everyone says the chicken at those stands is delicious, but I can't help thinking of the chickens as they were—full of life, skinny of shin, cheerfully stalking about, pecking and gabbling their way through a life that is short at best. Some of them may never have realized that they were alive at all. Some of them may even have been virgins!"[17] This is the stuff her readers adore. Who but Suwanee would call an intermission, in the midst of death and destruction, to speculate about the sex life of chickens? Her fictional women are straightforward, lusty, well meaning, and imperfect; we are sure that there is a warm female body beneath the silks and jewels—or the jeans and T-shirts. Suwanee demanded the right to give the authentic/nonideal woman center stage, rather than the role of the plain friend who scampers onto the scene from the wings, ungraceful but endearing, providing either comic relief or wise words. Her heroines do not dream demurely of love but obsess over it:

> I like love. I think of love as a classical art although it is true that I love in a casual, careless way; and that he was just another reflection fluttering across the surface of my pond.
> I like jealousy, too. It makes my heart dance, leap, and burn. I am not a stick or a stone, but a human being whose heart is full of cravings, and therefore I have loved whatever provoked jealousy, love, lust.[18]

It would be reasonable to assume that after Suwanee, who died at age fifty-three in 1983, women's writing would never be the same.[19] Yet, even though other women writers greatly admired her, most of them went on writing novels and short stories that were far less realistic and less revealing of female (or male) characters' deepest feelings. As the 1960s ended, an important new woman writer appeared, Botan, who was more interested in women's intelligence than in their emotions. Botan's goal, and that of her most memorable characters, is single-minded devotion to financial and social independence.

Botan: A Woman's Worth

Botan was born in Thonburi in 1947. She wrote the highly acclaimed autobiographical novel *Letters from Thailand,* a story of three generations in the life of a Chinese-Thai family living in Bangkok and Thonburi, when she was a twenty-one-year-old graduate student at Chulalongkorn University. She has been writing prolifically ever since, publishing and distributing her books through the company she founded and manages with her husband. She is the epitome of the self-made woman.[20]

Botan's novel *That Woman's Name Is Boonrawd* was written in 1981. It is set in the late 1960s, when, in the scrupulously descriptive words of the literature professor and critic Somporn Varnado, "it was a common scene to have a group of Thai women fraternizing with American Airmen for economic purposes."[21] Boonrawd, who works near an airbase, marries an American, but she is not—and this fact is of ultimate importance—a "rented wife," as such women were (and still are) designated.

Boonrawd has survived poverty, a supremely exploited childhood, sexual abuse, unrequited love, and numerous other misfortunes to become a successful businesswoman through determination, hard work, and sheer courage. The dutiful daughter of the traditional Thai novel is nowhere to be seen. Boonrawd turns on the mother who once sent her to work for a man everyone knew sexually abused his young female employees and charges: "You raised your sons to be princes and your daughters to be slaves!"[22] Somporn writes: "Her origin and her job . . . lowers Boonrawd's value in the estimation of . . . other Thais. Added to this is her 'ugly' complexion: a 'dirty-dark' complexion. Her features are unattractive and she distastefully wears 'loud colors.'"[23]

Boonrawd's material success—*money*—is almost entirely responsible for society's slow but steady revision of opinion of this poor, socially marginal, "dirty-dark" woman during the course of the novel. This is not an issue that Somporn directly expresses in her essay, but it occupies a central role in much of Botan's work. The primary issue for Botan has never been a "room of one's own"—she could write anywhere—but a bank account of one's own. I imagine that she would be either confused or irritated (in Botan's case, the latter seems much more likely) by, for example, Judith Grant's disapproving remarks about "those [feminists] whose only concern is that they be liberated into a free market economy where there is no glass ceiling, so that they can make as much money as the men of their classes. This is a tepid feminism indeed."[24]

Tepid perhaps, but Botan could never forget the poverty of her childhood or the fact that her father had refused to pay for her education past the mandatory fourth-grade level. That she was educated on merit scholarships from fifth grade through graduate school is a testament not only to her ability but to Thai society itself, which confers considerable social mobility on those who are able and diligent, regardless of family circumstances. Still, even if tuition is minimal or free, clothing and books never are. And Botan never forgot what it was like to be a poor child on scholarship, year after year, surrounded by children from well-to-do families. She understood from early childhood that autonomy and money, especially for women, are closely related.

The human body in Botan's fiction is presented in both a prudish and almost disconcertingly matter-of-fact way. However, the relative prudishness and pragmatism of her work, compared with that of writers such as Suwanee Sukhontha or, later, Anchan, has rendered Botan's work more approachable, and more comfortable, for conservative readers. As in all of Botan's novels, the rare love scenes in *Boonrawd* have a rushed, embarrassed, perfunctory quality. The consummation of Boonrawd and Robert's marriage is business-like, above all.

> She affected not to notice when he stroked her arm, or when his shoulder lightly grazed her own as they paced back and forth between the suitcases and the armoire. When there was nothing more to unpack, and the suitcases had been snapped shut, he put his arms about her, and hugged her tightly.
>
> "No, no," she mumbled, "I stink, Robert—I'm all sweaty. I've been hauling boxes all morning, and sitting in a hot truck, and—"
>
> "And I like it," he interrupted her, "I think you smell good, sweat and all. . . ." His hands grew bolder, but it was a loving urgency; he made her feel . . . swept along. . . .
>
> "Boonrawd," he whispered, *when it was over,* "did I make you as happy as you made me?"[25]

Immediately following this exchange, the talk turns, with notable relief, to important things: Robert's explanation of how much money he makes each month, how much he spends, and the couple's decisions as to how they will handle their money henceforth. Indeed, Boonrawd is astonished to learn the amount of her husband's salary and is stunned by his description of his weekly expenses, which seem shockingly wasteful to her.

Consummation of the marriage: one page. Discussion of money: the rest of the chapter. To Boonrawd, a body is a body. She is grateful for one that is healthy and functional. She reflects that she has the same number of hands and feet as a man, and she can use them just as well on behalf of her family and in pursuit of a safe future for herself and for them.

Aside from the importance of a woman's financial independence, two other themes are important in this novel: the emotional and social legacy of sexual abuse and the tragic results of the premium placed on virginity in Thai society. Both are present in this exchange between Boonrawd and her mother:

> "You [sent me to work for a] disgusting old man—what did you get in return for your daughter, eh? A few hundred baht, so he could treat me like a whore? You pushed me into the tiger's mouth."
>
> "You never said," her mother whined.
>
> "No, I never told you. But would you have cared? Why do you think I ran to [my old teacher] Kruu Orapin? Just because the old man didn't pay me my

salary? Face the facts, Ma. What are my prospects? No Thai man wants a woman who's been used, I've got a sister who's a rented wife, and then there are my nephews—a redhead, and the other one with kinky black hair. Do you think any decent man is going to come begging for my hand? Any Thai man who would marry me would know he could walk out any time, and nobody would think worse of him, because I was spoiled when he got me, and my family is nothing. So I've got a farang husband, and everybody says, 'Yah, Boonrawd—she sold herself.' Is it so impossible for you to imagine that we love each other? That this man really cares about me?"[26]

The mother's only reply is, "As dark as you are, I'm surprised a farang would go for you."

From the first page of the novel we are told (repeatedly) that Boonrawd prefers cheap, flashy, voluminous clothes in clashing colors and patterns; that she wears bright makeup over her "dirty-dark" complexion; and that she keeps her eyes covered with sunglasses much of the time. On the one hand, the reader may assume that the author intends this "covering up" of the body as a protective gesture, at least partially the result of the sexual abuse Boonrawd suffered as an adolescent. On the other hand, I believe that the constant references to Boonrawd's flashy appearance may be intended simply to emphasize her purposeful flaunting of convention. As for the critical glances thrown her way by more ladylike women, Boonrawd doesn't give a damn what people think as long as she gets what she's after—and what she deserves.

Sri Dao Ruang: Ordinary Women

While Botan was in graduate school on scholarship, writing her first novel, another young woman who had grown up in poverty was living hand-to-mouth in Bangkok, teaching herself to be a writer by making notes of her experiences in a series of menial jobs and gradually developing a style and a voice that would distinguish her from all other modern writers.

Sri Dao Ruang ("sri" is pronounced "see") was born in 1943 in Phitsanulok, the third of eight children; her father was a railroad worker, her mother made and sold sweets at the local railway station. Alone among the leading Thai writers, Sri Dao Ruang has only a fourth-grade education, the compulsory minimum when she was a child. As a young woman she worked in factories and as a household servant for both Thais and Americans.[27] She has often written that she feels uncomfortable among "the intellectuals," and once responded to a question I asked her in a letter with the uncharacteristically testy, "Why don't you ask one of the intellectuals [banyachon]?"

During the 1970s and 1980s, some members of the literary establishment hinted that Sri Dao Ruang's husband, the editor and writer Suchat Sawatsri, must have helped her write her stories because he has more education. One individual based this surmise on the fact that Suchat has read English translations of several modern French writers who have explored "absurdity," a fact that could explain how Sri Dao Ruang has been able to produce her more outrageously "absurd" stories. Within the last few years, however, many of her former doubters have begun to conclude that Sri Dao Ruang not only writes her own stories but is one of Thailand's most innovative and gifted writers—in part because she is not a product of the educational system that so strongly influenced virtually all the others.

The women writers whose work I examine here all admired and learned from each other. The ways in which Sri Dao Ruang portrays and makes use of the human body in her work reflect a debt to Suwanee Sukhontha, whom she greatly admired and who published several of her stories in *Lalana*. Because of Sri Dao Ruang's well-known shyness, the two women never met, a circumstance that is poignantly recounted in the short story "The Letter She Never Received."[28] Sri Dao Ruang's debt to Suwanee is evident in her eagerness to share her earthy sense of humor with her readers and in her willingness to sacrifice dignity and even privacy for the sake of her work. She often writes thinly veiled autobiography, as Suwanee did. Much of her writing is characterized by what Pam Morris calls "the wry self-parody of the comic image."[29] Morris continues: "The writing of [Anne] Sexton, [Sylvia] Plath and, I think, many other women can be seen to operate across the boundary site where a self constructs self as voice or performance, yet retains a comic cynicism—frequently of black humour—towards that construction of identity. It is this parodic resilience that constitutes the aesthetic control in their work, preventing any emotional excess or slide into a purely confessional discourse."[30]

"Parodic resilience" is exactly the quality that buoys and controls "Sai-roong's Dream of Love," a short story that is concerned—"consumed" might be more accurate—with sexual fantasies. Sai-roong, a respectable middle-aged woman whose neighbors all approve of her, begins to have amazing dreams shortly after a handsome young man moves in next door.

Unlike writers following the genteel traditions of erotic imagery, Sri Dao Ruang contributes something entirely new to modern fiction by depicting the female body in ordinary yet powerful visual images:

> What she saw made [Sai-roong's] uncombed hair stand on end, her skin tighten and shiver. Swiftly she drew back, hiding her unwashed face behind the door.
>
> What could have shocked her so? Only the sight of the new neighbor, the very young gentleman next door, striding past her gate. She was sure! How could she not be? Why, this was the very man from whose ardent embrace she had been dragged at dawn![31]

Sai-roong treats herself to a makeover: "These days she. . . . had even been seen wearing a Polo shirt and pants that were tight all the way up and down her legs. Most of her hair, which she had always worn long, suddenly disappeared, replaced by a short style that anyone would recognize who has seen the Princess from Wales. . . . In the mirror, she practiced making the wide-eyed, sparkly look of the models in the women's magazines. Ooy! She grinned at herself."[32]

"Sai-roong's Dream of Love" is a virtual celebration of bodies: good, bad, indifferent, and imagined. In waking life, Sai-roong is no graceful Thai maiden: "The raindrops were fat and clear, she noted, as she pushed the tendrils of sodden hair back from her face. She looked down, and saw that in only a moment the rain had soaked her, from the damp curves of her breasts down to her feet. Unfortunately the mud beneath her feet splashed up with each step, making ugly dark splatters on the backs of her calves, and her skirt."[33]

But in Sai-roong's dreams, a rainstorm is just another opportunity for erotic adventure:

> With a demure smile, she invites him to share her umbrella. They walk on side by side, but this umbrella is not large enough, not wide enough to cover two bodies. They are forced to press closer together. It is so cold, now; the wind blows, chill and clammy, but under the umbrella they breathe in the mingled, fragrant vapors of two warm, damp bodies. She wonders if he will encircle her waist with his strong arm and pull her close and if he does—yes, he has done it now—and she fits against him snugly, deliciously aware of the broad chest which, under his raincoat and shirt, is covered with fine, soft hair, and then, without a word, they pass the gate that leads to her house, and turn toward the gate to his own.[34]

When her dream lover takes a wife—in real life—Sai-roong imagines her revenge in starkly physical terms: "At first, her heart had withered like a flower ripped cruelly from its earthy bed. . . . And then, there was the horrible snake dream. *The huge cobra reared up, flared its hood, began undulating toward her. It was indescribably disgusting as it writhed about, coming ever nearer. She was petrified for a moment, then looked about wildly, her glance at last falling upon the garden spade. . . . She brought it down with all her might and smashed the hideous snake to a pitiful little pile of pulp.*"[35]

During the 1980s, Sri Dao Ruang wrote six stories based on characters and situations from the *Ramakian*, the Thai version of the *Ramayana*. She called them her "demon tales" (*ruang chaaw yak*). It is something of an understatement to describe these stories as "revisionist." Not only are they set in contemporary Bangkok but the identities and relationships of the characters are dramatically recast. In Sri Dao Ruang's stories, Sita rejects the virtuous Prince Rama, choosing instead Tosakan, king of the demons (from whose evil abductive clutches Prince Rama saves her, in the original *Ramakian*). She chooses the imperfect demon for her mate, rather than the pious prince, because Tosakan is a man who, for all his frailties and faults, his teasing and tantrums, she can understand and love—and rage at, when she suspects that he is having an affair.

> What is he doing now? Where is he doing it? (And . . . how, exactly?) He is in a room somewhere with this woman, and they are alone. A voluptuous scene unfolds in Sita's mind, a scene that cannot but end with Tosakan passionately embracing her. . . .
>
> After lying in her tears for a long time, painting various pictures in her mind that can only deepen her sorrow and vexation. . . . [Sita] goes to the bathroom, undresses, dips cool water from the earthen jar, and begins pouring it over her head. Dip and pour . . . dip and pour . . . the water streams down her body, and begins to wash away her sadness. Just a little cool water, pouring down from her head all over her body, and her tension, the giddy misery of her mind, begins to heal. Her skin feels clean and fresh, her thoughts are clearing, and the answers for which she had searched begin to come.[36]

Anchan: The Body Becomes the Metaphor

While Sri Dao Ruang was writing demon tales in the mid-1980s, a younger woman who much admired her was writing her own first short stories about women's lives. If critics, especially male critics, were sometimes perplexed or disapproving with regard to Suwanee's or Sri Dao Ruang's work, they were totally unprepared for the next feminist literary phenemenon, Anchan.

Anchan was born in Bangkok in 1953. She graduated from Chulalongkorn University and received a master's degree in English literature from the City University of New York. She currently lives and writes in New York State, because her husband has founded a business there. Although Anchan's stories have their foundation in kernels of life observed or fragments of her own life that throw her fervent imagination into gear and lead her in interesting directions, her work is not nearly as autobiographical as that of Suwanee Sukhontha or Sri Dao Ruang.

"A Pot That Scouring Will Not Save" caused controversy when it was first published in 1985 and won a "best short story of the year" award and a furor when the book of her collected short stories in which it was included won the SEAWrite Prize for Literature in 1990.[37] With this completely convincing depiction of the life of a battered wife and her sadistic husband, Anchan had not only transgressed the unspoken prohibition against writing (realistically, at any rate) about husbands who beat their wives but had also had the audacity to write a graphic description of sexual intercourse, which was promptly denounced as pornography in some quarters. It seems doubtful that this story would have received the "best short story of the year" award, much less that the collection would have won the SEAWrite Award, if determined women on both selection committees had not insisted that Anchan's important and beautifully written short stories be recognized, regardless of their social or sexual content.

In "Snakes Weep, Flowers Smile," Suwanee Sukhontha used images from nature to suggest the appearance of human bodies and their desires. But in Anchan's story, it is all reversed: the bodies themselves become metaphors for power and submission, dominance and fear, in a ghastly marriage between a bully and his terrified, fragile wife.

> She crossed the room, stopping just before her hip touched his, and glanced down at the damp, loose knot of the [towel] tied beneath his flat belly. She was intensely aware of the soft fragrance of soap that lingered in the creases of his body; and as he moved, despite herself Nien could not keep her eyes from the bewitching shifting of wet fabric that clearly revealed him. Astonished and disturbed by her feelings, she looked away quickly. But it was too late, he had caught her eye, and the corners of his mouth twitched into a grin. . . .
>
> He pushed her backwards onto the bed, fell over her, penetrated her at once. She wrapped her arms about him tightly, strained against him, greedy to absorb the delicious pleasure with her whole body. Breathless with excitement and the joy of his desire for her, she was barely aware of the whispering in her ear.
>
> "Little Nien had better be sure there's nothing on the stove, or she'll have to get down there and turn it off, little bare-tits Nien, bare-ass naked just like she is now—and who knows who might get a good look at her through the window, little Nien hustling her skinny bare ass around the kitchen . . ."
>
> Whispering, whispering as he always did, words to arouse not her passion but humiliation, which, reflected in her face, heightened his lust and his pleasure, as she well knew. But today, when he lifted his head to look down into her face, what he saw was not embarrassment but desire.[38]

Her reaction enrages him, but she chooses to interpret this sex act as proof of his love.

> Nien crawled across the bed to him, stroked him tenderly, scarcely daring to breathe lest the sweet moment be threatened in any way.
>
> "Get off me," he said. "Your hands are sticky."
>
> She rolled over onto her side and propped herself on her elbow. If only she could lie here all day, re-living at her leisure the pleasurable things he had done to her.[39]

Even the bodies of the tiny house lizards called *jing-jooks* assume importance in the story. In one scene, Nien's husband grinds a *jing-jook* beneath his sandal, mashing it into the kitchen floor and then ordering her to wipe up the mess as he leaves the room. In another scene, Nien identifies with a female *jing-jook* that skitters across her bedroom wall, hurrying after a male:

"'Don't follow him, you stupid thing! Don't screech and run away into your corner. Have you no shame, no shame?' She could neither bear the sight of the tiny lizard, nor take her eyes from it. She swayed back and forth on her knees like a madwoman, her mouth wide open, salty tears falling into it, howling soundlessly. 'Don't follow him! Get out! Get out, you stupid animal!' "[40]

It is bodies that tell the tale—swaggering, attacking, and brutalizing; or skittering, cringing, and hugging their agony in silence. This short story represents a landmark in Thai women's writing, not only because its subject matter is controversial and considered particularly unsuitable for a woman writer, but because in the final analysis Anchan succeeds on the strength of her talent and skill, regardless of the controversy. Remarks to the effect that "she just wrote those things to shock people" were ultimately unconvincing.

Recently, a Thai woman friend gave me a copy of *New York New York*, Anchan's humorous novel-as-memoir that chronicles her first year in the United States. My friend commented, "You'll see that she writes just like a man—you would never guess."

What is it that Thais mean when they say, "She writes like a man?" It means many things, including the use of straightforward language and realistic dialogue that may be rude, crude, and obscene—especially in writing meant to amuse. Earthy humor was a mainstay of Thai literature long before the modern period, and within limits it has remained so—especially what is called "bathroom" humor in the West—but women have been much less likely than men to write this way. "Writing like a man" also means writing without excessive regard for the eye of the critic or the prejudices of the market. By and large, however, most women writers have continued to be more sensitive than men to critical opinion and the prejudices of a still largely conservative reading public.

(Not) Writing like a Man

Modern Thai women writers have had to invent for themselves, over the last several decades, the ways in which they describe bodies, write about emotions, and present sexual behavior.[41] Perhaps they are now reaping some unintended benefits of long-standing, indirectly enforced taboos, for they have only a few old habits to break and many new ideas to try out.

Occasionally, a woman author does attempt to borrow themes and styles from men. Sri Dao Ruang has fallen between camps with a collection she calls the "Friday Club" stories. They are in a sense autobiographical but are written from a male perspective. A group of writer friends meets at the narrator's house each Friday night, swapping tales and drinking too much. One of the stories that is told one Friday night is about a woman with a mole on her genitals. The exact location or appearance of this mole is never specified, but the reader is given a politely rendered description of the woman's attempt to burn it off with a candle. No one wants such a mole. "According to the old ones, a woman or man with a birthmark in a particular place may have particular powers: a mole on the mouth, and one may be a great talker, or eater—a mole near a tear duct, and one's life may be unfortunate. . . . But— a man or a woman with a mole on the organs of reproduction! Such a man will 'devour' women, such a woman 'devour' men."[42]

What is meant is that, quite literally, the man so marked will be a "lady killer" and the woman will be a "man killer." Indeed, we learn that every man who has cohabited with this woman has—after the relationship ended—met an unexpected and disastrous end.

These stories are, I think, less successful than Sri Dao Ruang's stories told from a woman's point of view. There is something forced in the Friday Club stories, an attempt at "writing like a man," in a man's voice—a determined ribaldry that falls short, by comparison with the cheerful "body talk" that enlivens many of her other stories.

I have been reminded, writing this essay, of Carolyn G. Heilbrun's remarks on the growing feminist consciousness of American women writers during the 1960s:

> Until two decades ago, [the private lives of one-half of humanity] was the world's best-kept secret, and women were its best custodians, speaking for men. Louise Bogan, in the early 1920s, [wrote], "Women have no wilderness in them, / They are provident instead, / Content in the tight hot cell of their hearts / To eat dusty bread." Until Sexton, Kumin, Rich, Plath, and the others burst from their tight hot cell, to invent a new form—woman's truth—she was right. . . . The times helped. Women found the courage to demand what millennia had told them it was not reasonable to demand.[43]

Another American writer and critic, Elaine Showalter, has written: "In the 1960s, the female novel entered a new and dynamic phase. . . . [Female novelists] insisted upon the right to use vocabularies previously reserved for male writers and to describe formerly taboo areas of female experience. For the first time anger and sexuality [were] accepted not only as attributes of realistic characters but also . . . as sources of female creative power."[44]

Heilbrun's and Showalter's remarks could speak as well to the condition of Thai women writers in the 1960s and during the past thirty years. It is unfortunate that very few of these writers have been translated and therefore are unknown to their counterparts in the rest of Asia, much less in Europe, the Americas, or Africa.

Little has been written in Thai, much less in other languages, about the relationships of Thai women writers to each other, but there is substantial evidence that the women writers discussed in this essay have looked to each other for inspiration, gained courage from each other's experiments, and supported each other when necessary. Boonlua was the earliest champion of Botan's *Letters from Thailand,* staunchly defending both author and novel against those who claimed that the work was "anti-Thai" and "anti-Chinese" because it plainly revealed the social prejudices of both groups. Boonlua also admired the work of Suwanee Sukhontha, even though Suwanee's stories and characters seemed to inhabit a world that was very different from the world of Boonlua's fiction. Sri Dao Ruang looked to Suwanee as an example of what one could write if one had the audacity to expose one's own truths. Anchan looked to all these women for the courage to write stories her mind and heart told her needed to be written, whatever the consequences.

Individually and together, these women have raised, and sometimes answered, intriguing and provocative questions as to how, why, to what purpose, and by whom "the towel is to be dropped" in contemporary Thai fiction. Thai men and women writers who follow in their footsteps have much to learn from them and much for which to thank them.

Notes

1. These authors all write (or wrote) under pen names: "Boonlua" was M. L. Boonlua Thepyasuwan (1911–82); "Suwanee Sukhontha" was Suwanee Sukhonthiang (1932–84); "Botan" is Supa Luesiri Sirising (1947–   ); "Sri Dao Ruang" is Wanna Sawadsee (1943–   ); and "Anchan" is Anchalee Vivathanachai (1953–   ).

2. For further information on literature of the early modern period, see Mattani Rutnin, *Modern Thai Literature: The Process of Modernization and the Transformation of Values* (Bangkok: Thammasat University Press, 1988); Wibha Senanan, *The Genesis of the Thai Novel* (Bangkok: Thai Watana Panich, 1975); Susan Fulop Kepner, *The Lioness in Bloom: Modern Thai Fiction about Women* (Berkeley: University of California Press, 1996).

3. From the essentially religious work *Traiphummikatha,* composed during the fourteenth century, in *Thai Women in Literature, Book 1* (Bangkok: National Identity Board, Prime Minister's Office, 1992), 26.

4. Ibid., 23. This continues, "As human beings, they gave medicine to pregnant women to abort their babies. And then they falsely swore as follows: 'If I gave medicine to get rid of babies, may I become one of those ghosts who have bad-smelling bodies perpetually stung by flies. . . .' So they swore, and now they are naked, with flies eating them." Women who had committed the sin of cursing their husband also were punished by being reborn as ugly female spirits.

5. Ibid., 127.

6. Herbert P. Phillips, *The Integrative Art of Modern Thailand* (Seattle: University of Washington Press, 1992), 89.

7. Anthony Reid speculates on the origin and significance of this "unisex" hairstyle, which was shared by men and women and was common in Siam and neighboring kingdoms for a very long time, in *Southeast Asia in the Age of Commerce, 1450–1680,* vol. 1: *The Lands below the Winds* (New Haven, Conn.: Yale University Press, 1988), 79–84.

8. Kampoon Boontawee, *A Child of the Northeast,* trans. Susan Fulop Kepner (Bankok: Duang Kamol, 1987), 269.

9. R. J. Owens, *In Memory of Ajarn M. L. Boonlue Debyasuvarn,* a special issue of *PASAA* (Chulalongkorn University Language Institute, June 1983), 28.

10. Scott Barmé, *Luang Wichit Wathakan and the Creation of a Thai Identity* (Singapore: Institute of Southeast Asian Studies, 1993), 19 (emphasis added).

11. Thongchai Winitchakul, *Siam Mapped: A History of the Geo-Body of a Nation* (Honolulu: University of Hawaii Press, 1994), 133.

12. Boonlua, *Thutiya Wiset* (Bangkok: Prae Pittaya, 1968), 2.

13. It should be noted that the model for this character, Tanpuying La-iad, in fact was a strong partner to her husband and much more active in civic and cultural affairs than Boonlua's fictional "Cha-awn."

14. A translation of this story appears in Kepner, *Lioness in Bloom,* 107–14.

15. Ibid., 109.

16. Ibid., 111.

17. From my translation, "On a Cloudy Morning, in *Tenggara* 29 (1990): 90–99. This journal of Southeast Asian literature is published in Kuala Lumpur, Malaysia.

18. Kepner, *Lioness in Bloom,* 109.

19. Suwanee was murdered in her car during a traffic jam, apparently the result of a failed carjacking. Her death eerily reflects her short story "On a Sunny Morning" in which a woman stalled in a traffic jam is attacked by a man who darts into traffic from an alley and cuts off her finger to steal her diamond ring.

20. Botan, *jotmaai jaak muang Thai* (Bangkok: Duang Kamol Press, 1969); idem, *Letters from Thailand,* trans. Susan Fulop Kepner (Bangkok: Duang Kamol Press, 1977). Both the original Thai version and the English translation have been reprinted many times.

21. Somporn Varnado, "Social and Cultural Constraints on Modern Thai Women," in *Gender and Culture in Literature and Film East and West: Issues of Perception and Interpretation,* ed. Nitaya Masavisut, George Simson, and Larry E. Smith (Honolulu: University of Hawaii and the East-West Center, 1994), 76.

22. Botan, *phuuying khon nan chuu bunrawd* (Bangkok: Chomrom Dek, n.d. [early 1980s]). Translations of two chapters of this novel appear in Kepner, *Lioness in Bloom,* 143–63, quote on 159.

23. Kepner, *Lioness in Bloom,* 76.

24. Judith Grant, *Fundamental Feminism: Contesting the Core Concepts of Feminist Theory* (New York: Routledge, 1993), 188.

25. Kepner, *Lioness in Bloom,* 149.

26. Ibid., 160.

27. See Sidaoruang, *One Drop of Glass and Other Stories,* trans. Rachel Harrison (Bangkok: Duang Kamol, 1994).

28. My English translation of this story appears in *Two Lines/Tracks,* ed. Olivia Sears (Palo Alto, Calif.: Stanford Unviersity Press, 1995), 134–42.

29. Pam Morris, *Literature and Feminism* (Oxford: Blackwell, 1993), 155.

30. Ibid.

31. Kepner, *Lioness in Bloom,* 219.

32. Ibid., 220–21.

33. Ibid., 223.

34. Ibid., 223. The fantasies are italicized throughout the story.

35. Ibid., 224.

36. From my work in progress, "Married to the Demon King: Feminist Satire in the Thai Context."

37. Anchan, *anmanii haeng chiiwit* (Jewels of life) (Bangkok: Khombang, 1990). The story discussed here is included in Kepner, *Lioness in Bloom,* 172–204.

38. Kepner, *Lioness in Bloom,* 191–92.

39. Ibid., 192.

40. Ibid., 198.

41. This was not true, however, in premodern periods. Women who wrote classical poetry and dance-drama observed the same conventions as men. There is a brief discus-

sion of the career of Khun Suwan, an eighteenth-century woman who used earthy satire in her work, in Kepner, *Lioness in Bloom,* 9–11, 14.

42. Sri Dao Ruang, *The Demon Tales/The Friday Club* (Bangkok: Duang Kamol Wannakam, 1996), 99.

43. Carolyn G. Heilbrun, *Writing a Woman's Life* (New York: Ballantine Books, 1988), 70–71.

44. Elaine Showalter, *A Literature of Their Own: British Women Novelists from Brontë to Lessing* (Princeton, N.J.: Princeton University Press, 1977), 34–35.

Contributors

PHENG CHEAH, who earned a Ph.D. degree from Cornell University, is an associate professor of English at Northwestern University and a lawyer. He is the editor of *Thinking through the Body of the Law* and coeditor, with Bruce Robbins, of *Cosmopolitics: Thinking and Feeling Beyond the Nation.* He has also authored several articles on legal philosophy, neocolonial globalization, feminist theory, and contemporary critical theory.

WIMAL DISSANAYAKE is a professor of English at Hong Kong Baptist University and the author or editor of several books, including *Melodrama and Asian Cinema, Global/Local: Global Production and the Transnational Production* (with Ron Wilson), and *Narratives of Agency.* He is a leading poet in Sri Lanka who has published seven volumes of poetry in Sinhalese, his mother tongue.

SNEJA GUNEW is a professor of English and women's studies at the University of British Columbia and has taught for more than twenty years at various universities in England, Australia, and Canada. She has published widely on multicultural, postcolonial, and feminist critical theory and is the coeditor, with Anna Yeatman, of *Feminism and the Politics of Difference* and, with Fazal Rizvi, of *Culture, Difference, and the Arts,* and the author of *Framing Marginality: Multicultural Literary Studies.*

LAURA SCOTT HOLLIDAY grew up in Southeast Asia and is a Ph.D. candidate in English and women's studies at the University of California at Santa Barbara where she is writing a dissertation entitled "The Frying Pan and the Fire: Gendered Citizenship and the Kitchen from the Postwar Era to the Family Values Campaign."

SUSAN FULOP KEPNER teaches Thai language and literature at the University of California at Berkeley and has been translating Thai fiction and poetry for many years. She is the editor of *The Lioness in Bloom: Modern Thai Ficton about Women* and is working on a cultural biography of the Thai writer and educator M. L. Boonlua Thepyasuwan and a book entitled *Married to the Demon King: Feminist Satire in the Thai Context.*

FUKUKO KOBAYASHI earned a Ph.D. degree in English from Waseda University, Tokyo, where she is now a professor of American literature and women's studies. She has published extensively on American and Japanese literature from a feminist perspective. The translator into Japanese of Trinh T. Minh-ha's *When the Moon Waxes Red,* she is working on a critical biography of the Japanese woman writer Enchi Fumiko.

SHIRLEY GEOK-LIN LIM, professor of English and women's studies at the University of California at Santa Barbara and Chair Professor of English at the University of Hong Kong, is the author of four books of poetry, three collections of short stories, and two critical books on Southeast Asian literature. Her memoir, *Among the White Moon Faces,* received the 1997 American Book Award.

LARRY E. SMITH is dean of the Program on Education and Training at the East-West Center, Honolulu, Hawaii, and the cofounder and coeditor of *World Englishes: Journal of English as an International and Intranational Language.* An applied linguist interested in cross-cultural communication and the effects of the international spread of English, he conducts research on the intelligibility of different national varieties of English.

LYNN THIESMEYER is an associate professor in the Information Studies Program at Keio University, where she is also the director of the Women and Development Online Information Project and organizer of the Keio Symposium on Discourse. She previously taught at the University of Notre Dame, Georgetown University, and Japan Women's University. Her publications include two edited volumes, *Misrepresentation and Silence: Japan–U.S. and Nikkei Discourse* and *Discourse and Silencing,* and essays on the Nikkei internment (in *Discourse and Society*), on Mary Kingsley (in *Transforming Genres: New Approaches to British Fiction, 1890–1901*), and on Joy Kogawa and cultural theory (published in Japan).

ROLANDO B. TOLENTINO earned a Ph.D. degree from the Film, Literature, and Culture Program at the University of Southern California. He teaches in the Department of Filipino and Philippine Literature at the University of the Philippines.

C. J. W.-L. WEE, who taught British literature and cultural theory at the Nanyang Technological University, is a Fellow in the Institute of Southeast Asian Studies in Singapore. His essays have appeared in *New Formations, Public Culture,* and *positions: east asia cultures critique.* His research concerns modernity, gender, and national identity in the formation of late British imperial culture and the idea of East Asian/Sinic modernity, development, and culture as a proposed alternative model to Western modernity.

Rob Wilson teaches in the English department at the University of Hawaii at Manoa and has also taught at the National Tsing Hua University, the University of California at Santa Cruz, Korea University, and University of Massachusetts at Amherst. He is coeditor, with Arif Dirlik, of *Asia/Pacific as Space of Cultural Production* and, with Wimal Dissanayake, of *Global/Local: Cultural Production and the Transnational Production* and the author of *American Sublime* and the forthcoming *Reimagining the American Pacific: From "South Pacific" to Bamboo Ridge and Beyond.*

Index

Typeset in 10.5/12.5 Adobe Minion
Composed by Celia Shapland
for the University of Illinois Press
Manufactured by Versa Press, Inc.

University of Illinois Press
1325 South Oak Street
Champaign, IL 61820-6903
www.press.uillinois.edu